FIRST LADY OF LAUGHS

First Lady of Laughs

*The Forgotten Story of Jean Carroll, America's First
Jewish Woman Stand-Up Comedian*

Grace Kessler Overbeke

NEW YORK UNIVERSITY PRESS

New York

NEW YORK UNIVERSITY PRESS
New York
www.nyupress.org

© 2024 by New York University
All rights reserved

Library of Congress Cataloging-in-Publication Data
Names: Overbeke, Grace Kessler, author.
Title: First lady of laughs : the forgotten story of Jean Carroll, America's first Jewish
    woman stand-up comedian / Grace Kessler Overbeke.
Description: New York : New York University Press, 2024. | Includes bibliographical
    references and index.
Identifiers: LCCN 2023049559 | ISBN 9781479818150 (hardback ; acid-free paper) |
    ISBN 9781479818167 (ebook) | ISBN 9781479818181 (ebook other)
Subjects: LCSH: Carroll, Jean, 1911–2010. | Women comedians—United States—Biography. |
    Jewish comedians—United States—Biography. | Stand-up comedy—United States—
    History. | LCGFT: Biographies.
Classification: LCC PN2287.C287 O94 2024 | DDC 792.702/8092 [B]—dc23/eng/20240229
LC record available at https://lccn.loc.gov/2023049559

10 9 8 7 6 5 4 3 2 1

Also available as an ebook

To my parents, Kathy and Ned, for sending me down this path

To Matthew and Isadore, for being the people I was walking

toward all along

CONTENTS

TIMELINE OF JEAN CARROLL'S LIFE AND CAREER

1911: Jean Carroll born as Celine "Sadie" Zeigman

1912: Jean Carroll, her mother, and sisters immigrate to the United States

1922: Jean Carroll makes professional debut in Brooklyn as part of *Midnight Rounders*

1933: Jean Carroll meets Buddy Howe

1934: Jean Carroll leaves her Vaudeville partner to work with Buddy Howe

1936: Carroll and Howe are married and travel to the United Kingdom

1943: Buddy Howe is drafted

March 1944: Jean Carroll gets pregnant and makes her New York City stand-up debut

October 1944: Jean Carroll and Buddy Howe welcome their daughter, Helen

1946: Howe works for the Chicago office of General Amusements Corporation

1947: Carroll and Howe move permanently to New York City

1948: Jean Carroll debuts at the Copacabana

1949: Jean Carroll named "Female Comedy Discovery of the Year" by the National Laugh Foundation

1951: Jean Carroll is estranged from her husband

November 1953–January 1954: *Take It from Me*, Jean Carroll's sitcom, airs on ABC

1956: Jean Carroll reconciles with her husband

1956: Jean Carroll signs exclusive contract with Ed Sullivan

1960: Jean Carroll releases *Girl in a Hot Steam Bath* album

1964: Buddy Howe became dean of the Friar's Club

1966: Buddy Howe became president and chairman of the board of General Artists Corporation

1981: Buddy Howe dies

2006: Friar's Club hosts event honoring Jean Carroll

2010: Jean Carroll dies

FIGURE I.1. "A Tribute to Jean Carroll" at the Friars Club, November 6, 2006. (Private collection of Stephen Silverman)

Introduction

"The Mother of Us All": The Unwritten Legacy of Jean Carroll

A Night at the Friars Club

The night of Monday, November 6, 2006, the legendary New York Friars Club was bustling with camera crews capturing a gathering to celebrate the first Jewish female stand-up comic, Jean Carroll. Organized by Stephen M. Silverman and Diane Krausz in concert with their planned documentary, "Jean Carroll: I Made It Standing Up," the event was a special tribute to the then-ninety-five-year-old comedian. Hosted by the stand-up comedian and talk-show host Joy Behar, the evening featured speeches by comedians including Lily Tomlin, Caroline Rhea, and Freddy Roman, dean of the Friars Club (and, as Behar noted, "the only man we're letting speak tonight"), with video presentations by Ann Meara and Jerry Stiller and Rita Rudner.[1] The presenters sat alongside an audience of Carroll's family, Broadway performers, *New York Times* journalists, representatives from the mayor's office, and producers of *Saturday Night Live*, gathered together to honor—and hear from—Jean Carroll.

While Carroll's mental acuity was sharp, her vision was not—by the age of ninety-five, Carroll was mostly blind, and so she could not see many of the audience's upturned faces as she took the stage of the Friars Club—an association that had been off-limits to women throughout her career, even when under her husband's leadership. Clad in silk scarves and red lipstick, Carroll approached the microphone and launched into her machine-gun patter: "I'm only ninety-five years old. I know, I don't look a day over ninety-four. . . . I'm listening to all of this, and I'm not very emotional. . . . I had no idea that I was so good! You think I'm joking. I'm not joking. I had no idea that I would make the impact that I obviously made."[2]

And indeed, her impact that night *was* "obvious." Had the footage from the busy camera crews been used in the proposed documentary, it would have shown generations of comedians gathered together to attest to Jean Carroll's legacy and enduring influence. However, the economic tumult of 2008 resulted in the documentary losing its funding, and the project never came to fruition. The hours of interviews with Carroll and her family, friends, and fans instead went to the storage unit of the director's apartment building. The collapse of the documentary was a major blow to the visibility of Carroll's influence, rendering it not only less "obvious" but barely even evident in the extant media archive.

Given that so much of Jean Carroll's performance archive has been sequestered away in storage units and behind fee walls (her archive of almost thirty appearances on *The Ed Sullivan Show* was privately purchased by the corporation SOFA Entertainment), it is not surprising that she has been generally omitted from literature on comedy. Yet, although Carroll has been largely removed from the published narrative of American comedy, her lasting influence on stand-up is prominently evident in the "alternate archive" of performances by contemporary female stand-up comedians. Not all her protégés acknowledge or even realize the impact that she had on their careers. Nonetheless, Jean Carroll's stand-up career—and specifically her performance of Jewishness and femininity over time—has had an enduring and significant influence on modern stand-up.

In this book, I argue that Jean Carroll's absence from published history belies her significant impact on stand-up comedy and Jewish performance. Not only was she the first Jewish woman to do stand-up comedy, but in doing so, she set up a totally different model of "funny" Jewish women. She modeled a Jewish woman who had assimilated into American upper-middle-class, white, heterosexual, attractive, and even glamorous, society. At the same time, her persona retained something markedly Jewish to those who knew how to discern it. She had a subversive quality—not Lenny Bruce subversive but something more subtle—that nonetheless sparked inspiration among her fans.

The Cost of Mainstream Appeal

Carroll's material—riffs on the discontents of marriage, shopping mishaps, and parenting foibles—is not considered "edgy" by contemporary standards, particularly in contrast to the more overtly political work by later generations of stand-up comedians. As the popular understanding of stand-up evolved to what the Jewish female stand-up comedian Elayne Boosler called the "town crier" model, the political import of Carroll's work became less legible.[3]

Carroll's material came from situations that were recognizable to her audiences, prompting them to accept her content—and her—as "real." Jean Carroll staged a relatable facet of her reality: her perspective and experiences as a mother and wife. But her *total* reality encompassed her robust career: nightly performances, constant travel, and rigorous writing sessions, none of which became the subject of her comedy. As she was a Jewish woman, her reality also encompassed an ethnic dimension that was mostly coded onstage. The reality that Carroll's audiences were prepared to recognize as "authentic" and "universal" was actually extremely narrow: that of an upwardly mobile white (or not-quite-white) heterosexual woman, financially dependent on her husband. And so Carroll mainly stayed within those parameters, in spite of the fact that it was hardly an accurate representation of her life.

Critics describing Carroll's positive reception frequently attributed it to her jokes' universal familiarity. A trade magazine commended her for achieving "universality of material," with "personal identification so immediate that its commercial appeal is genuine."[4] The domestic travails of Carroll's jokes were deemed equally relatable abroad; a *London American* reporter explained that the reason "why so many of her gags hit home" is that she draws on "commonplace" experiences.[5] Of course, what Carroll and her critics deem "commonplace" experiences reveal their own biases regarding gender norms, motherhood, and other social roles. For instance, as she advocates writing jokes about "situations which everyone can recognize," her primary example is raising children.[6] In a similar vein, a review of Carroll's performance at Chicago's Palmer House Empire Room implicitly prescribes what ought to be "familiar" for the women in the audience: "Miss Carroll's comedy is found in events close to everyday living. She tells about buying a dress—or, rather, merely shopping—and she has a few verbal notations about love, PTA meetings, a day at the racetrack, the movies and dogs. Everything she relates is true-to-life, in conversational tone, and extremely hilarious."[7] The critic's sanguine praise of Carroll's experiences with shopping, parent-teacher associations, dogs, and other staples of 1950s suburban American existence as "true to life" and "familiar" to the "ladies in the audience" clearly delineates Carroll's imagined audience as white (or white ethnic), middle-class, heterosexual women occupying traditional gender roles. This limited repertoire is a double-edged sword when it comes to legacy, however, for the same material that was "relatable" in the midcentury is now dated and is conservative enough to be an outlier in the popular narratives of stand-up comedy as a subversive and progressive genre.

Although Carroll's domestic material makes her a difficult fit for more politicized and shocking histories of stand-up, it should not be fully dismissed as an engine of change. For her comedy sparked the creativity and humor of a generation of women comics, who termed her "the mother of us all."

"The Mother of Us All"

It is difficult to overstate the extent to which Jean Carroll paved the way for other women in stand-up comedy. The comedy legend Milton Berle called her "one of the great female stand-ups."[8] His praise is both effusive and oh-so-slightly marginalizing, qualifying her status as "one of the great stand-ups" with the pointed descriptor "female." But a more generous reading of Berle's words might see how he positions Carroll as a pioneer of her gender, carving out space in a male-dominated field.

Of course, Jean Carroll was not the first professionally funny woman. As a female comic monologist, Carroll was standing on the shoulders of the legendary Loretta Mary Aiken, a Black woman who performed monologues as Jackie "Moms" Mabley, an old woman in a floppy hat whose jokes about lusting for young men belied her subversive critique of racism and sexism. Although Aiken gained mainstream exposure through programs like *The Ed Sullivan Show* in the 1950s, she had been a huge success within African American media since the 1920s. One of the most remarkable elements of her work was the way that this savvy, queer young woman was able to inhabit the character of elderly, man-hungry "Moms." As *Ebony* magazine wrote, "Offstage, Moms Mabley is a striking figure in tailored slacks, matching sports shirt, Italian shoes. . . . She looks utterly sophisticated. Onstage, however, is a different story. She creates the impression that the theater cleaning woman has somehow wandered into the spotlight."[9] The clear distinction between the artist and her comic persona contrasts with the ambiguous, seemingly nonexistent boundary that characterized Jean Carroll's career—and those of subsequent stand-up comics like Joan Rivers and Richard Pryor.

Similarly, as a Jewish woman comedian, Carroll was part of a lineage that included predecessors like Fanny Brice. But the historic success of Brice's comedy was also a genre apart from what would now be called stand-up, due largely to the divide between artist and persona. While the offstage Brice was US-born and claimed not to speak Yiddish, the characters portrayed by Brice onstage typically featured a heavy parodic Yiddish dialect and expressive physicality that she referred to as "grotesque Yiddish steps."[10] Part of the virtuosic quality of solo comedians like Mabley and Brice was their ability to craft and inhabit a distinctive onstage character. What was notable about Jean Carroll—and what prompts me to position her at the beginning of a new stand-up tradition—is that she had no distinct stage character. Her jokes were framed as observations and anecdotes from her authentic experience. Her most remarkable trait was a breezy conversational style that was at the time deemed "too intimate" but that is now customary in stand-up comedy.[11]

Another distinctive trait was Carroll's commitment to a particular brand of femininity that she described as "dignified." As Carroll's career reached its peak in the 1950s, there were a number of other women comedians gaining acclaim and pushing the boundaries of "ladylike" behavior. Their humor was often dependent on what *Variety* called "extreme mugging and physical gaucheries."[12] Kaye Ballard, for instance, would do routines using her elastic features to make cartoonish funny faces. The musical comedian Beatrice Lillie would hike up her gown and roller-skate around the stage. Martha "The Mouth" Raye made her mark in comedy as "the go-to girl for loud and obnoxious characters."[13] Jean Carroll was publicly disparaging of these women, declaring in one interview, "I can't stand to see a woman lose her dignity."[14] Carroll admired the "dignified, genteel" persona of women like Ann Sothern and Eve Arden, asking, "Dignity and comedy—why not?"[15]

The answer to her query is, on one level, resoundingly obvious. Comedy is not the most dignified genre of performance. One of the most cited theories of humor proposes that a person laughs at what they feel superior to, so displaying inferiority is the quickest path to comedy.[16] Carroll's professed "aversion to seeing a woman make a buffoon of herself on the stage" effectively eliminated entire comic traditions—from slapstick to extreme self-deprecation—from her repertoire.[17] Her choice to limit her material so drastically (and to criticize other women who did not do the same) suggests that laughter was not actually her highest priority. Instead, she was invested in debunking some myths. The first myth was the prevailing stereotype, circulated by so many of Carroll's male stand-up colleagues, that Jewish women were homely and domineering. The second myth was that a conventionally "feminine" woman could not be funny. In response, she adopted the critics' moniker "The First Lady of Laughs" and established a persona as classy as she was comical.[18] Thus, while her brand of "dignified" femininity limited her material, it also allowed her to send some crucial new messages to her audience: a Jewish woman could be what a critic described as a "chic and well-poised" lady.[19] And a "chic and well-poised" lady could be hysterical.

When a journalist interviewing Carroll suggested that part of her legacy was more women, from all roads of life, pursuing stand-up, she responded, "I'm pleased about that, because I know lots [of women] with delicious senses of humor. And if stand-up is what they want to do, by all means, they should do it."[20] And indeed, they did. What began as Jean Carroll's job—one she took primarily to support her family— wound up paving the way for Phyllis Diller, Joy Behar, Lily Tomlin, and generations of women comedy professionals who saw her and dared to "stand-up" for themselves.

The women who followed in Carroll's career path show varying degrees of acknowledgment—or even awareness—of Carroll's work. Phyllis Diller—who became famous as a stand-up in the late '50s and '60s—is often miscredited as the first female stand-up comedian, an attribution that she seems to encourage. Diller flatly rejected Carroll's brand of "dignified" femininity, operating on the belief that "to be a female comic, you *can't* be a beauty. You *mustn't* be a beauty."[21] And so she dressed in wildly eccentric costumes that obscured her figure and spit out a rapid succession of one-liners berating her own hideousness. Diller's conviction that a female comedian "can't be a beauty" is odd, given that she was familiar with Jean Carroll, whom she described as "sophisticated and attractive." However, rather than positioning herself as Carroll's protege, Diller seems intent on minimizing Carroll's career in order to highlight her own achievements as unique. Diller writes in her autobiography, "Jean Carroll . . . specialized in witty one-liners about her husband and her home life. Carroll actually made several appearances on *The Ed Sullivan Show*, yet neither she nor any of the other women broke through on the scale that I did during the late fifties and early sixties—Jean didn't travel to build a mass audience, and [Belle] Barth and [Rusty] Warren were far too X-rated for television. So, for the first ten years, I had it all to myself."[22] Diller's words about Jean Carroll offer an interesting mixture of acknowledgment and dismissal. While praising Jean Carroll's "witty one-liners," Diller minimizes her nearly thirty appearances on *The Ed Sullivan Show* to the misleading "several." She also incorrectly asserts that "Jean didn't travel to build a mass audience" and therefore could not "break through on the scale that [Diller] did," when Carroll actually traveled extensively, with a following nearly as robust in England as it was in the United States. What Diller does capture accurately is the sense that the uniqueness of her own career is a matter of "scale." Building on the precedent for female comedians set by Jean Carroll (and subsequent musical comics like Rusty Warren and Belle Barth), Diller was able to achieve a level of recognition and success unavailable to her predecessors.

More eager to credit Jean Carroll as a pioneer of the field is Joy Behar, an Italian American stand-up comedian and writer who gained celebrity in the late 1980s. As both a comedian and a talk-show host, Behar had a persona that was outspoken, opinionated, confident, and poised. Starting in 1997, Behar became one of the original panelists on the popular women's daytime talk show *The View*, where she referenced Jean Carroll as an influence a number of times. When hosting the tribute to Carroll at the Friars Club, Behar introduced her as "the mother of us all," reflecting on her formative childhood experience watching Carroll on television:

> I remember being home at night as a kid, and seeing Jean on television—there she was, this beautiful, thin, good-looking woman who was very funny! She was Jewish, which made me think I was Jewish (I wasn't. I was Italian, but she looked like my relatives except better dressed and thinner). In a certain way, I think all women comedians owe you a debt. I didn't have any other role models to look at—she was it! Later, there was Joan and Phyllis, but Jean looked like a normal person! To be a normal person, wearing a regular suit, being funny the way she was, was simply spectacular and almost revolutionary. There was nobody else like that![23]

Behar's words speak to several elements of Carroll's legacy. First, she reflects how Carroll made Jewishness familiar and accessible to other white-ethnic populations. Behar saw a version of her own Italian relatives in Carroll, joking that this identification felt so strong that Carroll made Behar think she was Jewish. Second, she highlights Carroll's "revolutionary" embodiment of both comedy and beauty (what Carroll might call "dignity"). Behar goes out of her way to mention Carroll's svelte frame and "regular suit," in contrast to the later Phyllis Diller's fright wigs and outlandish costumes or Joan Rivers's hypercoiffed trendiness. Finally, and most broadly, she asserts Carroll's pioneering status as a woman stand-up comic, exclaiming, "I didn't have any other role models to look at—she was it!" and concluding that "all women comedians owe [Carroll] a debt." Speaking to that debt, the comedians Anne Meara and Rita Rudner made video testaments that they sent into the Friars Club event, thanking Carroll for paving the way. Rudner's message—"You were the first one to realize that men were just as funny as women!"— was a wittily succinct summary of Carroll's revolutionary act, transforming men from "funny" joke tellers to "funny" joke subjects.[24]

But the most influential figure advocating for Jean Carroll's legacy is the stand-up comedian and solo performer Lily Tomlin, who credits Carroll as a major reason she became a comedian. Often the token woman in anthologies of influential comedians, the Emmy-, Grammy-, Tony-, and Mark Twain Prize–winning Tomlin remains an undisputed staple of the American comedy canon. And in addition to praising Imogene Coca's character work and Lucille Ball's physical comedy, Tomlin has sung Carroll's praises as a sophisticated and subversive comic and major influence. In the *Windy City Times*, Tomlin painted a picture of her young self discovering Jean Carroll on *The Ed Sullivan Show*, remarking, "She was really kind of subversive and wonderful. . . . She was supposed to be sort of this middle-class housewife from Scarsdale and she always had a cocktail dress and a mink stole on . . . and she did all these jokes. I would just lift them right off of her act and do them! I would try on my mother's slip like an evening dress and do jokes on the back porch. . . . I was mad for her."[25] In addition to giving the young Tomlin an arsenal of jokes, Carroll also gave her a rare model of what Carroll called "dignity," showing a woman who was both feminine and (professionally) funny. In the *New York Times*, Tomlin was quoted observing, "Other women doing comedy were scatterbrained, fat, or homely. . . . Jean was very attractive. She was in control but not aggressive."[26] And so when Tomlin began her career as a performer and faced oppositional statements like, "How can you do comedy? You have to lose your femininity," or "You've got to be fat or ugly or you've got to make fun of yourself as a female," she was unfazed, explaining, "I didn't think any of that was true."[27] Perhaps Tomlin's most insightful words on the true depth of Carroll's influence and legacy took place at their first meeting—the November evening of Carroll's tribute. There, Tomlin gave a speech suggesting that in Carroll's work, she had caught her first glimpse of women's empowerment:

> Your manner was so confident and assertive, and these were all traits that I admired, . . . even though at the time, I didn't know that I did—I wasn't able to articulate that kind of thing to myself. Your material was smart, witty, and content-ful, . . . flat-out funny, but you would slip little things in. You were like a new type of person to me: a woman—charming, strong, very attractive, standing up there, talking directly to the audience about her life, which you never saw a woman doing. I mean, in my time, it was just like, breathtaking! You were like a precursor to the feminist movement, . . . although I couldn't possibly have articulated that at the time. . . . You cut such a path for women in comedy, whether they know it or not.[28]

The fact that Lily Tomlin, a major figure of feminist and queer performance, credits Jean Carroll with introducing her to "a new type of person," who served as a "precursor to the feminist movement," is a matter of no small significance. It attests to the empowering elements of representation. According to Tomlin, she and her mother saw themselves in

FIGURE 1.2. Jean Carroll and Lily Tomlin in "I Made It Standing Up" footage, 2006. (Private collection of Stephen Silverman)

Carroll; they felt she was "targeting [their] lives."[29] Perhaps this feeling helped Tomlin to envision herself not only in the role of comedian but also in the role of a woman who is both "attractive" and "strong."

On the subject of Jean Carroll's influence, the stand-up legend Joan Rivers plays the role of an enthusiastic gossip, passionately agreeing with whomever she is speaking to at the moment. When speaking to a journalist writing a feature on Phyllis Diller as the stand-up pioneer, Rivers dismissed Carroll as "a major schlep."[30] However, when interviewing Lily Tomlin on *The Tonight Show*, Tomlin recalled being inspired by Carroll's stand-up sets on *The Ed Sullivan Show*, and Rivers jumped on the bandwagon, crying that she too had watched and been influenced by them.[31] Notably, the comic elements for which Rivers became famous, like her conversational "talk style" and her move "away from punchline based comedy" in favor of "longer stories," were staples of Carroll's comic style.[32] Even a casual observer watching footage of Carroll can see how her chatty delivery set a blueprint for River's supposedly novel approach. In the words of a YouTube viewer commenting on newly unearthed footage of Jean Carroll on *The Ed Sullivan Show*, "I can see where Joan Rivers got her style."[33]

In sum, Carroll entered the male-dominated arena of stand-up comedy with an innovatively chatty delivery and a deliberately "dignified" femininity. Her public performance of a new kind of confident, attractive funny-woman helped to shape the field of comedy not only by inspiring Tomlin (and all those who were inspired by her) but by making room for a kind of figure that Tomlin could aspire to become. And in this sense, Carroll did indeed "cut a path for women in comedy, whether they know it or not."

"The Marvelous Mrs. Counterpoint"

In an unexpected way, Jean Carroll ultimately did make her way into the mainstream millennial media. For beyond functioning as a role model for actual practitioners of stand-up comedy, Jean Carroll also became a reference point for *The Marvelous Mrs. Maisel*, a period comedy released in 2017, depicting a fictionalized Jewish woman breaking barriers as a female stand-up comedian in the late 1950s and early 1960s.[34] Created by Amy Sherman-Palladino and Dan Palladino, and released by Amazon Studios, *The Marvelous Mrs. Maisel* was met with remarkable critical acclaim. The actress playing the titular role, Rachel Brosnahan, was especially lauded, receiving the 2017 and 2018 Golden Globe Awards for Best Actress in a Musical or Comedy, the 2017 Critics' Choice Television Award for Best Actress in a Comedy Series, and a 2018 Emmy Award for Best Actress in a Comedy.[35]

It was a well-publicized fact that Jean Carroll served Brosnahan as both an inspiration and a reference as she prepared for the role of Miriam Maisel. According to a profile in the *New York Times*, Brosnahan "studied the routines of the pioneering comic Jean Carroll," whom she described as "this beautiful, graceful woman who wore pearls and gorgeous dresses and sang a little."[36] To some extent, attribution of this kind revitalized interest in Jean Carroll. Comments from people viewing one of Jean Carroll's few YouTube videos began explaining, "I came here after seeing an interview with Rachel Brosnahan, who plays Mrs. Maisel, talk about Jean Carroll being an influence!"[37] A spate of articles promoting *The Marvelous Mrs. Maisel* appeared in the mainstream press referencing Jean Carroll. A piece in *Vulture* noted Jean Carroll's roots in a Vaudeville duo in "What *The Marvelous Mrs. Maisel* Gets Right about Early Stand-Up Comedy."[38] The feminist 'zine *Bustle* published a feature pondering, "Who Is Midge Maisel Based On? Amazon's 'Marvelous Mrs. Maisel' Draws Inspiration from Comedy Elite," which linked to a video of one of Carroll's earliest routines.[39] In coordination with the *New York Times'* feature on *The Marvelous Mrs. Maisel*, it released a profile called "The (Elegant, Brazen, Brainy) Pioneering Women of Comedy," crediting Carroll as a bridge between "the music hall comediennes of the past and the female stand-ups of the present."[40] And in the Jewish press, *The Forward* published my own article summarizing major findings on Jean Carroll, under the title, "Meet the Real Mrs. Maisel: Jean Carroll."[41] In that article, I wrote that the overlap between Miriam Maisel's story and Jean Carroll's history had an unnervingly obscuring effect. For, as the show's creators made clear, it was not intended to reflect the *actual* history of pioneering Jewish female comedians—either individuals or composites. At least one of the show's writers was not even aware of Carroll as a historical antecedent to the show's protagonist. When I spoke to Noah Gardenswartz, a stand-up comic and writer for *The Marvelous Mrs. Maisel*, he said that my email about Jean Carroll was the first that he had heard of her.[42] The show's real historical connection was to the creator Amy Sherman-Palladino's father, Don, to whom the show is dedicated. Don Sherman was a very successful stand-up comedian of the 1950s and '60s, and Sherman-Palladino "used to listen to him and his friends trading jokes in the backyard, absorbing the rhythms and tones as they tried to make one another laugh."[43] In an interview with the comedy writer Kliph Nesteroff, Don Sherman sounds like an encyclopedia of early stand-up references, riffing on Laff Records, Henny Youngman, Jack E. Leonard, Jackie Mason, and Flip Wilson.[44] It seems natural that growing up with him as a father, Amy Sherman-Palladino would be captivated by that moment in history when stand-up was first developing as a genre. However, in this fictionalized tribute to her father's era, Sherman-Palladino also retells the master narrative of male stand-up pioneers that makes Midge all the more "marvelous" and enforces actual women comics' erasure.

However, in the intervening years, I have come to realize that the two stories need not be in competition. Rather, the story *The Marvelous Mrs. Maisel* serves as a vital counterpoint for the history of Jean Carroll. At the beginning of the series, Midge embodies the persona that Jean Carroll tried to cultivate onstage; well heeled, Seven Sisters educated, a genteel wife and mother with a glamorous wardrobe and an indisputably American pedigree. But for Carroll, the truth was much less privileged. She had come to the United States as an immigrant with her mother, siblings, and abusive, alcoholic father. As a preteen, she kicked her father out of the house and became the family's primary breadwinner. While Miriam Maisel entered show business out of a love (and natural gift) for stand-up comedy, Jean Carroll entered show business out of economic necessity, well before stand-up comedy formally existed. Miriam Maisel was mentored by (and later romantically involved with) Lenny Bruce, portrayed as the patron saint of stand-up. Jean Carroll had been doing stand-up comedy before Lenny Bruce could speak.

The two women's marriages also stand in stark contrast to each other. Early in the series, Miriam Maisel's husband, Joel, tries to become a stand-up star, relegating his wife to the role of note taker, booker-briber, and doting audience member. Jean Carroll's husband, Buddy Howe—a fellow vaudevillean—openly admitted that she was the more talented of the two, even dropping out of their duet because he realized that he would be more successful managing than performing. When Miriam Maisel's husband commits adultery, the marriage is over. Even when he begs her to reunite shortly after his fling has fizzled, she refuses. When

Jean Carroll's husband committed adultery, she behaved in a much more typically midcentury manner: she stayed and put on a good face. Even during the years when they were separated (roughly 1951–1954), her daughter recalls that she would still make him dinner. After all, Howe was more than just her husband; he was her manager.

Even the two women's priorities point to the difference between a millennial reimagining of a 1950s comedian and the genuine article. Once Miriam Maisel begins pursuing comedy in earnest, she feels no compunction about blithely dropping her children with someone else while she goes to do a club gig or breaking an engagement to go on tour. Miriam's total—and anachronistic—commitment to her career contrasts starkly with Carroll's embattled relationship with her dual roles as caretaker and comedian. While Miriam's story ends with her as a living legend, estranged from her family but enthroned as comedy royalty, Jean Carroll's story ended with her show-business legacy mostly lost, surrounded by her family.

But the most revealing disparity between Miriam Maisel and Jean Carroll is their relationship to their own Jewish identity. As Samantha Pickette observes about *The Marvelous Mrs. Maisel*, "The series offers a post-assimilationist reframing of midcentury Jewish identity in its depiction of Midge's comfort with her Jewishness as an inherent aspect of her identity that she embraces without question, rather than as something that needs refining or hiding."[45] Antisemitism is not part of Midge's life, either onstage or off. From the very first season, she freely identifies herself as Jewish in her act and everyday life, without qualm. Jean Carroll's Jewish identity, both onstage and off, was much more complicated.

Jean Carroll evinced a complex combination of pride and guardedness regarding her Jewish identity. On the one hand, she married a Jewish man and raised her daughter as a Jew; she was active in philanthropy for Jewish causes, and in Jewish circles, she would make bold declarations like, "Long before it became chic to say that you were Jewish, I was a proud Jew" or "I'm so proud to be Jewish, I'd give anything to have my old nose back again!"[46] But in a shocking interview she gave toward the end of her life, a PBS reporter asked Jean Carroll whether being Jewish had influenced her comedy, and she replied, "No. No, nothing. . . . Nothing to do with it because I spent so much time with people who were not Jewish."[47] This disavowal, coupled with her assurance that she did not exclusively associate with other Jewish people, seems to suggest Carroll's anxiety about Jewishness limiting her in the public's eye. It is as if Carroll's ears distorted the reporter's question about Jewish influence into, "How would you like to be remembered as irrelevant to everyone except Jews?"

Counter to what the postassimilationist representation in *Mrs. Maisel* would suggest, Jews in the midcentury United States were in a socially contested place. They did not experience the dire levels of racism and disenfranchisement that Black people and other people of color endured, but they were still subjected to professional and social exclusion, rampant negative stereotyping, and the lurking possibility of violence.[48] Jean Carroll had grown up with children on the playground taunting her with antisemitic slurs, before graduating into a show-business world where Jewishness was mainly used as a punch line.[49] At the height of her career, network executives were giving speeches emphatically discouraging "New York" humor.[50] In every phase of her life, Jean Carroll was exposed to messaging saying that her Jewishness was a liability. It could threaten her ability to connect with her audience, depriving her of the laughter and empathy that were crucial to her success as a stand-up. In other words, it was something to be tamed, mitigated, and otherwise assimilated away.

This conflicted Jewish identity is evident in the ways that Carroll depicted Jewishness in her act. Like many Jewish performers, she changed her name and "bobbed" her nose. She almost never explicitly referenced Jewish holidays or practices onstage. She was far more likely to communicate her ethnicity in coded ways, using Yiddish linguistic structures or invoking (and deflating) well-known stereotypes of Jewish women. Even her meticulousness about her appearance and her intense commitment to embodying "dignified" femininity were connected to proving that a Jew could also be a successfully assimilated, glamorous, capital-*L* Lady. As both Shaina Hammerman and Roberta Mock have established, Jewish women performers often found their Jewish identities being subsumed and overshadowed by their female identities, and Jean Carroll certainly fits this pattern.[51] Throughout her life, she spoke about (and was spoken of as) being a woman far more than being a Jew.

However, some scholars would argue that Carroll's very presence, as a woman at the stand-up microphone, *was* an expression of her identity as a Jewish woman. For instance, in Sarah Blacher Cohen's pivotal essay "The Unkosher Comediennes: From Sophie Tucker to Joan Rivers," she argues that Jewish women who became comedians were reacting against both restrictive gender norms and religious mandates to embody *tzniut* (feminine modesty) and enforce *kashrut* (laws of keeping kosher, keeping clean).[52] Building on Cohen's work, the feminist Jewish studies scholar Joyce Antler observes that Jewish women were particularly well positioned to be comedians, since "their heritage as Jews, especially the Diasporic experience of living between two worlds, gave them a sharp critical edge," while their gender as women resulted in a "specifically female—and often feminist—point of view."[53]

This line of scholarship, positioning Jewish identity as intertwined with comedy, resonates strongly with the way that Jean Carroll's granddaughter Susan Chatzky describes her grandmother's Jewish identity.[54] "I don't think that she necessarily believed that being Jewish brought her any closer to God. . . . I don't know if she believed in God," Chatzky reflected. "Her Jewishness was social, not religious." Chatzky, who grew up largely with Carroll as her caretaker, described Sunday-night dinners at the Friars Club, where, in her perception, "everyone was Jewish." She remembered Passovers where the family rushed through the Haggadah to get to the food, describing their family as "food Jewish."[55] And she knew that her grandmother's long career of performing for and organizing charity benefits was intertwined with her Jewish identity. After Carroll's retirement from show business, she redoubled her efforts in Jewish philanthropy, which for her was inextricable from Zionist fundraising. She even won the Sullivan and Ulster County Israel Bond Committee's "State of Israel Bonds Woman of the Year" award in 1971 for her efforts to raise over \$175,000 for the "economic development of Israel."[56] "She was socially active, which I think she would connect to her Judaism," Chatzky reflected. "To her (and to me), I believe that it is part of a social tradition of Jews to care about their community."[57]

While Miriam Maisel's comedy routines included jokes about everything from Jewish holidays to concentration camps, Jean Carroll's stage persona typically left room for plausible deniability. It may be that for Carroll, years of antisemitism became internalized into the belief that Jewishness would shut her off from other people and was best kept private. However, by bringing together her identity as a Jew and her identity as a comedian, locating Jewishness in comedy and comedy in Jewishness, she was able to take it public.

Methods

While fictions like Miriam Maisel are built largely from the creative genius of artists like Amy Sherman-Palladino and her team, historical figures like Jean Carroll must be cobbled together into a kind of scrapbook story drawn from an eclectic patchwork of resources. The rarest and most significant sources of biographical evidence came from Carroll's friends and family. A combination of "Jewish geography" and Facebook led me to Carroll's granddaughter Susan Chatzky, a friendly upstate New Yorker who bears a striking resemblance to her grandmother. Chatzky had held onto Jean Carroll's personal scrapbook, in which Carroll meticulously saved selected press clippings. Carroll often marked these press clippings by underlining or circling her own name and occasionally scrawling the date in the margins. These recollections provide valuable insight, because of both the clippings themselves and the way that Carroll organized them to tell a larger story.[58] In addition to Chatzky connecting me with her sister, Andrea Ramos, and participating in several in-person conversations about her grandmother, she generously provided me with access to the scrapbook, which I was able to photocopy for further reference.

A Scrapbook Story

Thumbing through the brittle pages of Carroll's scrapbook, I felt invasive. My iPhone snapped photos, turning textured collages into weightless digital data. My academic gaze threatened to transform a family heirloom into something as mundane as research. At one point, when I unfolded a lengthy clipping that had been doubled over, it crumbled in my hand, and I gasped in horror. I imagined Carroll, carefully creasing the newsprint to fit the scrapbook page. I had desecrated the masterpiece she had so carefully prepared for . . . for whom? The scrapbook felt like Carroll extending her hand out through the onslaught of oblivion that comes with time, but who—or what—was she reaching toward?

The film and digital media scholar Amelie Hastie offers some insight on this question. In her study *Cupboards of Curiosity*, Hastie examines (among other texts) dozens of scrapbooks by and about women who worked in the silent-film era. The scrapbooks Hastie perused sound much like Carroll's, even down to the layout, with "multiple columns of stories that begin and end at various levels of the page" and some "folded up within the scrapbook, which creates an even greater sense of disarray."[59] Hastie sees these scrapbooks as curations of the self that allow their authors to reflect on themselves and their field. They are also "affective investments" that signify "a love for oneself, a love for one's past (her family, her memories, her work), and a fear of loss."[60] The author of a scrapbook both expects her artifacts to disappear (or she would have no need to preserve them in the first place) *and* anticipates their rediscovery. So too, Carroll's collection and curation of press clippings suggests that she expected her fame to recede but also that she hoped it would be recovered. Building this archive, this scrapbook, may have been her way to, as Hastie puts it, "transform memories (or acts of re-membering) into histories."[61]

Of course, the relationship between memory and history is fraught. Carroll's acts of remembering are not infallible: her scrapbook is not comprehensive, and the anecdotes she offers in her interviews are sometimes at odds with historical documents. But here, too, Hastie offers reassurance, pointing out that "the fallibility and fictionalizing function of memory" may be a small price to pay for the valuable trans-formation of history.[62] After all, the institutions that have produced "official" histories are no less infallible. Paraphrasing the silent-film star Lillian Gish, Hastie writes that "autobiographical accounts sown from memory might correct historical ones . . . especially in the case of those autobiographical subjects who have been silenced, marginalized, or otherwise misrepresented in official histories."[63] Both as a Jew and as a woman stand-up, Carroll certainly constitutes such a subject. So throughout this book, although I always note the moments in which Carroll's memory seems at odds with historical documents or other scholarly work, these disparities are not intended to discredit or un-dermine her account. Rather, the moments when Carroll takes creative liberties in her story offer crucial glimpses of her vision as a storyteller. They point to values she wants to highlight, circumstances she wants to address, and themes she wants to centralize.

Specifically, Carroll emphasized themes of overcoming hardship, undying devotion to her family, especially her mother (and, later, her daughter), and a naïve comic genius that belied the intense labor that went into getting—and remaining—in the public eye. As the feminist historian Susan Ware notes in *Letter to the World: Seven Women Who Shaped the American Century*, her analysis of the autobiographies of seven women from Jean Carroll's age cohort, "celebrity does not just happen."[64] Like Ware's subjects, Carroll was a dedicated and tireless self-promoter who nonetheless repeatedly deflected agency and claims to worldly ambition.[65] This trend of denying ambition sweeps across time periods in the study of women's autobiographies. Instead of focusing on

the work they did to promote their career, women like First Lady Elea-
nor Roosevelt (in Ware's work) or the silent-film star Colleen Moore (in
Hastie's) authored "star texts," which made their rise to stardom seem
like an effortless, inevitable consequence of natural genius. Or, like
"America's Sweetheart," Mary Pickford, they framed their drive for success as motivated by a need to support their family, often because of an
absent father.[66] These more conventionally "feminine" themes of naïve
genius and familial love allowed successful women telling the story of
their life and work to construct a protagonist that would be acceptable
to their (real and imagined) audience.

Hastie encourages the reader of a scrapbook to attend not just to the
contents of the clippings but also to the larger story woven through their
curation, explaining, "often such items are, in fact, structured as a sort
of historical collage, . . . which demands a reading of their arrangement
as well as of the information offered by them individually."[67] Paying attention to curation, rather than just content, can prompt significant rev-
elations. In Hastie's work, it shows how her subjects used the narrative
structures and cinematic conventions of silent movies in their recollections. For instance, actress Colleen Moore's "Fairy Castle" dollhouse and
collection of miniatures was not meant to be played with like a typical
dollhouse but to be consumed visually and marveled at for its extrava-
gance, much like an early Hollywood film. Similarly, the director Alice
Guy-Blaché's memoirs, which on the surface are a series of unrelated
"anecdotes and personal memories," are more meaningfully read using
Eisenstein's theories of "montage," in which separate units "collide" to
create new forms and ideas.[68] Through the technique of montage, Guy-
Blaché is able to convey a sense of rage and disenfranchisement that she
never articulates. In sum, these female pioneers of cinema echoed the
storytelling structures of their films in their memoirs.

In Carroll's field of stand-up comedy, the dominating structure is the
joke. The most common joke structure establishes expectations (setup)
and then subverts them (punch line). For example, see Carroll's joke,
"I went to see a big throat doctor. Only big throats he saw." The first

sentence establishes the expectation that Carroll went to see a prestigious throat doctor. Then, the second turns on the alternate meaning of "big" to subvert those expectations for a humorous surprise.

This same structure of setting—and then subverting—an expectation is played out in Jean Carroll's scrapbook. The first ninety-five pages consist of documentation of her career: booking information in trade papers and advertisements and reviews in the popular and (rarely) Jewish presses. Then, in an abrupt subversion of expectations, the final thirty pages chart not her work but her family life. It is a notable difference that may not be a punch line, per se, but certainly packs a punch. The comedy routines that Carroll did onstage were famously autobiographical and revolutionarily personal. So the idea that Jean Carroll's scrapbook—her most thorough account of her life and work—echoes joke structure offers an appealing symmetry: not only do her jokes tell a kind of autobiography, but her autobiography tells (kind of) a joke.

Thinking along these lines, it is hard not to wonder if Carroll is "in" on the joke. Did she notice the incongruity between the scrapbook's early clippings, praising her turns at the Palace Theatre and the Copacabana, and the later ones, documenting her daughter's dance recital? Who had the last laugh? The entertainment industry, which fawns and then forgets in the blink of an eye (or the turn of a page)? Or Carroll, who took the spoils of show business and ran, leaving the nameless audience for her beloved family and friends?[69]

The weight of the scrapbook in my arms is a physical reminder of what I owe to Jean Carroll as a subject and collaborator. I want to honor the stories that she is trying to tell. But I also explore the stories that she was not trying to tell but that nonetheless emerge from her collection of clippings and conversations.

* * *

Another treasure trove of Carroll's life and work came from Stephen Meredith Silverman, who had been referenced in Carroll's obituary as the writer/director of the work in progress "I Made It Standing Up," the documentary about Carroll. A well-known Manhattan-based author, Silverman had let go of the documentary after it lost its funding in the economic crash of 2008. He generously agreed to share the hours of footage of interviews with Carroll; her daughter, Helen Tunick; and her high-profile fans like Lily Tomlin, Alan Zweibel, and Jane Wollman Rusoff, as well as the entirety of the 2007 event at the Friars Club honoring Carroll's career.

Of course, a major roadblock to reconstructing Carroll's life is that the live performances that constituted the bulk of her career are gone. What currently remains of Jean Carroll's work is only a fraction of the repertoire she performed in comedy clubs. Carroll's nightclub routines take the ephemerality of live performance to its fullest extent, for unlike plays, they have no scripts, and unlike film or radio, they have no recording. The nightclub forum in which Carroll could be at her most subversive is also the least accessible to contemporary scholars. A live stand-up comedy set is a different animal from a televised set and one that refuses to be domesticated by historical documentation.

An imperfect, but still valuable, resource in this respect is the recordings of Carroll's live appearances. Footage of Carroll's twenty-six appearances on *The Ed Sullivan Show* is fairly difficult to access. The complete archive of *The Ed Sullivan Show* is owned by a private corporation, SOFA Entertainment, which has a policy against sharing its footage. However, it was willing to make an exception for research purposes—for a "modest" fee of fifty dollars per clip. Other available recordings of Carroll performing for a live audience include two clips of Jean Carroll on *The Gary Moore Show* at the Paley Center Media Archive, a rare bootleg recording of Carroll live at the eleventh annual Crystal Ball Dinner in Detroit, Michigan, at the New York Public Library Performing Arts Research Collection, and her record *Girl in a Hot Steam Bath* (1960), released by Columbia Records.

Another imperfect but useful resource in piecing together Carroll's life and work is the reviews, advertisements, features, and other print media artifacts that have been digitized and made available through online archival databases. Sadly, historical periodicals are often dominated by the narrow perspective of white men who were working in journalism and advertising. Still, they offer valuable—if limited—information on how Carroll was advertised, where she performed, and how those performances were received. My method of data collection involved research using three different online archival databases, exploring three distinct types of publications: trade publications, Jewish publications, and mainstream newspapers.[70] After reading each article and advertisement, transcribing each recording and interview, and examining each publicity shot and playbill, I annotated them with notes on recurrent themes and nonverbal performance elements (e.g., costume, tone of voice, physicality) and then coded those notes in an Excel database using three-letter codes.

I recognize that because Carroll's live performances are only available in mediated form, there is some slippage chronologically. For instance, in order to discuss a nightclub act that she did in the 1940s, I might have to refer to the version of it that she performed on *The Ed Sullivan Show* in the 1950s. Each of these instances is clearly acknowledged in the text.

Methodologies

The most common research methodology used in this book is performance analysis of Jean Carroll's television appearances and live recordings. Performance analysis examines both the jokes and commentary as well as embodied elements including tone of voice, gestures and nonverbal communication; costume, production design, and external frames such as venue and audience response. For instance, I chart her negotiation of Jewishness by attending to her changing vocal mannerisms, such as accent and Yiddish linguistic devices. I trace her gender performance through her body language, costume, and makeup choices. And I gauge audience response by noting (and occasionally timing) the audience's laughter and applause.

The archival methodologies of this book owe a great deal to Susan Manning's *Modern Dance, Negro Dance*, in which diverse sources of evidence are read "against gaps in documentation."[71] For instance, comparing Jewish periodicals to trade and mainstream papers revealed that Jewish periodicals were more likely to cover her benefit appearances for Jewish and Zionist organizations than were their mainstream or trade counterparts. This comparison also revealed that Jewish periodicals tended to feature Carroll's life and work less frequently than did mainstream and trade publications. Trade magazines like *Variety* and *Billboard* provided far more insight into the backstage politics surrounding Carroll's casting (or lack thereof) in television sitcoms.

When examining Carroll's scrapbook, I paid special attention to the differences between the press clippings curated by Jean Carroll herself and those that emerged from my own archival and database research. For instance, while the clippings folder from the New York Public Library contained a series of articles detailing Carroll's alleged attack on the model Dorothy McHale, her scrapbook contained nothing about this event.[72] These divergences speak to the way that the scrapbook was, in a way, another one of Carroll's carefully curated performances.

Significance

This book engages with a variety of disciplines, many of which already intersect with one another. Jewish studies is a particularly broad field, encompassing everything from sociological studies on synagogue affiliation to historical studies of race and gender to a small but robust collection of Jewish performance studies. Theater studies is equally capacious, including subjects ranging from the history of stand-up comedy to the role of the audience in theater for social change. And the relatively new field of comedy studies transverses comic media to examine the mechanics and social import of comedy.

This book makes two main contributions to these overlapping fields. In the field of Jewish studies, it offers a new way to read Jewishness in performance. While scholars including Julius Novick, Harley Erdman, and Heather Nathans have explored theater about Jewish characters and subjects on the American stage, and Henry Bial and Andrea Most have examined subtle, "coded" performances of American Jewishness on-stage and on-screen, this volume examines the performance of Jewish-ness in a new way: by attending to the outer frames of the performance, such as its venue and financial beneficiaries.[73] For instance, although a musical revue featuring the Rockettes, Frank Sinatra, and Desi Arnez may not intuitively be considered Jewish American performance, the musical revue featuring the Rockettes, Frank Sinatra, and Desi Arnez that took place in 1949 to raise money for the Actor's Temple Synagogue could be.[74]

Similarly, even discounting Carroll's frequent but coded references to her Jewish identity, she could be considered active in Jewish Ameri-can performance by virtue of her frequent public appearances to benefit Jewish causes and organizations. Like many other Jewish entertainers of the post–World War II era, Jean Carroll did not distinguish between domestic Jewish philanthropic organizations and money raised to support the new State of Israel, and she was extremely active on both fronts. Jewish American celebrities like Carroll and her colleagues such as Eddie Cantor, Georgie Jessel, and Molly Picon raised large sums of money by performing at charitable benefits and lending their celebrity to fundraisers. My intervention offers another way to read Jewishness in performance: as a cause to champion, not a character to inhabit. Rather than look exclusively at Jewish content—or even for codes of Jewishness like dialects, behaviors, and mannerisms—scholars can turn to other frames of performance, including the venue and financial ben-eficiaries, to look for signs of Jewish identity.

But, like Carroll, this book also aims to expand popular notions of the kind of femininity that is legible as "Jewish." The marginalization of Jewish identity into "parenthetical Jewishness" when considering female comedians is a problem that Shaina Hammerman explores at length in her study of the contemporary comedian Amy Schumer, noting that "gender and sexuality keeps trumping Jewishness for women."[75] Roberta Mock's study *Jewish Women on Stage, Film, and Television* shows that this problem can be traced as far back as the mid-seventeenth century with Jewish actresses like Rachel Felix.[76] And so, too, in the midcentury United States, women in comedy were made to choose between being read as Jewish and being read as attractive and feminine. Those who were successfully read as Jewish, like Totie Fields or Sophie Tucker, were not considered conventionally attractive women. Those Jewish female entertainers who did "pass" into the realm of the attractive, such as Judy Holiday or Dinah Shore (both of whom were more actresses than comedians), were often discounted as contributing to Jewish representation. Jean Carroll, I argue, should not be dismissed as part of the canon of Jewish comedy. Rather, the category of "Jewish comedian" must be capacious enough to accommodate even this feminine, glamorous, double-coded version of Jewishness.

Perhaps the more pressing intervention of this volume is in the still-emerging field of comedy studies. Within the past ten years, this still-nascent field has seen the emergence of the Comedic Arts majors at Emerson College and DePaul University, Comedy Studies majors at Columbia College, and the Comedy program at the School of Cinematic Arts at the University of Southern California. However, before comedy studies becomes a standard department of study within universities, it demands some major adjustments to the canon, which currently has an overwhelming bias toward white, male stand-up comedians. This work has been taken up with skill and passion in recent monographs such as Beck Krefting's *All Joking Aside: American Humor and Its Discontents* and Katelyn Hale Wood's *Cracking Up: Black Feminist Comedy in the Twentieth and Twenty-First Century United States*, theoretical texts like Cynthia and Julie Willett's *Uproarious: How Feminists and Other Subversive Comics Speak Truth*, and collections like Linda Mizejewski and Victoria Sturtevant's *Hysterical: Women in American Comedy*, all of which reclaim the place of women and people of color in the history of stand-up. In the tradition of these contemporary female scholars, this text intervenes against the false portrait of stand-up comedy as a genre dominated by men and also therefore as aggressive, dominating, and inherently masculine. This volume, showing that a member of the very first cohort of stand-up comics was a woman, takes important steps toward removing the unjustly gendered perception and study of stand-up comedy. Just as Jean Carroll "pushed her way" to the stand-up microphone, this book must push its way into the masculine historiography of stand-up comedy, to contribute a new archive, new history, and new perspective.

Chapter Overviews

Overall, I argue in this book that Jean Carroll, the first Jewish woman stand-up comedian, made enduring changes to the genre of stand-up comedy by carving space for women, innovating a newly conversational, gossipy style of delivery, and modeling a new form of Jewish femininity with her glamorous, assimilated, but still legibly (to some people) Jewish persona. Moreover, her four-decade career, which spans a wide variety of comic media, provides important insight into the shifting modes of comedy circulation in the United States. Therefore, the book is generally organized chronologically, separated into chapters focused on the dominant medium of comedy circulation. Like the genre of stand-up comedy, the book begins with vaudeville, then moves into presenting houses and radio. It then shifts to comedy clubs, "party" records, and television variety programs like *The Ed Sullivan Show* and next moves into half-hour television sitcoms. In each of these media, Carroll made her mark and illuminated the changing negotiations of Jewish femininity—to varying levels of critical success.

Chapter 1 tells the story of the transformation from the Jewish immigrant Sadie Zeigman to the solo star Jean Carroll, against the backdrop of larger histories of immigration, show business, and American Jewry. Close readings of Carroll's carefully curated personal scrapbook, interviews, and reviews of her early work coalesce to create both an important historical archive and a compelling rags-to-riches tale. Like many Jewish immigrants in the early 1900s, Carroll came to the United States from eastern Europe (by way of Paris) and grew up in Brooklyn, New York. Her father was an abusive alcoholic, and so by the age of eight, Carroll was determined to rid her family of this dangerous patriarch. She began performing in amateur talent shows to win prize money to support her family. This impulse to protect her family launched Carroll into a career in vaudeville, where stand-up comedy was born. Moving from amateur talent shows to touring musical revues to husband/wife double acts to USO tours and finally to stand-up, Carroll's own performance history mirrors major trends in vaudeville comedy.

Chapter 2 examines the last days of vaudeville, as stand-up comedy was raised by a cohort that *Variety* termed the "Younger Fraternity," with Carroll as "the one and only lady monologist."[77] In her early work, Jean Carroll set out to prove that she could hold her own. This chapter examines one of her first stand-up successes, the "racetrack" routine, in which Carroll took on the "male sphere" of playing the ponies with an insider's savvy (it helped that she was an avid gambler at the tracks). As she toured around the country, from the Borscht Belt to the presentation houses, critics praised her skill but always kept her at arm's length from the stand-up genre she was helping to pioneer.

Chapter 3 charts the boom in nightclubs and how the changing venues altered Carroll's work and the overall genre of stand-up comedy. This portion of the book uses performance analysis of Carroll's nightclub acts to explore how she responded to prevailing negative attitudes toward women and even used them to her advantage. Taking on the stereotypes about materialism, she wrote a series of routines about shopping for everything from dresses and furs to apartments and décor. However, she revised and humanized the stereotype of the consuming Jewess, leveraging her conventionally attractive face and figure to disrupt images of Jewish women as vulgar, homely, and unappealing. Her comic persona demonstrated that Jewish femininity *was* compatible with sophistication and even glamour. Also, she addressed the audience with the distinctively intimate tone that I call *confidant comedy*. Unlike the presentational "setup, punch!" delivery that characterized so many of her contemporaries, Carroll used a more anecdotal, gossipy form of storytelling humor. This cozy, confidential approach to stand-up bonded Carroll with her audience, turning her from a stereotype into a friend— and comedy legend.

Chapter 4 zeroes in on comedy's midcentury shift to television sitcoms—a turn that proved harrowing for Carroll's career. It analyzes the unearthed scripts of *Take It from Me*, Jean Carroll's short-lived ABC sitcom, delineating how the show undermined the persona she had worked so hard to craft in her stand-up comedy. While Carroll's stand-up persona was a well-dressed, upwardly mobile lady with a touch of glamour, her sitcom character was a lower-middle-class housewife beset by endless household drudgery and a miserly, gluttonous husband. Reception analysis in trade publications shows a decidedly lukewarm response. These tepid-to-scathing reviews reveal that the television show failed to establish the same bond between Carroll and her audience that her stand-up had so easily formed. This chapter raises questions about the show's brief run, asking to what extent the show's unspoken but coded Jewishness and embattled backstage culture contributed to its demise.

Chapter 5 follows Carroll's comeback. Rather than dwell on her lost sitcom, Carroll spent the rest of the 1950s and 1960s embracing other popular forms of comedy media: televised variety shows and comedy albums, sometimes known as "party records." For many Jewish comedians, the national reach of these platforms meant that they were representing Jewishness to a much larger population. They faced the danger of alienating audience members if they appeared "too ethnic." As Carroll made the shift into national television and records, she was careful to modulate her performance of Jewishness in response to broader national attitudes toward Jews. This chapter argues that Carroll's mainstream performances are a reflection of the complex negotiation of assimilation and difference that American Jews were enacting after World War II.

Chapter 6 examines Carroll's onstage representations of parenthood in her "rotten kid" routines, her offstage relationship with her daughter, and her efforts to reconcile the two. Carroll's publicity clippings are haunted, brief but painful references to the conflicts between her roles as mother and celebrity comedian. Carroll even attempted to get her daughter, Helen, cast to play her daughter in a new sitcom for Associated Television. The project did not go forward and signaled the end of Carroll's career. After she retired, Carroll devoted herself to Helen, as well as to Helen's two daughters. Her scrapbook—once a meticulously annotated document archiving publicity shots and reviews—morphed into a collection of family mementos, like a photo of her granddaughter smiling alongside a horse. Carroll's caretaking role in her retirement may seem anticlimactic or insignificant compared to her time as a headlining celebrity stand-up, but it highlights obstacles to balancing comedy and caretaking that continue to dominate the comedy industry.

The conclusion examines Carroll's legacy through the work of contemporary women stand-up comedians. While Jean Carroll's comic intervention expanded Jewish femininity to encompass white upper-middle-class status, today's Jewish female stand-ups are working to expand that identity still further, destabilizing Ashkenormative and heteronormative limitations.[78]

1

"You're Jean Carroll"

From Immigrant Daughter to American Vaudevillian

In a grand mansion in Westchester County, thirty miles north of New York City, Jean Carroll's granddaughter kept an old scrapbook bound in green leather. Its pages were yellowed with time, but the marginalia and order revealed a meticulously organized creator. Clippings of reviews of vaudeville lineups often had the words "Jean Carroll" underlined, as if urging the reader to disregard descriptions of less important acts on the bill. In later pages of the scrapbook, reviews and performance ephemera gave way to family documents: a program from a daughter's dance recital, a newsletter featuring a picture of a smiling granddaughter with a horse, a note from a neighbor thanking Ms. Carroll for her letter of recommendation. The collection told a jumbled story without a clear chronology or commentary but with traces of curation that revealed the scrapbooker's hand.

Meanwhile, in a posh apartment in the Financial District of New York City sat more than six hours of footage of interviews with Jean Carroll, her family, and her friends. Stephen Silverman, the pop culture historian and former entertainment correspondent for the *New York Post*, showed me the trailer to his erstwhile documentary film "I Made It Standing Up," while his Havanese-Schnauzer Kingston ran around the living room. With these interviews, Silverman and the crew attempted to fill in some of the scrapbook's holes. Each subject—a daughter, a friend, a protégé—offered a different perspective, but none was more striking than those offered by Carroll herself. A masterful raconteur, Carroll wove tales of growing up in the hardscrabble Bronx of the early decades of the twentieth century, the immigrant child making her way up the show-business ladder, kicking her abusive father out of the house and providing for her beloved family, and becoming an unrivaled star comedienne.

Taken together, the interviews with Jean Carroll and her personal scrapbook offer a vivid account of a turbulent period of US history, one that witnessed large-scale immigration, a world war, and major shifts in the media. But this material also offers a kind of memoir by a consummate storyteller. The footage had been collected for "I Made It Standing Up," a documentary film intended for mainstream audiences. And so Carroll used all of the dramatic skills at her disposal to craft a rags-to-riches story that would entertain her audience. Although the documentary was never produced, due of a loss of funding, the interviews and material gathered for the project constitute both a robust archive and a creative performance.

Coming to America

Jean Carroll, or, as she was known in her youth, Celine Zeigman, was part of what is often known as the Third Wave of Jewish immigration to the United States, which consisted mainly of eastern European Jews who arrived during the late nineteenth and early twentieth centuries, many of whom were driven from their homes by violent pogroms. Carroll, her parents, and her sisters were among the two and a half million Ashkenazy Jews, mostly from Russia, Romania, and Austria-Hungary, who flooded the United States between 1880 and 1924.

Not a great deal is known about the family's early lives. Carroll's mother, Anna, was a devoutly religious Russo-Polish Jew who had been orphaned at birth. Her father, Max, had been a soldier in the Russian army. Both had survived pogroms, famines, and Czar Nicholas II's brutal antisemitic policies before deciding to emigrate.

However, the young couple faced another obstacle when Max deserted his post with the Russian army and was jailed in Paris. "I always thought he was a war hero," Carroll said in an interview with Stephen

Silverman. "I found out years later that he was a deserter from the army, and they caught up with him and they put him in jail. Oh, so much for my heroic father!"[1] In Paris, Anna gave birth to three girls: Rachel in 1907, Mary in 1909, and, on January 7, 1911, Celine, quickly nicknamed Sadie.

Carroll's father was not there to witness her birth. By 1910, Max Zeigman had arrived in the United States and settled in New York, intent on finding a job and earning money so he could send for his wife and children. Carroll's account of her father's immigration was cursory: "I guess he served his time. Went to America. Got a job. He was a baker. . . . We stayed until my father sent for us."[2]

About two years later, Anna Zeigman, answering her husband's summons, set out from the port of Le Havre in Cherbourg, France, with her three young daughters. Carroll recalls her mother confessing that there were many times aboard the ship when she was so nauseated that she contemplated drowning herself and her children. Finally, on July 20, 1912, after weeks at sea, the SS *Philadelphia* arrived at Ellis Island.

The young family soon included two more children, Will, born in 1916, and George, born in 1920. They followed Max Zeigman's employment, hopscotching from place to place during their first few years in the US. "In those days," Carroll recalled, "wherever there was a job is where the family lived."[3] The moves were facilitated by special promotions from landlords offering the first two months' rent free.[4]

Like many immigrant families of the day, the Zeigmans moved around a lot. Their first home was in Harlem, at the time a mixed-race community. They then moved to Englewood, New Jersey, and then New Britain, Connecticut, where, Carroll said, she "really grew up." It was there that she stopped using Yiddish as her primary language and, as she put it, "learned to speak English properly," although she and her mother continued speaking Yiddish privately throughout their lives.[5]

In 1920, when Jean was eight and a half years old, the family moved back to New York, settling in the Bronx.[6] For the most part, she had positive associations with her time there. "It was a happy time," she recalled, adding, "Nobody was afraid to be outdoors. When it was hot, we didn't have air conditioning. We had Crotona Park."[7] However, she also spoke of the prejudice she encountered. "That's where I learned about antisemitism," she said. "I couldn't understand it."[8]

Antisemitism was hardly unknown when Jean Carroll came of age in the 1920s. The United States had seen a large influx of Jews, many of whom settled in the South Bronx, where Carroll's family lived.[9] And with this surge of immigrants came nationwide backlash, notably in the form of the Johnson-Reed Act of 1924, which limited immigration from southern and eastern Europe.[10]

Jews were only one of many immigrant groups affected by the anti-immigration legislation and sentiment of this period. However, as Russian-Jewish immigrants, Carroll's family may have faced a particular hostility. The years from 1917 to 1920s were the era of a Red Scare, in which Jews were the favored targets.[11] In *The Jewish Americans: Three Centuries of Jewish Voices in America*, the Jewish American historian Beth S. Wenger notes that "in the wake of the Bolshevik Revolution, and given the overrepresentation of Jews in leftist politics, the KKK and other hate groups portrayed Jews as dangerous radicals."[12] Perhaps understandably, even later in her life, Carroll preferred not to describe herself as Russian American, noting instead her technical birthplace, Paris, France.

Mama's Girl

Although Carroll's father's work determined where the family lived, it was clearly her mother, Anna, who was the more animating force in her life. When speaking of her mother, Carroll revealed a fierce affection and loyalty. "I adored my mother," she often said. "I loved her with such an overwhelming love that it's impossible to describe to anybody." Carroll often spoke with a romantic quality of her mother's Old World ways, reminiscing about nights when she was allowed to "sit quietly and listen" to Anna and her friends in their tenement apartment. "They weren't educated," she said of these women. "They weren't literate. They weren't well read. But they had such wisdom. Life had taught them such lessons."[13]

It was to her mother that Carroll attributed her earliest experience at mimicry. "I wanted to give this wonderful person a reason to smile," she explained. "When I'd imitate the old ladies, she'd say, 'You shouldn't make fun of other people.' Then she'd crack up and tell all the neighbors."[14]

Anna was her daughter's first and most important audience. In an unreleased 2007 interview with the Public Broadcasting Service, Carroll shared another story about how she fell in love with entertaining others, one that also centered around making her mother laugh. "Friday night, my mother made Shabbos, with the beautiful white tablecloth and the candles, and all the members of my family seated around the table," she said. "The minute my mother would light the candles, it was as though a spotlight suddenly was on me and I became the clown." Carroll crafts a poignant image of herself as both Mama's girl and star-to-be: her mother's Shabbos candles her first spotlight, her mother's breathless cries of "Der naar shtupt dir!" her first ovation.[15]

But the most potent example of Carroll's love for her mother is her assumption of the role of protector against her father's emotional and physical abuse. "My father was . . . he was a baker, but he was also a drunk," she recounted. "[He] worked nights and came home in the morning. We lived in a two-family house in New Britain, with a separate staircase. When he came home in the morning, that was his big meal." She continued,

> My mother was a wonderful cook. And she had put down the dinner for my father. I looked up in time to see my father take this boiling hot food and fling it at my mother, who was standing up against the back wall cowering like some trapped animal. And I sat there and watched her. And he did it more than one time. And I thought, "Oh God, I gotta stop him. I gotta stop him. What can I do to save my mother?"

And there in those few minutes of horror . . . I realized that the only reason my mother was trapped in that horrendous situation . . . well, she had no place to go. She had three children and herself . . . to feed and to clothe, and to try and bring them through life. And I made up my mind. I was only eight years old, but I made up my mind at that moment that never, ever ever in my life would I be beholden . . . to a man . . . or a woman, but mostly to a man. NEVER would I be subjected and accept what he was doing to my mother.[16]

Carroll's description of this event captures her perception of the power dynamics at work in many Jewish immigrant families. As she explained to the journalist and friend Jane Wollman Rusoff, "In a Jewish family, if you brought home the pay, you ruled supreme."[17]

This linking of Jewish family culture and financial power exemplifies how the eastern European Jewish background of Carroll's family was at odds with US gender roles. In *Gender and the Shaping of Modern Jewish Identities*, the social historian and Jewish feminist scholar Paula Hyman argues that Jews from eastern Europe were accustomed to a system of gender roles in which the ideal husband was a scholar and the wife was in the marketplace.[18] Women were accepted as economic agents and major decision-makers. However, in the United States, men were regarded as heads of the household and women as subordinate, even if women were the ones who provided for the family. In Riv-Ellen Prell's seminal study *Fighting to Become Americans*, the cultural anthropologist found that daughters in Jewish families commonly produced an average of 40 percent of the family's yearly earnings, but their financial contribution was not rewarded with commensurate power.[19] So too, in Carroll's family. Regardless of her role as a breadwinner, it was her father's name listed in census reports as the head of the household.

Nonetheless, Carroll thought that she could protect her mother if she was financially independent. "I realized it was all economical," she once said. "I was only eight years old. But at the finish of that episode, I was no longer eight. . . . I was an old woman. Old in my thoughts. . . . I knew I had to grow up quickly, quickly, quickly. Grow up. Get a job. Take care of your mother. Take her out of this."[20]

And so Carroll pushed herself to graduate from school early, zooming through grades due to a policy called "Rapid Advancement."[21] She was ten and a half years old when she finished eighth grade at PS 55 in 1922, the same year she launched the show-business career that would soon bring her economic autonomy.

A "Natural" Entertainer

Jean Carroll's account of her first big break in show business reinforces her image as an indomitable, if naïve, genius. After being mocked by her oldest sister, Mary, for being too "yellow" to audition for their school's production of *Peter Pan*, Carroll allegedly snapped, "Oh, don't say that to me. I'm not yellow. . . . I'll take your dare." As her story goes, she appeared at the audition, dowdy in her "standard dress for school" alongside "all these pretty little girls in their pretty little dresses."[22] But by the end of the audition, the dramatic coach, Miss Dawson, had proclaimed her "a genius."[23] In a separate telling, Carroll embroidered the event with her naïve response, "I don't even know what 'genius' means!"[24] "That started it all," Carroll said. "The lead in the play. . . . Scholarships. Helen Muller School of [Interpretive] Dancing. The Perkins School of National Speech. . . . Dramatic training that would have cost a fortune, but [Dawson] gladly gave it."[25]

That same mixture of talent and fearlessness characterized the story that Carroll told to explain her first foray into performance, in which she won an amateur talent competition for children. Amateur talent shows preceding silent films in local movie theaters were a common form of entertainment, a good way for ethnically diverse metropolitan communities to offer local talent "a moment in the limelight."[26] According to Carroll, school friends told her about one of these shows, held at the local Crotona Theater. As she described her performance,

For my big debut in show business, for the amateur contest, I did the Italian laborer who comes home and finds his little girl—dead. I put on mascara. And I'm doing this recitation. I'm down on my knees, and I'm holding the Rosa, my little girl, in my arms, and I'm saying (FAKE AC-CENT) "Who killed my little Rosa? Who killed my little Rosa?" I started crying, and the black mascara and the tears are running into my eyes—I'm rubbing my face.

And the guy in the front row stands up and he says, "I did! What are you going to do about it?" So I rubbed off this smudgy black gook from my eyes and my face, and I go down to the footlights, and I look down, I said, "Ah! I know you! You used to take my sister to the movies, and she dumped you." So, of course, the audience laughed. They thought it was part of a gag.

I go back. I get back down on my knees, finish the thing. And now, I have an encore, and someone in the galley howls, "No! Oh no, oh no! You stink!" I said, "Nevertheless, I have an encore!" So of course, the audience is laughing. This is when the first sweet sound of laughter came into my ears. And I was only saying what I thought. I wasn't saying it to be funny. I was saying it because it was so.[27]

Whether or not Carroll's story is an accurate account of the event or an exaggerated version is less significant than what is revealed by her storytelling choices, which suggest a desire to depict herself as both an empowered performer and a naïve vessel of comic genius. By choosing a tale of overcoming a heckler as her entrée to show business, Carroll presented herself as an underdog whose fierce determination and pluck won over her audience. However, by explaining that her jokes were both improvised and unintentional, said not "to be funny" but "because it was so," she emphasized the spontaneous quality of her humor.

The emphasis on spontaneity and natural genius that characterized Carroll's "origin story" would continue throughout her career. Describing her early performances, Carroll said, "I'd tell the band, 'Wait! Wait! I've got something to tell the people.' And I'd walk down to the footlights [and begin] saying what I was thinking."[28] Again, she discusses her comedy as a kind of unfiltered honesty—or "saying what I was thinking"—rather than putting it in terms of technique or craft.

This element of spontaneity would become a defining characteristic of stand-up comedy and solo performance. The comedy theorist and author of *Stand-Up Comedy in Theory* John Limon, for example, describes the stand-up condition as a space in between nature and artifice, explaining, "They are neither acting nor conversing, neither in nor out of costume."[29] A stand-up comic—unlike an actor in a traditional play—does not have to inhabit a "character" whose name and circumstances differ extensively from their own. This proximity between the stand-up comedian and their stage persona can create the illusion that the comic is fully "authentic," simply bringing themselves to the stage and spontaneously reacting to the audience. It is a pleasurable illusion, for it suggests a direct and intimate connection between the audience and the comic. However, this illusion also obscures the craftsmanship that goes into cultivating and maintaining the persona. Interacting with an audience is a different skill from interacting with an individual, and so Carroll's crowd work required a more technical expertise than simple conversation. To put it in Limon's terms, she may not have been in a costume, but she also was not out of costume.

As Carroll concluded the description of her first foray into the world of amateur talent contests, the portrait of a naïve genius child gave way to emphasize a fierce and empowered advocate:

They line you up, and they say, "And the winner is," and they hold a hand up over you. Whoever gets the most applause wins. Well, it came to me, and I got the most applause. So, the announcer said, "Sadie Zigman [*sic*] is the winner!" Okay. Come off stage, and my eyes are burning like crazy. And I went over to the announcer. . . . He was the one in charge of this. And I said, "Where's my money?" He said, "What are you talking about?" I said, "I want my money. I won. You said so." He said, "Oh, you're not from the office?" I said, "No. I'm not from an office, I'm from P.S. 55. And I want my money." He said "You don't understand."

Then I found out that really out of maybe eight contestants, only myself and one other person were really amateurs who had submitted their names. The rest was all professional people. . . . It was a business!

I said, "If you don't give me my five dollars, I'm going out on that stage and tell the audience that this is a fake!" He said, "You wouldn't." And he didn't give me my five. The movie was on. I didn't care. I walked right out on the stage right in front of the movie screen. I said, "Ladies—aaaaah!" I got the hook.[30]

He said, "You were telling them!" I said, "I told you I would tell them. I don't say anything I don't mean." He gives me five bucks. I said, "I'm still going to tell them." He said, "Well, if I let you do every night, will you promise not to tell?" I said, "How much can I get?" He said, "Well, it's five, three and two. And there's a two-dollar guarantee." I said, "I'll take it."[31]

This (probably embellished) tale describes an amusing anecdote that is also a reminder of Carroll's precocious yet hard-nosed business sensibility, part of her continuing mission to protect her mother and wrest familial control from her abusive father.

The financial autonomy that Carroll gained through the amateur-show racket also came with an increased level of assimilation. In her account of how she got her stage name, it is clear that the specter of anti-Jewish sentiment was never entirely absent from her career. She described one of her childhood talent competitions thus: "The announcer says, 'What is your name, little girl?' I said, 'Sadie Zeigman.' He said, 'Oh no—all the German Bunds are right here, 86 Street and Yorkville, they'll kill you.' He said, 'You're Jean Carroll.' I said, 'I am?' 'Yeah, you're Jean Carroll.' 'Okay.'"[32] While the earlier story shows Carroll rejecting the announcer's refusal to pay her, the latter shows her amenably agreeing to his refusal to introduce her by her real name. She was willing to defy an authority figure to keep her paycheck but not to keep her name. Even as a child, Carroll knew there were social and material advantages to "passing" as non-Jewish.

The story of Carroll's career placed her family, particularly her mother, at the center. In her early days doing amateur shows, she recalled, "Night after night, I'd come home and my mother . . . she'd wait up for me."[33] At one of these shows, a talent scout named Joe Wilton from the powerful Shubert Organization saw Carroll perform, and he and his wife came to her house in the Bronx to add her to their roster. In Carroll's telling, the anecdote centers around her mother: "He spoke to my mother and said he had seen me in the amateur shows, thought I was very talented, and would she be interested in having them, more or less, take me under their wing? I was still going to school. He said they would treat me as their own daughter, they would see that I didn't make any wrong associations, and they would train me. . . . Oddly enough, my Mom agreed to let me go, which floored me because there was nothing more important to my mother than my education."[34]

In another interview, Carroll revealed that Wilton's show-business niche was burlesque, and Carroll would be performing in a show called *Joe Wilton's Girlie Review*. However, she would be receiving "thirty-five dollars a week," which to her mother "was a lot of money."[35]

But Carroll's burlesque career was short-lived. "I was homesick," she explained. "I had never been away from home before. So that only lasted three or four months."[36] She returned home, where she hit a different kind of milestone. Her school, Walton High, had a job-placement program that employed her in a real estate office off East Tremont Avenue, where she made the remarkable wage of ten dollars a week. Her family's rent was only about eight dollars a month, so this income meant one thing to Carroll: "I was finally reaching a point where I could get my mother out of her entrapped situation with my father."[37]

In Carroll's account, by 1922, her father came and went as he pleased, until she put her foot down. As she described that moment, "He came and he said [to my mother], "You're looking too good— and you're having too good a time. I think I'll move back in." And I said, "No, you won't. You're not moving into this house. Not ever again."[38] This story seems unlikely, especially given the great number of absentee fathers in immigrant communities of this period. The American Jewish historian Pam Nadell's history *America's Jewish Women* points to the National Desertion Bureau, an organization founded by Jewish communal leaders, which testified to more than twelve thousand cases of desertion by 1922.[39] Yiddish newspapers like *Der Forverts* published names and photographs in a grim "Gallery of Missing Husbands." These men abandoned their families for myriad reasons, but as Nadell succinctly puts it, "divorce cost money," while desertion was free.[40]

This historical perspective offers a slightly different explanation for Carroll supporting her family. It may have been less about deciding to conquer an abusive predator than about compensating for yet another in a long list of absent fathers. In US census data, Max Zeigman was listed as the head of his household until his death. But Carroll's account of the episode makes it clear that for whatever reason, her father was not paying the bills. Moreover, her decision to present herself as a heroine forcing out a villain, rather than a victim abandoned by her father, helps paint a portrait of a person whose life was always defined by the desire for independence. "I went from age 11 to age 40," Carroll once reflected. "I really never was a child."[41]

Comedy in the Variety Theater

The same year that Carroll allegedly banished her father from the family home, she was also beginning her career in variety theater. Vaudeville and variety theater, a nationwide network of theaters that presented family-friendly shows, was the primary form of entertainment in the United States from the mid-1890s until the early 1930s.[42] Although acts varied dramatically, ranging from animal tricks to dancing duos, they differed from burlesque by eschewing vulgar language and overtly sexual humor.[43] Yet despite the restrictions, variety theater gave women considerably more than the legitimate stage in the way of creative freedom and financial control.[44]

Carroll's variety career began in 1922, when she appeared in a touring musical revue called *Midnight Rounders*, which opened at the Shubert-Crescent in Brooklyn.[45] One review described the show as "a flash act . . . chockful of meaty entertainment, comedy, clever people, pretty girls and snappy action."[46] The act had previously toured starring the famed comedian Eddie Cantor, the review noted, and was "somewhat condensed for Vaudeville usage."[47]

It seems that Carroll joined after Cantor's departure, as the show was being reworked for its tour on the Shubert circuit. Garbed in "black net skirts and silver bodice," the young Carroll performed in a "brief dancing interlude" and a "fast little stepping bit."[48] As most of the reviews noted, it was male performers doing comedy sketches and monologues, while female performers appeared in musical and dance numbers.[49]

In Carroll's first major exposure to show business, she was cast as a dancer and singer, while the lion's share of the "talking acts" and monologues were given to men. The underlying message of this casting suggests that men will speak and be funny—while women will sing and dance and be spectacular. This division, taken for granted at the time, was noted in an article in the *Jewish Criterion*, which contrasted men in the act, like "clever Jewish comedian" Jack Strouse, with the female "collection of beautiful and blushing buds selected personally by Messrs. Shubert from the New York Winter Garden."[50] Yet Carroll's time as a "beautiful and blushing bud" served as her education in the basic mechanics of comedy. The elements of comic performance that critics highlighted, such as comic monologues and "impromptu manner and ad-libbing" the "comedy along Yiddish lines," would profoundly shape Carroll's later work.[51]

"Comedy along Yiddish Lines": "Jew Comics" on the Vaudeville Stage

To understand the trajectory of a young Jewish performer like Jean Carroll, it is necessary to understand the stereotypes of Jews that were circulating on and off the variety stage at the time she was learning the ropes of show business. The vaudeville stage that made Carroll a star had long been a place where ethnic stereotypes were profitable comedy acts. As the historian Michael Rogin noted in *Blackface, White Noise*, blackface minstrelsy, the practice of covering one's face with burnt cork and affecting a cartoonish imitation of an African American, had been both precursor to and mainstay of vaudeville, serving as "the first and most popular form of mass culture in the nineteenth century United States." Rogin traces the influence of blackface minstrelsy through the twentieth century, observing, "Blackface . . . presided over melting pot culture in the period of mass European immigration. While blackface was hardly the only distinctively American cultural form, . . . it was a dominant practice, and it infected others."[52]

The theater historian Barbara Wallace Grossman explains some of this spread of "infection," writing of the proliferation of ethnic humor from blackface minstrelsy to other ethnic types: "During the nineteenth century, when vast numbers of immigrants flocked to the United States, the country's population exploded as 'potatoes, politics, and pogroms' created millions of new Americans. . . . Comedians in vaudeville and burlesque were quick to transform the traits of the new Americans into readily identifiable types. Irish and German (or Dutch) comics soon became stage favorites. The 'Jew comics' appeared later because the great mass of Jewish immigrants did not arrive until the 1880s."[53]

By the turn of the twentieth century, there was a wide variety of "Jew comics." In *World of Our Fathers*, the Jewish historian Irving Howe found "literally hundreds of Jewish acts listed in the weekly trade papers."[54] Some of these "Jewish acts" were probably performing blackface minstrelsy, because the early twentieth century was also the period when Jewish entertainers superseded Irish as the major blackface performers.[55] Rogin argues that this was a strategic move on the part of Jewish performers, for blackface minstrelsy helped Jewish immigrants facing "nativist pressures" to Americanize themselves "by differentiating them from the black Americans through whom they spoke."[56] As

Americans grappled with who was granted the privileges of citizenry, much of the Jewish assimilation, both onstage and off, came by Jews defining themselves as "not Black." Yet the repertoire of comic tools that "Jew comics" deployed drew heavily on those used by their blackface minstrel antecedents and colleagues. And one of these tools was the use of an exaggerated Yiddish dialect.

While blackface minstrelsy was characterized by southern-inflected pidgin English, early Jewish American comedy was characterized by an eastern-European-inflected Yiddish dialect. The vaudeville legend George Burns recalls the dialect comic Lou Holtz, whose "classy Jewish accent" made him the first comedian to book the Palace for ten consecutive weeks, at $6,000 a week.[57] The popular culture author Joseph Dorinson also describes how dialect humor was used in vaudeville by such Jewish celebrities as Eddie Cantor, Fanny Brice, and the duo Weber and Fields. Before Cantor started his film career, he made a splash in vaudeville by interspersing his act with "Yiddish words and Russian phrases, . . . anything for a laugh."[58] Fanny Brice had her first hit with Irving Berlin's heavily accented song "Sadie Salome, Go Home!," which jump-started a series of Yiddish-inflected musical parodies in the early 1900s. Joseph Weber and Lew Fields were also known for their dialect humor, as in the following bit:

FIELDS: Vot are you doing?
WEVER: Voiking in a nut factory.
FIELDS: Doing vot?
WEVER: Nutting.
FIELDS: I know, but vot voik are you doing?
WEVER: Nutting, I tole you.[59]

The wordplay-driven misunderstanding presages the "Who's on First" sketch used by Abbott and Costello in the late 1930s. But as the comedy scholar Lawrence Mintz points out in his work on humor and ethnic stereotypes in vaudeville and burlesque, the wordplay and dialect humor also functions as a "reference to problems of language acquisition, a serious matter for immigrants, who realize constantly that understanding and misunderstanding vocabulary and pronunciation can be crucially important."[60] Jewish comedians using dialect humor were both opening themselves to mockery and expressing their frustration at a situation that made communication and comprehension a daily struggle.

A Budding Comic on the Road

By the time Carroll was a teenager, her assorted incomes made her a breadwinner for her mother and four siblings. In addition to taking a leadership role in the family finances through her work on the variety stage, she continued her studies so that she could graduate and then work full-time. In 1925, the fourteen-year-old high school graduate was eager to begin touring.[61] However, according to Carroll, she felt tremendous pressure to marry. "In those days, the Jewish girl, . . . you had to be married when you were fourteen or fifteen or sixteen at the most," she said. "I was not interested in anything like that."[62]

However, this statement recalls Carroll's tendency to exaggerate the truth for the sake of the audience. It is unlikely that girls of the era were expected to be married by age sixteen. Even judging by memoirs of other Jewish immigrant girls at the turn of the century, ages fourteen to sixteen were still considered young for marriage. Rather than seek a mate, Carroll spent her teenage years on the road, learning to become not only a performer but also a fierce advocate and leader. By 1927, she had left *Midnight Rounders* and was part of a dance act that featured the dancer Pearl Saxon and two men.[63] She also served as the act's manager, because, as she explained, "I could talk longer." But Carroll took her role as leader seriously. "Since they appointed me manager," she said, "I decided I would really manage!"[64] She described going to the booking office of "Harold Eldridge, 1650 Broadway," recalling, "They would give you your itinerary, and you would travel maybe four, five hundred miles overnight, to get to the next town. And each town only had one

Vaudeville theater, so you pretty much travelled all over the country."[65] From a girl who had left the burlesque circuit due to homesickness, Jean Carroll was becoming a seasoned traveler.

In these appearances, Carroll experimented with comedy, calling out to the band and speaking to audiences directly with snatches of comic patter. An early line she recalled was, "I like this little town. When I first came here I didn't think there was much going on, but I've been watching the grass grow, and it's very, very exciting."[66] While it was not stellar material, the setting offered a training ground for Carroll to develop her skills working a crowd. Characteristically, Carroll put it in less professionalized terms, saying simply, "I liked them, and I wanted to talk to them to tell them how much I liked 'em."[67]

Carroll's relationship with some of her fellow performers was not particularly amicable. The entertainment journalist Bill Smith's oral history *The Vaudevillians* includes one of Carroll's own stories from this period, about a time when she and Pearl Saxon were sabotaged by her male colleagues:

During a show I saw one of the fellows flirting with some girl and carrying on a little conversation. I was angry. You can't carry on a conversation doing unison dancing! So when we came offstage I told that guy, "I don't want that to ever happen again." It wasn't fair to the three of us. I guess he became angry. Anyway, come pay night and instead of going with us he said, "You girls go ahead to the next stop. We'll be there tomorrow morning." His excuse was they had something to do.

So Pearl Saxon and I went ahead. We checked into a small hotel we had been told about and went to the theater and waited for them to show up. They had the music and the wardrobe. When they didn't show, I did what any normal American girl would do. I bawled. . . . The manager asked, "How good are you?" I forgot my tears and said, "We're really two great hoofers. We dance as well as any two men." He said, "I'll tell you what we'll do. Can you manage without music? I said, "Sure, if you have a good piano player." We opened as a duo, she and I. I did my "five-foot-two with eyes of blue" with just the piano, and we managed to do six numbers. We really did a fine act. We never saw the fellows again. I don't know what happened to them. I think they put on our dresses and went away.[68]

Carroll's story clearly positions herself as a plucky leader, outsmarting the male saboteurs. Rather than weep like a wilting flower, she snapped back into her managerial role and asserted her skills. As a parting shot, Carroll painted the men as both superfluous and effeminate: while they "put on . . . dresses and went away," the women of the act stayed and put in their work.

The Comedy Double Act

Carroll continued to perform as a musical theater dancer through the late 1920s, appearing in short-lived two-person acts with Carl Shaw, known as the "comic tanglefoot," and Jules Edward Lipton, aka "Saranoff the Violinist."[69] But her entrée to comedy began in earnest in 1930 with her double act alongside the comedian Marty May. According to Carroll, May, a seasoned performer, had seen her "horsing around backstage" and chose her to be "his little stooge."[70]

By 1937, such man-and-woman acts were already a long-running form of entertainment. The *Variety* columnist Joe Laurie Jr. characterized the early days of variety by crediting man-and-woman acts with helping "to start vaudeville on its golden journey." Early on, Laurie noted, these acts "consisted of the man doing the comedy and the woman contributing good looks." Citing partnerships like Wilbur Mack and Nella Walker, Laurie and Bronson, and Ryan and Lee, Laurie described "flirtation acts" in which the couple would exchange comic banter, with the women "picked for their beauty and their ability to wear clothes" and the "burden of carrying the act on the man's shoulders." These roles seem to have held for May and Carroll, with Carroll initially playing the role of the straight man. However, Laurie noted that starting in the 1890s and continuing through the 1930s, "funny women were in great demand." Citing comediennes like Lulu McConnell, Gracie Allen, Marion Cleveland, and Blossom Seeley, he observed that "all the female members of teams 'in one' were keeping a nation laughing with their clowning."[71] From 1930 to 1934, when Carroll and May worked together, a similar trend played out, and Carroll's role in the man-and-woman acts shifted to be more comedic.

Carroll told the story of how she began her partnership with Marty May, highlighting her own irreverence:

> I was on a bill working with a man, Saranoff, and in those days some theaters used to have what they called Green Rooms. This theater we were in had one, a sort of lounge where the performers could sit, read, and play—they had a piano. I had a ukulele. I used to love to strum that uke and sing. Make up songs. So we are sitting there one day, all of us, kibitzing, and I'm playing the uke, and this chap, Marty May, he was the star on the bill, says, "You know something, you're really a talented girl and you're really funny."
>
> I used to do imitations of the Kentucky Colonel. I'd stick a pillow on my belly underneath and do the fat colonel and stuff like that. So May says to me, "How would you like to work with me?" I say, "Aw, come on." He's a star, and how would I like to work with a headliner? I say, "You're joking." He says, "I'm not joking at all, I mean it. You're one of the cleverest girls I have ever seen and you're funny. I could use someone like you."
>
> I went to Saranoff and I said I had an offer to do a double act with Marty May. He told me May couldn't mean it. I said I wanted to take it and Saranoff became angry because he also wanted me. He said, "Why don't you stay in my act and we'll also do some talking?" but I said no. That is how I really started doing comedy.[72]

In this account, Carroll again used the theme of "natural genius," an unintentional but eminently observable comic talent that came out as she was naïvely "kibitzing." She also emphasized her audacity in the face of her male partners. Not only did she greet May's proposition with an irreverent, "You're joking," but she also refused Saranoff's offer to modify their act to keep her on board. For a relatively unknown young dancer, she behaved with boldness bordering on chutzpah.[73]

By 1930, May was bringing Carroll to Chicago to give a "guest appearance . . . warbling and hoofing" in his act.[74] In its embryonic form, the act was a blend of jokes, fiddling, and dance that often evoked comparison to Jack Benny. As one review put it, "Marty May . . . not only looks, acts, and plays a fiddle like Jack Benny—he uses a few of Benny's gags."[75] The same critic also noted that Jean Carroll "comes on for a number and a little gab."[76] As Carroll reflected on her routine with May, she provided some insight as to the kind of material that constituted this "little gab." Her remembered version of the act positions her as a driving force, speaking most of the dialogue and delivering all the punch lines:

> I'd say, "I haven't seen that suit. . . . I bet whenever you're down in the dumps you get a suit."
> He said, "Yeah."
> I said, "I wondered where you picked that one up!"
> . . . Then he said something about "Well, with my broad shoulders . . ."
> I said, "Broad shoulders? You forgot to take the hanger out"
> . . . And he said something about, "You're very unfriendly."
> I said, "I'm not unfriendly. I just . . . you haven't paid me in three weeks."
> He said, "I paid you last week."
> I said, "In bottle caps? You call that getting paid?"[77]

However, Carroll's account is at odds with those of *Variety* reporters, one of whom described the piece as a ten-minute "patter act with the girl doing the dumb cluck and May wiseguying."[78] A more detailed review described the pair's entrance, noting that "May unloads a flock of instruments, but makes little use of them outside of the violin for several clowning bits."[79] As May unloads the instruments, Carroll delivers a monologue, a segment critics often disparaged as "long winded auto-flirtation," a "long-winded tale," or "dumb patter."[80]

One reviewer described how May would interrupt Carroll's "naïve patter," to undermine her with derisive comments, which resulted in audience members doubling up with laughter.[81] Some of the banter between Carroll and May leaned toward the risqué, as several reviews referred to "blue" material such as the "nudist tweezer gag" and the "baby on the arm gag."[82] Another element of the act revisited familiar territory with a "brisk hoofing windup by Carroll" and May's "hoke fiddle playing."[83]

Critics mainly praised Jean Carroll as "a looker and a smart tap dancer," effusing, "Her dancing is plenty hot, and guarantees a good finish."[84] A photograph from the act shows that Carroll wore a revealing dance costume (figure 1.1). These early reviews established a trend in which reporters from various spheres of journalism—Jewish press, mainstream press, and trade press—repeatedly emphasized Carroll's appearance and dancing ability over her comic skills.

This trend continued even as their act became more egalitarian in its title and pay scale. November 24, 1931, marked the first issue in which *Variety* advertised an act with both May's and Carroll's names on the bill: "Meet Marty May, Friend of Thousands, Annoyed by Jean Carroll."[85] Carroll's explanation of this development revealed that even this comically disparaging billing constituted a hard-won victory:

> It used to be Marty May & Company. And at one point the devil entered the scene with the two horns and he said to me, "Do you realize that you are the major player in this little act?" I said, "No, I didn't realize that." I said it was his act. He asked me if I'd work for him, in it. [The devil] said, "Well, you're the act, kiddo."
>
> . . . So I went along with that and then I said to Marty one day, "Why does it have to be & Company? Why can't it be my name?" He said, "Because it's Marty May. It's my act." . . . And I began to think about it, and I realized that his salary had skyrocketed after I became a part of the act.

FIGURE 1.1. Carroll and May. (*Spokane Chronicle*, February 4, 1932, 15)

. . . I said to him, "It has to be a totally different arrangement. Here's my proposal. It's going to be "Marty May & Jean Carroll, and I get half the salary."

He said, "Oh, you cra . . . [*sic*]"

I said, "That's my proposal. You have a choice. You worked by yourself before. You did very well. You can go back to doing that! I feel that I'm grateful that you did ask me to work with you, but I still have to think of myself and my contribution to the act and to the success and to the increase in salary."

He said I was taking advantage. I said, "I'm making a proposal. You can turn it down. I'm not taking advantage of you. You still can go back and do your Marty May act, which was very entertaining." So he accused me of all kinds of things, and I said, "Well, in that case it's just Marty May from now on because no longer will it be '& Company,' and on a salary of—I don't know what I got, $70 a week or something like that—while he was raking it in!" And that was it.[86]

Again, Carroll narrated her story as an underdog advocating for herself in the face of a hostile man. And though she comically cast her desire to renegotiate her salary and billing as the work of "the devil," she was actually describing a very feminist action and one that would become more commonplace only several decades later: seeking equal pay and recognition for equal work.

Despite Carroll's improved billing, critics seem to have discouraged her from stepping further into comedy. For one thing, there is a sharp disparity between the frequent praise given to Marty May for his comic skill and the rarity of praise to Carroll for hers. And while many critics praised May's "nonchalant" comic delivery, critical response to Carroll's work as a comedian was distinctly lukewarm.[87] As one reviewer declared, "Miss Carroll's chatter is not sufficiently surefire, nor loud enough to be socko."[88] Another accused her of causing the act to "drag badly," and a third damned her with the faint praise of being "a good foil."[89]

Reviewers were considerably more enthusiastic when describing Jean Carroll's dancing ability and physique. As one critic wrote, "Her personality is pliable, but her feet have a firm touch when tapping out a routine upon the cleats."[90] Her appearance as a "nifty looker" would occasionally take bizarre prominence in the review, as was the case when a critic complained that she "evidently has gone in for extra modesty. . . . It was the payees' loss," adding, "Perhaps the chilliness of the weather had something to do with it."[91]

On the basis of the reviews in *Variety*, it seems that Carroll's role in her partnership with Marty May was to be attractive but silent, expressing herself through dance but speaking only as a way to make May look as funny as possible as he interrupted her. After four years of this role, Carroll left the act. A three-line article in *Variety* titled "Jean Carroll on Own" reads, "Jean Carroll leaves Marty May after the current week at the Palace. She has been foiling for the light comedian for the last four years. Miss Carroll will essay a comedy set of her own."[92] Her choice to "essay a comedy set" is remarkable, given the press's subtle discouragement of her efforts as a comedian.

A New Double Act: Carroll and Howe

Another factor contributing to Carroll leaving her act with Marty May was her romantic relationship with Buddy Howe, born Benjamin Zolitan, a dancer whom she met on the vaudeville circuit.[93] Their meeting resulted in courtship, marriage, and a stage act that lasted roughly from 1935 to 1943, in which they toured vaudeville, British music halls, and the United Service Organizations (USO).[94] And although in marrying a "nice Jewish boy," Carroll was in one way conforming to the prescribed path for a Jewish woman, she described the romance in a way that suggests that her relationship with Howe was very consistent with her core determination not to become subordinate to a man.

Carroll's account of her relationship with Howe makes it clear that her feelings toward him were always related to her commitment to autonomy.

FIGURE 1.2. Jean Carroll and Buddy Howe on the vaudeville stage, n.d. (Travelanche.com)

For instance, the first time they met, Howe was smitten by her wit, and she was disgusted by his dominating behavior. It was 1933, and Howe was performing in a dance act with "Fat Jack" Leonard and Elise McLaughlin at the Oriental Theater in Chicago, where he shared a bill with May and Carroll.

"He made a comment to Jack that he thought I was the funniest and the cleverest and the bah bah bah," Carroll said of Howe.[95] The feeling, however, was not mutual, primarily because of a backstage exchange that Carroll witnessed in rehearsal in which she perceived Howe as domineering. "I didn't like him because at rehearsal time, in a very loud voice so that everybody could hear it, he said, 'Jack, wash my stairs!'" He used to do a little stair dance, a tap dance. He was asserting his supremacy and I didn't like that."[96]

A year later, however, Carroll and Howe met again in Toronto, where his troupe was performing and Carroll was trying out her solo act.[97] Howe seemed different, stripped of his domineering quality. Carroll described, "Jack came to visit me, . . . and he brought Buddy with him. And this Buddy was nice. He was pleasant, he was gentle and he wasn't trying to show his insecurity by being Mr. Big."[98] Her use of the words "pleasant" and "gentle" and her dismissal of "being Mr. Big" make it clear that only by shedding the traits stereotypically associated with toxic masculinity was Howe able to reverse Carroll's animosity. Even Carroll's anecdote about professing her romantic interest in Howe reveals ambivalence between affection for him and aversion for his gender: "He [Buddy] got up and came towards me. I could tell that he was going to come over to try to kiss me or something. . . . I put my hand up and I said, 'Listen, I don't like men. I have no respect for most men. I don't like them. I didn't like you when I met you, but I like you now. I like you a lot.'"[99] Ever the entertainer, Carroll could not resist adding, "It took him three years to get into my drawers."[100] She did not specify what she meant by "I have no respect for most men. I don't like them," but her words suggest that the qualities that she initially found repulsive in Howe, his "supremacy" and affectations of being "Mr. Big," are the ones that made men in general lose her respect. In choosing to be with Howe only after he stopped displaying these qualities, Carroll showed a continuing determination to maintain her own autonomy.

Another way in which Carroll's union with Howe demonstrated her commitment to autonomy is the way she leveraged the partnership to gain the creative control that she had been denied by Marty May. Shortly after forming a relationship, Carroll and Howe began working on an act together. In Carroll's telling, their love and their desire to spend time together was the key reason for the shift. "We were in love and we wanted to be together," she explained. "So I sat down and wrote an act, and that's how the act of Carroll and Howe began." Howe's account of the event is similar but with slightly more emphasis on the professional considerations of their partnership: "She was then very successful working with

Marty May in a very fine comedy act. We started to see each other, go out together, fell in love, and decided maybe we could work together. That was about 1933–1934. So Jean wrote us an act and taught me to read lines. I had never done any lines before. Jean was very experienced. She was also a good writer who knew the business. . . . I was essentially a hoofer."[101]

Howe's words suggest that by trading in Marty May for Buddy Howe, Carroll was doing more than trading a colleague for a lover. She was also trading the status of the naïf for that of the veteran. Howe's recognition that "Jean was very experienced" and "knew the business," coupled with his self-proclaimed lack of acting experience, suggests a kind of professional deference on his part. Furthermore, he took on the very role to which she had been relegated in her act with May—a "hoofer"— allowing her to become the writer.

Even the billing "Carroll and Howe," in which her name is listed first, points to the new dynamic. Typically, male-female comedy duos gave the man the first billing, as was the case in "Shaw and Carroll" and "Marty May Annoyed by Jean Carroll." More important, while Carroll had been the foil to May, she said of her partnership with Howe, "He was my straight man; I was his funny lady."[102]

The Carroll and Howe act gained increasing success as it moved from smaller to more mainstream venues. "We broke in the act on the state fairs," Howe recalled. "If the state fair wasn't too big, we did the talking act. In others, we just danced." He also noted a key shift taking place in Jean Carroll's career. "Jean could dance, sing, and do a little of everything. But she was essentially a comedienne."[103] This shift in viewpoint marked a significant turning point for Carroll and constituted a fairly radical move, given critics' attempts to recognize her as a dancer more than a comic.

Carroll and Howe continued touring between 1934 and 1936, garnering positive reviews and ultimately playing the legendary Palace Theatre, the pinnacle of vaudeville success. A critic for *Variety* praised the duo for "showing promise, especially the wacky femme."[104] And Howe

ON STAGE AND SCREEN—Dick Powell, the Hollywood Blondes, Jean Carroll and Buddy Howe are seen in person on the stage of the RKO Boston Theatre where the film feature is "Ride 'Em Cowboy," with Abbott and Costello.

FIGURE 1.3. Illustration of Carroll and Howe. (*Boston Globe*, March 2, 1942, 4)

recalled that as soon as they "brought the act into New York," they were "immediately bought by all the circuits": "We played the Palace a couple of times and every major theater from coast to coast," he said.[105] Carroll added, "Milt Berger—he was then with Jack Davies—got us booked into Loew's State when Sid Piermont was the booker. Then came the RKO theaters, the Pantages, there was so much work. Then finally, the Palace."[106] In 1936, the team of Carroll and Howe took a big step both personally and professionally: they married and embarked on a performance tour of England.

The story, or rather stories, of Jean Carroll's wedding to Buddy Howe reveals the ways that family mythology embroiders and distorts events over time. When telling the story of her wedding for "I Made It Standing Up," Carroll recalled,

My husband lived in Flatbush, Brooklyn. And the wedding took place in his mother's living room. And the rabbi had another gig. After he married us, he was going to audition for a job in one of the shuls there, one of the synagogues.

. . . So he's there, and he starts the davening type of thing. And my nephew whines, "I want to go home!" So the rabbi says, "We'll start over again. Now, da da da . . ." "I want to go home!" The third time the rabbi says, "That damn kid is ruining the whole ceremony!" So we ended up doubled up in laughter. That was my wedding. It was so romantic, you have no idea. And how did we spend our wedding night? There was a prize fight on television and we sat in the living room and watched it![107]

According to official records, the marriage did indeed take place on June 16, 1936, in Brooklyn. However, in the version offered by Carroll's granddaughter Susan Chatzky, Carroll was basically tricked into marrying Howe.

Chatzky describes the story of their wedding as a surprise affair aboard a ship bound for Great Britain. "He booked them voyage to England on some ship," she recalled. "And when she got on the boat, she said,

"OK, where's my cabin?" And he said, "We're in the same cabin." And she said, "We can't be in the same cabin, Buddy, that's ridiculous! Where's my cabin?" And he opened the door to the cabin that they were going to share, and her whole family was there with a rabbi. And that's how they got married." "She was not going to marry him," Chatzky added. "She was being a pain in the ass about getting married, and that's how he solved that problem. . . . After thirty years of marriage, she thought it was funny, but having known her, I'm guessing she did not think it was funny at the time."[108]

The two accounts are as notable for their consistencies as their differences. While the granddaughter's story presents the wedding as a kind of nautical-nuptial ambush, Carroll's leaves out this element of surprise. However, both versions specify that a rabbi officiated and Carroll's family attended. This suggests that Carroll viewed these two elements— religious tradition and family—as key to the story, regardless of the particular location of the ceremony. And even though it seems highly unlikely that there would be an ordained rabbi and Carroll's family hiding aboard a ship about to set sail for the United Kingdom, telling the story to her granddaughter in this way suggests a desire to emphasize both Jewishness and family.

Carroll's account of the next three years of her life—traveling through England with Howe as a newlywed couple and increasingly popular comedy team—continued to emphasize her personal and professional self-determination. First, she established their success as "the darlings of the British people."[109] She effused, "We were supposed to stay in England four weeks. We stayed there three years! We worked the London Palladium. We were just a little number-two act. But we were an instant smash and we became headliners. We played all the provinces, nightclubs, made a couple of little movies, some shorts, and we became the big thing. After Burns & Allen, we were *the* big thing. We loved the people there and they loved us."[110] Carroll's comparison to the vaudeville comedy duo of George Burns and Gracie Allen was evidently one that she maintained for many years, for her daughter,

Helen, also described the routine, which she had never seen, as "a kind of George Burns / Gracie Allen Act."[111] This comparison is key both because it provides a sense of the genre of their act and because it implicitly positions the woman as the breakout talent. In George Burns's memoir reflecting on the forty-year life of the Burns and Allen act, he cites a series of reviews that make it clear that his partner (and wife), Gracie Allen, was the undisputed star. Burns accepts and even confirms the audience's preference, declaring, "She was the whole act."[112] The legacy of Burns and Allen, then, includes the rare instance of a female comedian outshining her male partner. And so comparisons between Carroll and Howe and Burns and Allen carry with them the ghost of comedy success springing from the woman's, rather than the man's, comic chops.

And in the case of Carroll and Howe, it is even more true that "she was the whole act," for unlike Gracie Allen, Carroll both wrote and performed in the act. Her husband, by his own account, would often stand by while Carroll went onstage and improvised ten minutes' worth of new material. Howe recognized his wife's gift for spinning everyday occurrences into comedy. "Jean wrote many, many pieces, developed them, and performed them, starting many of the things that comics are doing today," he said, continuing, "The thing that was so good about our act was that I was lucky enough to find a girl who could write material that was so distinctive they had to play us. We did material that nobody had ever heard before. All fresh. We seldom, if ever, resorted to an old joke. In fact, it was never a joke, it was always a 'bit,' a routine. It was never 'Two Jews met on a corner' or 'Two Italians met in the street.' I think Jean got her comedy out of natural happenings."[113] In Howe's telling, he was happy to cede authorial control to Carroll. "I was strictly a straight man," he said. "If she wrote, 'When are you coming to dinner?' that's what I said every show, exactly as written."[114]

But however empowered Carroll was within her relationship and her act, the outside world continued trying to demean her. She offered one backstage anecdote from her time in England:

We were in England, at the Palladium theater. And I'm up on the stage and the pit band is down there. And as I'm leaning over to talk to the conductor, one of the British acts comes along and gooses me!

I turn around, I said, "Did you just accidentally bump into me?"

He said, "No."

"You mean you did that on purpose?"

"He said, "Of course. We know how you American girls are."

I said, "Listen, you!"

Now, we had been prompted, you know, prepped to go to England. Ambassadors of good will. And they resented American acts coming over there and performing, they're taking work away from their British performers.

I said, "I want to tell you something. If you ever, ever come close to me or put your hand on any part of my body, I will knock your teeth down your throat. Do you follow me?"

He laughed. . . . This idiot walked over to my husband, whose back was turned, hadn't seen any of this, and he says, "Your wife has no sense of humor. . . . All I did was grope her, and you know what she did? She said if I ever touched her again she would knock my teeth down my throat."

And my hero who had just married me squared his shoulders, stood up and looked this guy in the eyes and he said, "And if my wife says she'll do it, she'll do it."[115]

Carroll cheerfully downplayed the more disturbing elements of the harassment and offered a delivery that could be pulled from a stand-up routine. But the story also asserts Carroll's growing American identity. Not only was she perceived by the British actor as being promiscuous due to the reputation of how "American girls are," but she was specifically cast as an "Ambassador of goodwill." Although she would not become an official citizen for several decades, she was nonetheless a proud representative of the United States.

An excerpt filmed at London's Pathé studios in 1937 has preserved at least a fragment of the comedy routines that Carroll was writing and

FIGURE 1.4. Jean Carroll and Buddy Howe in *Pathetone Presents Carroll & Howe*, 1937. (British Pathé Studios)

performing with Howe on their tour of the UK.[116] The scene begins with Howe wearing a three-piece suit and sitting alone on a set featuring a small table with a wine bottle and two empty glasses. The table is surrounded by other empty tables, chairs, and a potted palm, suggesting a nightclub atmosphere.

Carroll rushes in. Her nose has a more pronounced bend in the bridge than in her later images, revealing it as preoperative. She is glamorously attired in black T-strap heels, a long, fitted coat with a ruffled collar, matching pocketbook, leather gloves, and a satin hat.

"Hurry up, will you? What's the idea of making me wait?" Howe demands, as Carroll breathlessly takes her seat.

"I can't help it," she replies. "I was talking to a man out there—you know, that man out there [she extends her arm, gracefully gesturing offstage], he almost gave me an automobile for nothing!" Her tempo is quick, her voice high and birdlike, her gestures frequent and animated. If you listen closely, you can catch a hint of a Brooklyn accent as she pronounces the words "talking" and "automobile." "Whaddya mean for nothing?" is Howe's gruff reply. "Really, it's true!" Carroll chirps, dissolving into giggles as she nods eagerly. "It is!"

Howe fills in dubiously, as Carroll explains, "Yes, he was out there, and it was a beautiful car! I walked up to him, and I said, 'Are you the owner of this car?' He said, 'Yes.' I said, 'Well, I like it very much—give it to me?' He said, 'No!'" Her eyes widen with incredulity as she repeats his rejection.

Howe squints, unfazed. "He said, 'No.' So you almost had an automobile for nothing."

"Sure!" Carroll replies with a giant grin and a little laugh. "Imagine if he'da said yes!"

Howe grunts and holds his head in his hand with despairing incredulity as the scene continues.

Carroll's opening chastisement and giggling demeanor belie the tremendous amount of control that she has in the scene. On the surface, the sketch bears similarities to the many "Dizzy Dame" and "Dumb Dora" scenes circulating vaudeville. As George Burns observes in his memoirs, "There had been a long line of 'Dumb Doras,' as 'silly' women were called. Harriet Lee had worked with Benny Ryan. Gracie Deagon. The 'Martin Family' had a 'dumb' mother."[117] The comedy historian Susan Horowitz also writes about "Dumb Doras" who "deny their intellect," extending the lineage from Gracie Allen to Fanny Brice, on through Lucille Ball and Goldie Hawn.[118] In some ways, Carroll's stage persona fit into this model. She had the same giggly, childlike mannerisms of Allen and other Dumb Doras. And she responded to Howe's setup conundrums with the same kind of comically outlandish solutions. For instance,

HOWE: I'm troubled with insomnia.

CARROLL: Well, why don't you send her home? Hah hah! Some joke—I like that!

HOWE: Some joke . . .

CARROLL: [putting her hand on his shoulder, concerned] No, seriously, can't you sleep nights?

HOWE: No, I can't!

CARROLL: Well, I'll tell you what you'll do! [her hand still on his shoulder, moving to his lapel] You'll go out and get yourself a nice big bottle of scotch, like that you see? [gesturing to the bottle on the table] And um . . . [she grabs her hat, momentarily puzzled], at night, when you can't sleep, pour yourself a big tumbler of scotch every half hour. . . . And you see what that'll do for you!

HOWE: Will it make me go to sleep?

CARROLL: No, but it'll make staying awake a pleasure! [giggles]

Carroll's persona's impractical solution again recalls the kind of material Gracie Allen often performed, which Burns and Allen termed "illogical logic." This allowed Carroll, like Allen, to deliver the lion's share of the punch lines and made her the focal point of the sketch. Even within the act itself, Carroll comments on her own wit, following up her more risqué (and thus risky) joke on the "lady" insomnia with a faux self-congratulation and giving Howe the chance to shift her status with a dismissive, "Some joke."

Without a studio audience, it is difficult to judge how Carroll and Howe were received in this particular performance. The jokes are followed by a rather conspicuous silence. And so the clip cannot confirm whether Carroll's use of "illogical logic" stole the scene in quite the same way that Allen's did. However, it may be revealing that the camera spent much more time in close-ups of Carroll's animated face than it did on Howe's or on wider shots of the two of them. And upon their return to the United States, it became clear that Burns's comment that "she was the whole act" was as true for Carroll and Howe as it had been for Burns and Allen.

World War II and the USO Circuit

In February 1938, the increasing threat of World War II prompted Carroll and Howe to leave England. Although there was not yet military action in Britain, there was talk of impending war and an upswell in antisemitism. According to the historian Aaron Goldman, antisemitism in Britain had reached new heights in the mid- to late 1930s, spurred on in part through propaganda disseminated by the British Union of Fascists.[119] While Carroll and Howe may have been relatively insulated from this prejudice due to their celebrity, it is unlikely that they were wholly oblivious to the wartime-exacerbated antisemitism. Moreover, the dangers of being in a country that had formally declared itself at war were considerable. By January 1940, well before any of the bombings on England began, Carroll and Howe returned to the United States.

Back in the US, reviews show their growing success and also an increasing preference for Carroll, celebrating her comic skill even at the expense of her partner's. Critics praised her as "especially clever with comedy" and "always a surefire comedienne."[120] A particularly effusive critic wrote, "Jean Carroll is one of the best comedy femmes in the business, and with half a break she will score in a big way. She has a way of working, a style of delivery that is top-notch in any league."[121] In contrast, Howe's comic ability was generally unremarked upon, other than the reviews when critics complained that he "seemed tired" or "might perk up a bit."[122]

By the end of 1941, Carroll had become so recognized for her comic skill that she was performing as an emcee at Baltimore's Hippodrome Theatre. Typically, the emcee was a male performer—in fact, only in 1928 did Gracie Allen became the first female emcee (dubbed "femcee") ever to work the Palace Theatre.[123] However, Carroll's critic praised the "nice switch," commenting that she was "holding down an emcee spot and doing all right."[124]

Like many of the popular American vaudeville acts of the 1940s, Carroll and Howe made the transfer to the United Service Organizations tours. As tensions surrounding World War II escalated and US military involvement seemed increasingly likely, both army enrollment and the need for morale boosting increased. In 1941, President Franklin

Roosevelt formed the United Service Organizations by urging private groups like the Salvation Army to merge with religious groups like the Young Men's Christian Association, the national Catholic Community Services, and the Jewish Welfare Board to pool their resources and produce "Camp Shows" and other recreation for the growing number of soldiers.[125]

Conditions on the USO circuit were rough for the performers. A critic from *Variety* commended cast members of the Camp Shows not only for their performances but also for being "troupers" and "taking everything in stride: one day a tent, the next a theatre; long distance bus hauls from downtown to camps; bad hotel accommodations with raised rates."[126] But another *Variety* writer noted the benefits of performing on the circuit, such as covered costs for transportation and especially "a chance to get in a solid 24 weeks of work without worrying whether or not they are doing any business at the box office."[127] Carroll herself wrote, in an article for *Billboard* magazine touting the benefits performers accrued on the USO, "From a purely business standpoint, one cannot help feel that many acts will benefit financially from USO dates after the war. We have been stopped in the streets by greeting soldiers, remembering the act from a camp showing. This type of reaction is bound to prove of some benefit to acts."[128] Howe explained how he and Carroll got involved: "Abe Lastfogel, who was then the head of the USO and also the William Morris office, asked us to go on USO and we did. We stayed on it for two years until I was called up."[129]

Carroll and Howe participated on the USO's Red Circuit in such revues as Unit 52's "Looping the Loop."[130] By *Variety*'s account, Carroll and Howe's USO act continued to mix dance and comedy. It began with comic dialogue or "smart crossfire."[131] The standout number was Carroll's performance of "Lady Be Good," in which she did an imitation of a trumpet player "using only her hands."[132] Carroll and Howe appeared alongside the "Line Girls" dance troupe, "The Four Macks" roller-skating act, "The Lane Brothers" acrobatic dancers, Chester Dolphin the comic juggler, and the Randall Sisters singing trio. The tour hit around seventy camps, performing for up to twelve thousand soldiers at each one.[133]

By building a reputation with the USO, Carroll and Howe were able to position themselves as both entertainers and patriots. However, as the draft went into effect, Buddy Howe went from entertaining troops to serving in them. Show business was no exception to the wartime phenomenon of young men being taken from their careers and recruited to the military. *Variety* began publishing a column called "Uncle Sam's Callboard," listing the many performers who had been drafted that week. On October 6, 1943, that column noted, "Carroll & Howe, standard act for 10 years, has been broken up with the induction of Buddy Howe into the Army. Jean Carroll (Mrs. Howe) will continue as a single. Team did its last date together two weeks ago at Camp Grant, Il., when Pvt. Buddy Howe was called up from the audience and did the old routine, in uniform, with his wife."[134] After training at Camp Grant, Howe spent two years in Camp Lee, just south of Richmond, Virginia. Carroll described their farewell in terms that mix romantic melodrama with professional strategizing:

> When he was drafted, I said to him, "Don't worry about it. When you get out after you serve, or even if you have to go overseas, when you come back, we'll continue with the act."
>
> He said, "No . . . I've held you back long enough. You're great. You will do great things on your own."
>
> I said, "No, no, no. I married you to be with you, not to be without you. We will do an act."
>
> He said, "No, *we* will not. *You* will do an act."[135]

Like so many wives of the period, Jean Carroll found an increased level of professional autonomy as a result of her husband's military service. What was less common was that Carroll's newfound professional independence confirmed a trend that had been growing increasingly evident to audiences: in Carroll and Howe, she was the whole act.

From Double to Single

The early years of Jean Carroll's solo career saw her transitioning from the "Dumb Dora" character of Carroll and Howe to the savvy persona who eventually held court on *The Ed Sullivan Show*. When writing for Carroll and Howe, Carroll had drawn a great deal of humor from incongruity and status shifts between the two partners. The incongruity mainly sprang from making use of gender differences. Her persona was distinctly feminine: light, bubbly, and eager to please, full of lively stories and absurd plans (e.g., get a free car by asking for it, cure insomnia with whisky). Howe's persona, in contrast, was more stereotypically "masculine": truculent, wry, and resigned, speaking only to chastise her or to offer tersely delivered feed lines. Even without any actual jokes in the dialogue, the incongruity of their energies provided a comical friction. Moreover, the quick exchanges between the two people allowed for their status to shift back and forth relative to each other, with one person cutting the other down, only to be swiftly undermined themselves. Without Howe, Carroll had to figure out how to create these incongruities and shifts in status within herself.

On the basis of her account, given to Stephen Silverman, Carroll's first step in trying to develop her own solo act involved intense self-reflection. "I stood for hours and hours in front of the mirror," she said. "I used to do mimicry. . . . I'd listen to radio and I did takeoffs. I would lampoon the different radio shows, especially the giveaway shows, . . . and I sang and I did imitations, and I put together an act."[136]

Carroll's first review as a solo performer, published in *Variety*, confirmed that her nascent act experimented with a range of voices and bits. As the emcee at the National Theatre of Louisville, she was praised for her "good impression of various radio announcers delivering trite commercials." The review also noted that she told stories, "a couple in Yiddish dialect."[137] It seems that this first stab at solo performance was experimental in nature, casting about for a persona that could stand on her own. By her next solo engagement, this time in Baltimore,

Carroll seems to have settled on impressions as her winning gambit. The trumpet-player impression that had so impressed audiences from her Carroll and Howe days resurfaced, though to remain topical, she switched it from Louis Armstrong to Harry James.[138] Without the incongruity of an actual man to play off, Carroll drew on the incongruity of a singing woman performing the role of a trumpet-playing man.

In interviews, Carroll reflected on this period of her life—finding her voice as a burgeoning stand-up comedian—with nearly reverent fondness. "My first time really where the burden of success was on my shoulders alone," she said. "I get goose flesh now just thinking about it."[139] The satisfaction she gained from this independence provides an important parallel to her childhood vow in which she declared that she would never be dependent on a man.

Carroll's excitement at the prospect of independence also points to a defining feature of the genre that would come to be known as stand-up comedy: the focus on individualism. In the words of the stand-up comic Emily Levine, "You're in charge. If you fail, it's your fault. If you don't, it's your credit."[140] The theater scholar Eddie Tafoya argues that the emphatic individualism central to stand-up comedy makes it a uniquely American genre, writing, "It is an art form which, at its very core, is about pluralism and individualism and thus could have been born only in the United States. It is the singular person standing against the crowd, exercising the right to free speech and sinking or swimming (or killing or bombing, as it were) on unique merits."[141] This emphasis on independence may also be why so many comedy theorists are eager to masculinize stand-up comedy. Although the gender politics of a woman valuing her own autonomy and individualism is not quite as revolutionary now as it was in the midcentury, it has remained a countercultural position.

Throughout the literature about stand-up comedy is the claim that individualism, and the assumption of individual agency, is built into the form. The story of Jean Carroll's life and career similarly underscores emphasis on individualism and self-determination. Her personal narrative makes it clear that from the very beginning, her career in show business was rooted in a desire for self-determination; she performed in order to be free of financial dependence on her father. As a stand-up comic, she performed in a way that mimicked the fierce autonomy of her personal life.

By the time Buddy Howe returned from the war, Carroll had settled into a solid comedy act that used her unapologetic woman's perspective to provide a resonant and wry new subject of mockery: men. Specifically, she riffed on the men in her love life, both her husband and past boyfriends:

Love! Does anybody know what love is? That's a moot question.
So I asked Moot. Moot was my first boyfriend.
I was crazy about him.
Our romance was one of those triangles.
You see, he and I were both in love with him!
Then there was Jack.
Oh, let me tell you how I met Jack.
I was standing on the corner—as usual. . . .
We went out and lemme tell you something, he was a real sport. Money? Money meant nothing. Nothing! He didn't have any.
I shouldn't make fun of him. After all, he is my husband.
Nothing bothers him. . . . He drinks.
Well, he doesn't drink because he likes it. He drinks to steady his nerves. The other night his nerves got so steady he couldn't move at all![142]

An early reviewer of Carroll's solo act wrote that her "monolog [sic] is really pretty sharp, but possibly too intimate."[143] While women had long been lampooned by male comedians, Carroll's jabs at "Moot's" vanity and "Jack's" drinking problem were relatively novel. Perhaps the author critiquing Carroll's "too intimate" content was unprepared to hear men's private foibles and flaws mocked in such a public setting. Buddy Howe, however, recognized how marketable this new approach was, and far from being upset, he decided to become her manager. Throughout her career, mockery of her husband (whose pseudonym "Jack" soon disappeared) became the bedrock of Carroll's act. And as her words put him down, her popularity bolstered them both.

* * *

The toddler Sadie Zeigman became "Jean Carroll" as a child, a pioneer stand-up comic as an adult, and a masterful autobiographical performer as an elder. In her recollections of stories and scrapbooks, her biography is the triumphant tale of a poor Jewish immigrant whose familial devotion and naïve comic genius propelled her to riches and fame. However, the yellowing reviews carefully pasted in her tattered green scrapbook could just as easily describe an ambitious young dancer whose comedy aspirations were barely evident until she took action, strategically cultivating her skills and profile and seeking partners who would do the same. In Carroll's telling, her first steps toward show business were rooted not in starry-eyed dreams of glory or even in a particular interest in comedy. Rather, they came from a determination to provide for herself, her mother, and her siblings. This tale of family devotion has historically been a way for successful women to downplay their ambition and thus to be more appealing to mass audiences. The study of vaudeville by the popular culture scholar Alison Kibler finds in the art form a history of "depictions of actresses as reluctant stars, turning to the stage out of family loyalty, not personal ambition."[144] Like the women at the center of Kibler's research, Jean Carroll made use of careful storytelling techniques, emphasizing themes like familial devotion or irrepressible, unbidden genius, as a way of making their success more palatable to a broader audience. An ambitious woman may have been—may still be—unacceptable. But no one will begrudge a "natural" who loves her family.

2

A Woman in the Stand-Up "Fraternity"

Jean Carroll and Stand-Up Comedy in the Post-Vaudeville Era

By the 1930s, vaudeville had been dying for so long that by the time it finally flickered out, American show business had already moved on. Many vaudeville acts transitioned to radio or continued touring the country at presenting houses, sharing the stage with motion pictures. Jean Carroll was also transitioning, although there was no word yet for what she was transitioning into. What would now be called "stand-up comedy" was in the 1940s and early '50s still a nascent, as-yet-untitled genre. Critics fumblingly referred to stand-up comics as "monologists," "single comedy acts," or "joke guys." And they were—with the exception of Jean Carroll—guys. As countless press outlets chorused, Carroll was the lone woman in the United States' first cohort of "stand-up" comedians.

In 1952, the comedian Joe Laurie wrote a profile in *Variety* on these pioneering comics, which he called the "Younger Fraternity," naming (among others) Sam Levenson, Steve Allen, and Jack Carter, with Carroll as "the one and only lady monologist." Laurie charted the shift in comedy from the vaudeville generation, whose "great funmaking will always be sealed in the memory of old troupers," to the next generation—a set of "kids who have broken into the laugh-getting ranks."[1]

Joe Laurie never discussed the ethnicity of this "Younger Fraternity," but the subject does come up—albeit indirectly—in another *Variety* state-of-the-industry perspective on the changing landscape of American comedy in 1952. Oscar Hammerstein, the famed lyricist from the musical comedy duo Rogers and Hammerstein, cheerfully debunked the morose eulogizing of post-vaudeville American comedy:

Where are our great comedians going to come from now that we no longer have burlesque and vaudeville? This is a question you often hear and
read. . . . It's an impressive and a frightening question—unless you take
the trouble to look for an answer. You don't have to look far—a few miles
north to the Catskills and the Adirondacks, a few miles west to the Po-
conos. In these borscht-tinted hills, many a belly-laugh has budded and
bloomed, and many of our funniest men have sharpened their jokes on
summer campers. Danny Kaye, Sid Caesar, Sam Levenson, Jerry Lester,
Red Buttons, Henny Youngman, (Miss) Jean Carroll and Julie Oshins
all owe at least a part of their development to the Mountain Time. . . .
So if two of our old meadows lie fallow, we have found fresh fields that
are producing promising crops of comics—TV, radio, pictures, niteries
[nightclubs], the "Borscht Circuit"—that is where our new funny men are
coming from. . . . There is very little left of vaudeville as we know it. . . .
But the ingredients that flavored these mediums are showing up in other
mediums, and so it will always be.[2]

By positioning the "borsht-tinted" Catskills as the primary incubator
of comedy, Hammerstein was not so subtly recognizing the way that
Jewishness "flavored" mainstream American comedy.

Taken together, these accounts of comedy in the post-vaudeville era
paint the picture of a cadre of innovative young Jewish men creating a
new form of American comedy—a cadre of innovative young Jewish
men *and* an innovative young Jewish woman named Jean Carroll.

From the Catskills to Madison Square Garden:
Carroll on the Borscht Circuit

Oscar Hammerstein's characterization of the Catskill Mountains resorts
as post-vaudeville "talent incubators" was only one of the glowing testimonials waxing poetic on the famed Borscht Belt hotels. The Catskills
were sometimes referred to as the "Jewish Alps," and these hotels initially gained popularity in the early 1900s because of antisemitism

among country clubs and other vacation destinations in upstate New York. The documentarian Ian Rosenberg recalls that through the 1930s, restricted hotels would bear signs reading, "No Hebrews or Consumptives."[3] So enterprising Jewish innkeepers set up "self-contained hospitality fortresses" where Jews could enjoy accommodations and kosher food.[4] Over the next few decades, these inns expanded, incorporating luxury amenities like golf courses, swimming pools, and—of course—entertainment venues.

The theaters of the Catskills became places where comedians who were unemployed by the death of vaudeville could get steady work. Hotels capitalized on entertainment as yet another reasonably priced amenity. One advertisement promoting Jean Carroll's appearance at Grossinger's Hotel featured the thrifty encouragement, "See Broadway stars you'd pay a fortune to see in town."[5] The entertainment agent Charles Rapp, sometimes known as "The Ziegfeld of the Catskills," built a successful agency almost exclusively representing talent for Catskills resorts.[6] These comics kept a grueling pace. Jerry Lewis, who got his start as a Catskills comic, reflected, "We had the opportunity of working a hotel at seven o'clock and driving to another hotel for an eight-thirty show, and another show at eleven."[7]

Here in this *haimish* haven, Jean Carroll developed her comic skills and built her audience. She appeared in many Borscht Belt hotels, ranging from Wentworth Hall and the Stevensville Lake Hotel to the Laurel Club, but the two with which she had the strongest affinity were the Concord and Grossinger's.[8] Carroll referred to Grossinger's as "THE place" where she expanded her repertoire, remembering that she had to come up with "a whole bunch of new stuff because [she] appeared there so many times."[9] Indeed, Carroll's personal scrapbook suggests that over time, she developed a friendly relationship with the Grossinger family, as it features a photograph depicting Carroll grinning alongside Mrs. Elaine Grossinger Etess.[10] Carroll's daughter, Helen, also remembers Grossinger's and the Concord by name, recalling their "huge showrooms . . . kind of like Vegas."[11]

Helen's Las Vegas comparison seems apt based on other comics' recollections of the showrooms. The stand-up comic Jack Carter bemoaned the vastness of the Concord, complaining, "It used to be a cute little job when it was a couple hundred, but then it became a massive arena and it was really tough to handle. Thirty-five hundred seats. You had to have a powerful act to capture that group."[12] Another comic, Marilyn Michaels, declared that "if you headlined at the Concord, . . . it was like you 'made it.'"[13]

Jean Carroll was determined to prove that her act was powerful enough to "make it" with an audience of over three thousand people. And to do that, she started in some well-trod territory, building "a whole routine about [her] mother, . . . a Jewish ham."[14] Although her Catskills routines were never recorded, Carroll paraphrased some in an interview at the Friars Club in 2007. The "Jewish ham" routine seems to be a rather unoriginal Myron Cohen–style smorgasbord of Jewish mother stereotypes and dialect humor, pandering to her audience with tried-and-true gags about trying to cover up the telltale immigrant behaviors of her parents' generation. In the following bit from the routine, Carroll describes her failed attempts to keep her mother from embarrassing her in front of a gentile dinner guest:

> "Ma, just put the food on the table, serve it. Don't bug him. Don't stand in back and watch every spoonful of soup go to his mouth like you do with us. And don't tell him he has to finish 'cause children are starving in Europe!"
>
> She says, "I vouldn't, I vouldn't, I vouldn't say a vord." She didn't say a "vord" for a little while.
>
> She brought out the vegetable soup, . . . and she's standing in back of him, and I think she had a slingshot, because out of nowhere comes a flying piece of butter. It had to be a slingshot!
>
> He looks up, and she says, "The soup is too skinny."[15]

The dialect humor used in Carroll's imitation of her mother had already proved its popularity in the musical parodies of Carroll's antecedent

Fanny Brice. And the mother's food-based pushiness had proven its comic mettle with Carroll's contemporary Gertrude Berg, to say nothing of the slew of Jewish male comics mocking their force-feeding mothers. In a separate interview, Carroll performed a different bit about visiting her impossible-to-please Jewish mother in Arkansas: "My mother had me take a plane, come from New York City to Hot Springs with a kosher chicken, because there was no kosher butcher in Hot Springs, Arkansas. . . . Now, you go to Little Rock and you take a cab from Little Rock to Hot Springs. The chicken was beginning to smell, because I didn't have it in ice. And when I got to the Arlington Hotel, in Hot Springs, and knocked on my mother's door, my mother opened the door, looked at me standing there with the shopping bag and said, 'Eh, I ate already.'"[16] This kind of fish-out-of-water Yiddishkeit is markedly different from the kind of comedy that Carroll would perform on television or in more mainstream venues. The Catskills was clearly not the place where Carroll developed the material that made her a stand-up legend, but it was the place where she developed the ability to work a crowd. Keeping a stadium-sized venue entertained takes practice.

Even more significantly, the Catskills was a place where Jean Carroll could express her Jewish identity—not just in the familiar "Jewish mama" jokes but in the choice to devote her talents to entertaining her own people. In these Borscht Belt resorts, Jews went from being a minority group to the primary audience. So whether or not the stand-ups and tummlers onstage were Jewish themselves—whether or not they made references to Jewish practices or culture—they were participating in Jewish comedy.[17] The Jewishness lay in what the theater scholar Susan Bennet would call the performance's "outer frame," which includes "all the cultural elements which create and inform the cultural event."[18] In other words, regardless of the content, the Jewishness was embedded in the venue.

The kinship that Jean Carroll signified by performing in Jewish venues is especially clear in an anecdote she shared about bringing her mother to the Borscht Belt to see her perform. Carroll recalled, "I once took her with me to Grossingers. This was war-time, I believe. . . . And after the show, my mother said, 'I'm proud from you.'" Given Carroll's characterization of her mother as a loving but tough immigrant not given to effusive praise, such a declaration of pride must have been deeply meaningful, if surprising. Perhaps this is why Carroll responded, dumbfounded, "You're proud from *me*? Why?" Her mother answered, "That there's such trouble in the world, and you're able to make people laugh."[19]

The subtext of this story seems to be Carroll's claim that the work she was doing as an entertainer contributed to her Jewish community by providing much-needed levity to a people traumatized by history and current events. The act of allowing Jewish people to respond to depictions of themselves with laughter at a time when most of the world was responding with vitriol took on a political cast. While propaganda machines churned out derogatory stereotypes in the service of exterminating Jews, comedians like Carroll could use more playful stereotypes in service of entertaining them.

Carroll told a similar story of comedy as catharsis as she reflected on her performance at a different Jewish venue: a 1948 celebration of the State of Israel being recognized by the United Nations, held in Madison Square Garden. Carroll recalled,

> [They had] the rabbi, and a choir did Hatikvah!
>   How you could keep from weeping, I don't know.
>   . . . And then he introduces *me*. . . .
>   I defy anybody to go out and be funny following that!
>   [But] I went out, and I said to the audience, "Tonight I'm so proud to be Jewish, I'd give anything to have my old nose back again!"[20]

In the scant biographic record of Carroll's career, this quip about missing her old nose is legendary: it appears in a joke book, comedy anthologies, and even her obituary in the *New York Times*.[21] According to Carroll, the joke was an instant hit. As she described it, "At first there was silence.

Then there was a ground swell of laughter that started. And 20,000 people got up off their feet. . . . Right now, I'm finding it tough not to cry. In my life, I will never know that kind of a sensation. To be able to make people laugh in the face of such horror, that they were able to wrest victory out of the horrors."[22] To Carroll, the audience's laughter also signified a greater truth: laughter as a mode of empowerment, of "wresting victory out of horrors," the same sentiment as her mother's response to her show in the Catskills. This act of laughter as resistance to horror is precisely the way Carroll positioned it in her autobiographical narrative. In the grand tradition of Sholem Aleichem and Yiddish comedy, Carroll used laughter as a way to avoid tears and overcome obstacles. Laughter was the way that she wrested financial autonomy and acceptance from a patriarchal society that had little interest in welcoming Jewish women. It was how she had escaped her father, faced down the prejudices of her colleagues, and now, flown in the face of the horrors of World War II. It was her show of kinship—her personal contribution to her people.

Jean Carroll's mode of expressing her Jewish identity by choosing to lend her talent of live performance to Jewish venues and causes became a pattern that would repeat throughout her career.[23] Performing at Jewish charity events and benefits was an important way that she could express her Jewish identity at a historical point when such expression was unwelcome in mainstream entertainment. And she was not alone in this métier—many of her male colleagues traveled this Borscht Circuit of live comedy fundraisers and benefits alongside her. The Jewish comedy legend Georgie Jessel boasted that he raised $25 million in bonds for the new nation of Israel by leaving "no Cohen unturned."[24] There was also a social element to it: it was a way of establishing community or, as Laurie put it, a fraternity. The comedian Eddie Cantor explained, "Another good thing about charity—it brings Jews closer together. Gives one a chance to say to the other, 'Here, you son-of-a-gun, you can't let us down on this cause.'"[25] Like many American Jews of the era, Carroll made little distinction between American Jewish causes and American causes to benefit Israel. And so in the late 1940s, Carroll, Myron Cohen,

Danny Kaye, Red Buttons, and many more of the "Younger Fraternity" became staples in one of the most high-profile Zionist events for entertainers: the "Night of Stars" from the United Jewish Appeal for Refugees and Overseas Needs (UJA), an organization that helped Jewish refugees from central and eastern Europe to relocate to Palestine.[26]

The "Night of Stars" was a variety show mainstream enough to be covered by both the Jewish press and trade publications, which charted its headliners with great detail. In 1948—the first year of Israel's statehood—*Variety* boasted a celebrity-packed bill that included Jean Carroll, Red Buttons, Milton Berle, Myron Cohen, Danny Kaye, Mickey Rooney, Henny Youngman, and even the Rockettes.[27] The Radio City Rockettes, best known for their annual *Christmas Spectacular*, are a particularly noticeable attestation to the event's mainstream status. The next year, however, *Variety* noticed that the event was "marked by extreme difficulty in getting many performers to respond." Offering reasons ranging from lacking new material to union restrictions and weariness of working without pay, many of the big stars opted out.[28] Those who remained, such as Jean Carroll, Henny Youngman, Harry Hershfield, and Joey Adams, were predominantly Jewish and expressed personal commitment to Israel. By 1950, *Variety* did not even cover the "Night of Stars" event, though the *Jewish Advocate* confirmed the continued participation of devotees like Carroll, Youngman, and Adams.[29] Carroll continued to participate in the UJA "Night of Stars" for years after and saved the UJA's thank-you notes in her personal scrapbook.

These scrapbook clippings and archived news reports shine a light on the overwhelming maleness of the Jewish benefit performance circuit. For instance, in the *American Jewish Outlook*, there is article promoting a benefit for Hillel Academy, a prestigious Jewish school in Pittsburgh, which managed to turn the school's anniversary fundraiser in 1951 into a premier event featuring headlining comics like Jean Carroll and Georgie Jessel. The article recognized Carroll's anomalous status as the lone Jewess jokester: "When hardened theatrical men take time out to hail a new star, that's news. And when that star happens to be a young comedienne, that's headlines."[30] A photograph in the *Jewish Advocate* documenting her performance at the "Celebrities Night" benefit for the Boston Jewish Memorial Hospital in 1951 shows Carroll surrounded by the (all male) chairmen of the event.[31]

Six years later, the *Jewish Advocate* promoted Jean Carroll's participation in another "Celebrities Night," where she appeared alongside Jackie Miles, Barry Gray, and the Winged Victory Chorus, before a crowd of thirteen thousand people.[32] That article was also illustrated by a photograph that depicted Carroll surrounded by an overwhelmingly male crowd of performers and hospital executives. These images draw attention to how conspicuous Carroll's female body was among the male performers. Even when she was in a Jewish space expressing the Jewish identity that she shared with costars like Myron Cohen and Red Buttons, Carroll was still set apart by her gender. This otherness was not lost on Jewish critics. A reviewer from the *American Jewish Outlook* opined that Carroll "defies every ancient law of show business by working with material usually associated with male comics."[33] While these critics' intent may have been to recognize her achievement as a comedy pioneer, it also had the effect of pointing to Carroll's singular status as a woman stand-up. Even among insiders, she was outside.

In Carroll's 2007 retrospective interview, she reflected, "Long before it became chic to say that you were Jewish, I was a proud Jew."[34] Indeed, in the 1930s through the early '50s, it was hardly chic, or even safe, to say that you were Jewish. And so Carroll expressed her pride by seeking out Jewish venues and audiences, giving her people the gift of laughter. Fortunately—and not coincidentally—these Jewish venues were often profitable and productive places to hone skills and build an audience. Kliph Nesteroff's history of comedy names a litany of comics who made a full career without ever leaving the Catskill Mountains: "Larry Best, Larry Alpert, Jackie Miles, Jackie Winston, Jackie Wakefield, Mal Z. Lawrence, Pat Cooper, Morty Storm. . . . These guys never really made it, but always worked the mountains."[35] Jean Carroll could easily have followed the Larrys and Jackies and made quite a comfortable living staying on the Borscht Circuit of Catskills resorts and Jewish charity benefits. But her trajectory was much larger than that. The Catskill Mountains may have served as a post-vaudeville talent incubator, but once that talent hatched, there was a much broader entertainment industry to explore. Carroll was determined to have the kind of appeal that could cross over, shifting nimbly from Jewish to mainstream audiences. Mainstream comedy was moving to new forums like radio and presentation houses. And Jean Carroll would be part of it all.

Radio Killed the Vaudeville Star: Jean Carroll on the Air

If the Catskills resorts were the inheritors of vaudeville, radio was its conqueror. According to Nesteroff, "there were three million radio sets in 1923 when vaudeville was still humming," but by 1936, "there were thirty million radio sets in American homes and everyone had forgotten vaudeville ever existed."[36] The vaudevillean-turned-radio-star George Burns recalls the transition anecdotally, remarking, "Gracie and I knew that vaudeville was finished when theaters began advertising that their shows would be halted for 15 minutes so that the audience could listen to 'Amos & Andy.' And when the 'Amos & Andy' program came on, the vaudeville would stop, they would bring a radio on stage, and the audience would sit there watching the radio."[37] The period between the 1930s and 1940s is often thought of as the United States' "Golden Age of Radio." In this period, Americans had unprecedented access to news and entertainment from the comfort of their own homes. Franklin D. Roosevelt broadcast his famous "fireside chats," advertising agencies discovered a whole new way to market to customers, and comedians flourished. Many established vaudeville comics like Fanny Brice, Eddie Cantor, Burns and Allen, Jack Benny, Ed Wynn, Bob Hope, and even the ventriloquist Edgar Bergen made the shift into radio. NBC abounded with hit comedies like *Fibber McGee & Molly* and *The Fred Allen Show*.

Like most of the US, Jean Carroll was an avid radio listener. She was a particular fan of the serial dramas *Stella Dallas* and *Our Gal Sunday* (the latter of which featured a staff writer also, confusingly, named "Jean Carroll"). *Our Gal Sunday*, a rags-to-riches story of a young woman engaged to a rich and handsome English lord, struck such a chord with Carroll that she could quote it nearly word-perfect almost fifty years after it went off the air. She even claimed to have bought the fictional heroine an engagement present.[38]

Carroll got her first opportunity on the airwaves in 1940, when she and her husband were still in the comedy duo Carroll and Howe. Capitalizing on the media shift from vaudeville to radio, NBC aired the Saturday-morning program *Vaudeville Theatre on the Air* at 11:30 a.m. on WEAF. Carroll and Howe were initially booked as a guest act for three weeks of the program. However, the duo made a strong impression, prompting the radio critic Ben Gross to exclaim, "Jean Carroll and her boyfriend Buddy Howe—they're a sort of embryonic Burns & Allen outfit—convulsed us," and even rating a mention in Dorothy Kilgallen's famous "Voice of Broadway" column.[39] Their popularity made them "the first to land an extended contract," as NBC kept them on for another six weeks as regulars.[40]

Carroll's most notable experience with radio as a solo comic was connected with the NBC comedy *The Village Store*. Originally hosted by Rudy Vallee, the show transformed radically when Joan Davis joined the cast in 1941. Davis's character of the man-hungry she-wolf became a huge hit and established her as a major comic force. In 1943, when Rudy Vallee left to serve in the Coast Guard, Davis found herself and new addition Jack Haley promoted to cohosts of the newly named *Sealtest Village Store* (sponsored by the Sealtest Dairy Company). The show continued to garner good ratings, and Davis's popularity soared. In 1945, she left *The Village Store* for her own show, *Joanie's Tea Room*, on competing network CBS, leaving the store-manager role open for an up-and-coming comedienne.[41]

For a moment, it looked as though Jean Carroll would be the successor to Ms. Davis. Bea Pepan of the *Milwaukee Journal* reported that an ad man who caught Carroll performing at Washington's Capitol

FIGURE 2.1. Jean Carroll promotional headshot, NBC Western Program Service newsletter, July 15, 1945, saved in Jean Carroll's personal scrapbook. (Private collection of Susan Chatzky)

Theatre praised her as "a kind of female Bob Hope with a bit of Frank Fay added" and signed her on the spot to appear on *The Village Store*.[42] The *Hollywood Reporter* gave a different account, mentioning that "the pact was reportedly set by MCA and McKee & Allbright, a Philadelphia ad agency."[43] An NBC Western Program Service newsletter from a month later broke the news with a front-page photograph. A large glamour shot of Carroll was captioned by the announcement, "Jean Carroll is the lovely comedienne who helps Jack Haley in the fun department of NBC's 'Village Store' every Friday night over NBC-KFI" (figure 2.1).[44]

However, Jean Carroll's time in the "fun department" was short-lived. One account pinpoints Carroll as a replacement for Joan Davis only from July to mid-September 1945. Starting on September 20, 1945, Carroll was replaced by Eve Arden, who would go on to play the role for three seasons before starring in the beloved sitcom *Our Miss Brooks*.[45] Arden left a lasting impression on Carroll, who gushed, "Her persona was dignified, genteel, always. And she was very clever. Dignity and comedy—why not?"[46]

A brief glimpse of Carroll's July 26, 1945, appearance on *The Village Store* shows that her character—also named Jean Carroll—has the same she-wolf tendencies popularized by Joan Davis. Carroll enters by colliding with and being knocked down by a man who chivalrously extends his arm and asks, "May I pick you up?" Carroll quips, "Why not? That's the best offer I've had since the last time I was at the Paris Inn!" In the next scene, Carroll confronts Jack Haley:

> JEAN: I want to talk to you about a love scene you and I are supposed to do tonight at Camp Elliot. I refuse to get up on a stage and make love to you with 3,000 sailors watching. I demand a change!
>
> JACK: What kind of a change?
>
> JEAN: *You* sit in the audience and watch and let the 3,000 sailors make love to me.
>
> JACK: But Jean, 3,000 sailors kissing you, wouldn't that be a little tiring?
>
> JEAN: Nah, those guys are in good shape; they can take it![47]

Carroll's character is clearly well stocked with boy-crazy gags but little else. A critic from the *Hollywood Reporter* called her performance "great" but also felt that "she is just too funny for the part she was expected to play."[48] It appears that the show that launched Joan Davis and Eve Arden was merely a brief gig for Jean Carroll. Carroll's big break into mainstream comedy was happening off the airwaves, in the world of live performance. And the world of live comedy was increasingly moving toward presentation houses.

Palace Is Out, Paramount Is In: Jean Carroll at Presentation Houses

The medium that made Jean Carroll a star—and in which she made lasting innovations on the form of stand-up—was live performance. And in the post-vaudeville era, mainstream live performance meant presentation houses. These massive one- to five-thousand-seat theaters were either owned by or had a deal with a major film studio, so an hour of live entertainment preceded a new motion picture. Typically, a show program at a presentation house would feature a live band with a singer, along with a dance team and a comic doing about twelve minutes of stand-up. Each program would run anywhere from four to six times each day, beginning around 10:00 a.m. The engagements were long, and the money was excellent. Although presentation houses could be found in every major city, Nesteroff asserts, "it was Broadway presentation houses that offered the comedian's largest payday." Major New York City presentation houses included Loew's State, the Capitol, the Music Hall, the Roxy, the Strand, and the Paramount, which had the prestige of slightly more expensive tickets, at fifty-five cents a piece.[49]

It was here that Jean Carroll and the other members of the "Younger Fraternity" really established the genre of stand-up comedy. Unfortunately, one of the new genre's most defining elements was misogyny. Many of the most successful presentation-house comics bonded with their audiences using a seemingly endless supply of jokes complaining about their wives. Led by comedians like Henny Youngman, Alan King, and Shecky Green, stand-up comedy became in large part a forum for men to complain about the women in their lives. Since the first cadre of stand-up comics was disproportionately represented by Jewish men, stand-up comedy was filled with negative stereotypes of Jewish women as consuming, demanding, and aggressive. For example, a staple of Youngman's act was his series of gags at the expense of his (presumably Jewish) wife, including,

"My wife has a black-belt in shopping."
"My wife went to the beach. She talked so much her tongue got sunburnt."
"Do you know what it means to come home at night to a woman who'll give you a little love, a little affection, a little tenderness? It means you're in the wrong house, that's what it means!"
"My wife said to me, 'For our anniversary I want to go somewhere I've never been.' I said, 'Try the kitchen!'"[50]

Youngman's jokes highlight his wife's insistence on material consumption, speaking too much, and resisting her roles as lover and cook. In this way, they paint a picture very much in line with the ongoing stereotype of Jewish women as materialistic, dominating, bottomless pits of consumption.[51] This picture, insulting as it is, provided Carroll with plenty of comic fodder. Later in her career, she would take on many of the charges leveled by these stereotypes of Jewish American women and humanize them with her disarming friendliness and wit.

But in her early days, Carroll found a neat workaround for her lack of a wife to complain about: she complained about her husband. "My mother likes my husband—she says he's better than nothing" was one of her characteristic quips, along with, "I was always attracted to my husband because of his pride. I'll never forget him, standing there with his hair blowing in the breeze, and he too proud to run after it!"[52]

As if to help the medicine of jokes from a woman's perspective go down, Carroll interspersed her one-liners with the more traditionally feminine repertoire of musical numbers. Bill Smith, a vaudeville critic who had been a fan of Carroll and Howe, reviewed her at the Loew's State presentation house doing "a single," for the first time with reticent praise. He acknowledged that she was a "show stopper" who "got the yocks" but criticized her songs for being "pseudo-comic." He advised, "more singing and less mugging, particularly to emphasize punch lines, would help the act."[53]

Carroll's turn at Loew's State was quickly followed by one at the State Theatre, where she was hailed as "boff" and distinguished as "the only turn on the bill to encore."[54] But it was clear that her comedy was still at least partially musical, as a review from her show at the Strand in October 1946 mentions a song parody about the housing shortage called "Sleeping on a Bus."[55] Gigs at major presentation houses across the country came steadily, and Carroll held the crowds with a combination of one-liners and funny songs. Her success as a joking comedy singer was remarkable but not revolutionary. As one critic from this period noted, "There's a lot of the Fanny Brice approach in the work of Jean Carroll."[56] It was only by giving up the songs and leaning into her unique point of view that she would go from a performer who could stand on the shoulders of others to a genuine stand-up. But that was soon to come.

Carroll also spent her time at presentation houses refining her look as a comedienne. Carroll's appearance was part of the equation in a way that her male colleagues' was not. The feminist cultural theorist Linda Mizejewski calls this phenomenon "the historic binary of 'pretty' versus 'funny,'" pointing out that "women comics, no matter what they look like, have been located in opposition to 'pretty.'"[57] Mizejewski charts a long lineage of women comics who have exploited "notions of pretty" to be funny, making lemonade from sexist lemons.[58] Reviews from Jean Carroll's early days as a solo act suggest that she initially held to this misogynistic binary, downplaying her attractiveness with bizarre costumes. A review from 1943 stated that Carroll referred to herself as "a pin-down girl"—a self-deprecatingly comic contrast to the glamorous "pin-up girls."[59] In 1944, a reviewer commented on Carroll's odd apparel, describing her as "off-beam" and adding, "Her costume fits her act."[60] A separate review mentioned that she performed wearing a "business suit," while a critic in 1945 pronounced her "dressed like a yokel."[61] Although I have not found photographs of her act in this period, the reviews suggest that her clothes were intended more for comic effect than glamour.

A women's column by M. Oakley in the *Hartford Daily Courant* sheds more light on how Carroll was presenting herself in the early 1940s. In unabashedly sentimental language, the columnist depicted Carroll as a sort of "weeping clown" character, who relied on her sense of humor because she was too afraid to "show off her prettiness":

> If you were a girl who could keep the boys (and the girls) in stitches, laughing gaily and continuously telling stories with the joke on yourself. If you were pretty but didn't dare show off your prettiness but went strictly for laughs, even though you'd rather have the boys ooh-and-la about you. If you knocked them in the aisles, so to speak, but didn't make yourself happy in making others that way. . . . If when the party was over you went home alone? What would you do about it when you saw yourself as others saw you? . . . Gosh, we're asking you? But that's the act Jean Carroll has at the State Theater and is so good in it that she has the standout name on the bill. She got it watching such gals (and maybe hearing them cry afterwards). And if you're that kind of a gal, be sure and see the act. Barbara Stanwyck [glamour girl] used to be that way before she got smart. Did you know that? . . . Gee, it has set us thinking. Jean, by the way, is on her own now. Her husband is in the service. They used to be a double act.[62]

On a descriptive level, the article reveals that Carroll's act consisted of self-deprecating "stories with the joke on [her]self." But the assumptions about "pretty" and "funny" in the piece are even more telling. On the one hand, there are the girls who "knocked [boys] in the aisles," and on the other hand, there are those on whom boys "ooh-and-la." And the favor falls squarely on the "ooh-and-la" side. Those women unfortunate enough to choose "funny" over "pretty" are doomed to go "home alone."

Barbara Stanwyck is praised for her decision to "get smart," stop being "that way," and become a glamorous actress and model. The underlying message seems to be that—at least based on this critic's interpretation—Carroll's act reinforced the divide between funny and pretty women, with humor stemming from Carroll's pathetic embodiment of the former. In an interview from this period, Carroll commented on her efforts to downplay her looks, stating, "Look, if I wanted to look like a toothpaste ad, I'd become a professional model. My field is comedy."[63]

However, the period between 1945 and 1950 seems to mark a turning point, during which Carroll discarded her pretense of homeliness. Her reviews began commenting on her attractiveness—often with regard to how unusual it was for a comedian. In 1946, a *Variety* critic who praised her as a "show-stopper" also saw fit to remark that she was "a cute-looking trick with a load of acsexories [*sic*]."[64] Another critic, Mal Hallett, commented, "A rarity in the comedy field is Jean Carroll, who is as attractive as she is funny."[65] Carroll's contemporary the comedian Freddy Roman recalled her as a "standard bearer in the field of stand-up comedy," exclaiming, "She was not outrageous! She was not dressed with the flaming hair! She dressed magnificently."[66]

In Carroll's personal scrapbook, these effusive descriptions are illustrated by a series of plastic-encased headshots from this period, each showcasing her glamorous good looks (figure 2.2). One photo, used to promote an upcoming appearance on the stage of the Capitol, is a headshot in which Carroll peers out from under heavily lidded eyes with meticulously manicured brows. Her expression is softly pensive, and the lighting makes it seem as though her carefully coiffed finger waves are encircled by a halo. The other picture—saved without comment or context—looks like it would not be out of place on the cover of a romance novel. The shot displays Carroll's torso in profile, with her head tossed back, her eyes downcast toward her prominent décolletage. The bodice of her dress and its short sleeves are pleated and ruffled, and her dark hair is worn long, spilling down her back in romantically unkempt curls. Her features are heavily defined by dark makeup, with her brow

FIGURE 2.2. Jean Carroll promotional headshots saved in Carroll's personal scrapbook. (Private collection of Susan Chatzky)

heavy and her lips pouted, giving a brooding effect. Both seem curious images to promote a comedian in a society where beauty and comedy were thought to be mutually exclusive.[67]

Women came to rally around Carroll as source of sartorial and cosmetic authority. A reporter for the women's column "Chatter!" commended her "talent for dress that is the last word in chic." Another "Chatter!" column was devoted to Carroll's cosmetic hints, such as her advice to follow a traditional 1950s regimen of "ordinary stage makeup" and her hint that "omitting the rouge makes a woman look prettier."[68]

It may seem backward to interpret a woman dressing glamorously and trying to appear attractive as way of undermining misogyny. However, in the topsy-turvy world of comedy, it was a considerable intervention.

Carroll's embrace of cosmetics and fashion was not simply aesthetic. By proving herself a master at pretty, she was able to claim one of the few modes of power and authority available to women. Later female stand-up comics like Joan Rivers and Phyllis Diller would famously subscribe to the idea that pretty women could not be funny. "God divides!" Joan Rivers repeatedly lamented, bemoaning the mutual exclusivity of female brains and beauty.[69] But Jean Carroll, years ahead of her time, threw the misogynistic binary of pretty versus funny out the window, along with her sheet music.

Aside from misogyny, the defining element of nascent stand-up comedy was speed. Success was measured in how many jokes you could spit out as quickly as possible. The cultural scholar Henry Jenkins views this quality as a holdover from the vaudeville days, explaining that "vaudeville bookers paid for the number of jokes per minute."[70] Even after vaudeville, a comic's jokes-to-minute ratio became a defining element. Henry Youngman's obituary in the *New York Times* eulogized him with the telling metric, "He could tell six, seven, sometimes even eight or more jokes a minute, 50 or more jokes in an eight-minute routine."[71] A tribute to Bob Hope was rendered in similar terms, memorializing his ability to "rattle off jokes at a rate of six per minute."[72] Carroll shared this metric for success. In one interview, she even referenced practicing at home doing "time tests" to make sure that she was maintaining enough jokes per minute.[73]

Reviews of Carroll's early-career appearances at presentation houses approvingly noticed her confident and swift wit. However, critics consistently paired praise with sexism, offering Carroll's success as a freakish anomaly due to her gender. For instance, a critic watching one of her first shows at the Capitol Theatre praised her "speed, assurance, and originality." However, the compliment was buried in an article titled "Jean Carroll Does a Man's Job as a Comic," which reads like a cascade of condescension: "Jean Carroll, clever young comedienne on the Capitol Stage has gone a step farther in the Freedom Drive of Females, proving that a woman can handle comedy lines with the speed, assurance, and originality usually associated with male funsters. Till now the distaff side in the comedy field has more or less contented itself with pat routines as befits the 'weaker' sex. But such is not the case with Jean Carroll. She murders hecklers and is an ad libber par excellence. Pretty, she tosses female tranquility to the winds."[74]

Likewise, the reviewer from *Variety* who caught her debut at the Paramount Theatre commented on her "skillful rapid-fire timing." But he went on to observe that her quick tempo was "unusual delivery for a femme comic, handling the audience exactly like one of her male counterparts."[75] One of Carroll's colleagues on the presentation-house circuit, Jan Murray, echoed the critics, praising her skill at one-liners by declaring that she "banged out jokes like a guy."[76] Of course, there is no reason that speaking with a quick tempo should be essentialized as masculine. A rapid tempo is not so much a product of gender as it is of genre— the emerging genre of stand-up comedy. But time and again, critics and comics viewed Carroll's pace and energy as anomalous for a women. Rather than acknowledge that men did not have special claim on rapid-fire delivery—and the confidence that it suggests—critics instead chose to focus on how her comedy painted her as "masculine."[77]

Another highly gendered element of Carroll's comedy is the content of one of her most popular presentation-house offerings: the racetrack routine. The first published reviews of the racetrack routine start appearing in 1947, right around the time when her bookings at presentation houses really picked up steam.[78] Again, there is nothing inherently masculine about a racetrack. In the 1950s, horse racing was widely popular, ranking as the number-one spectator sport in the United States.[79] Throughout Carroll's life, she was a well-documented racing enthusiast and gambler. An image published in the *Middletown Daily* depicts Carroll happily collecting her winnings after picking a horse with 60–1 odds (figure 2.3).[80]

However, restrictive gender norms masculinized this arena and gambling more generally. The film scholar Julie Assouley demonstrates that media depictions of women gamblers in the late 1940s emphasized

FIGURE 2.3. "Racing at Monticello," *Middletown Daily Record*, July 13, 1960, saved in Jean Carroll's personal scrapbook. (Personal collection of Susan Chatzky)

addiction, loose morals, and sexual depravity.[81] Gambling, it seems, suggested a comfort with risk that men found threatening in women. One study from 1952 found that "women who took chances were less popular."[82] And so it is ironic that by taking an enormous chance—starting her career in the overwhelmingly male-dominated stand-up comedy genre, with a routine about "manly" subject matter—Carroll's popularity soared.

The racetrack routine helped put Carroll on the map—making her a fixture at presentation houses and even leading to an early spot on *Toast of The Town*, the 1949 televised variety show that would later become *The Ed Sullivan Show*. The piece exemplified both Carroll's high jokes-per-minute ratio and her ability to transgress some of the restrictive norms of 1950s femininity.

Unfortunately, the earliest iteration of the racetrack routine has not been thoroughly documented, since presentation houses did not record their live entertainment. The best documented version is a 1949 televised version. However, it is useful to keep in mind that stand-up comedy is a dialogic form, and therefore it changes in subtle but substantive ways based on each individual audience's response. So the "takeoff of a racetrack announcer" that she performed at the State Theatre in 1947 would not be precisely the same as the "race track routine" that critics praised the next night at Loew's State or the "race track routine" that got "yocks" at New York's Capitol Theatre after that.[83] The racetrack routine that Carroll performed at the Olympia in Miami in 1948 would be different from the racetrack routine she did at the Paramount in New York in 1949.[84] And none of them would be identical to the version of the racetrack routine that Carroll performed for a live studio audience at the January 30, 1949, broadcast of *Toast of the Town*. For one thing, every comedy routine changes over time. For another, Carroll had far fewer restrictions without the censure of television executives, even *before* the implementation of the National Association of Radio and Television Broadcasters' draconian "Television Code" in 1952.[85] However, the televised version does offer a glimpse into the general content and style of the routine that gained her such acclaim in the presentation houses.

Carroll began the routine by striding onto the stage with purpose, leading from her shoulders and swinging her arms with just a hint of swagger. She then turned to the audience, one hand planted firmly on her hip, the other gesturing animatedly as she addressed them, exclaiming, "People say I make a lot of money!" Drawing her chin to her chest into a sort of shrug with a disbelieving raise of her eyebrows, she continued,

> Well I *make* it, but I haven't *got* it, because everything I have I give to Charity—that's the name of my bookmaker. As a matter of fact, I went to Eddie the other day. . . . I went to him, and I said, "Ed, this is a little em-barrassing, but I'm broke!" He said, "Well, don't be ashamed. How much do you want? Fifty? Sixty? Eighty? A dollar?" Well, look, he's telling you about how I'm a great handicapper? Don't you believe it. It's not true. The way I've been picking those horses lately, I don't bet them win, place, or show. I bet them to *live* now.[86]

Already, by opening with a bit about finances, loans, and gambling, she placed herself squarely in transgressive territory by taking on material rarely publicly discussed by women. And in her next bit, she continued stepping into men's territory, actually embodying a masculine-presenting character. She first complained about the unsavory men who hang out at racetracks, including "a tout" with a chain: "a real hep shmoe."[87] Then, she assumed the stance of said tout, pursing her lips, pulling at her col-lar, and periodically jerking her shoulders up to her ears. She mimed his nervous tic, continually twirling an invisible pocket chain with her left hand and adjusting her pants with her right. Each time she twirled the pocket chain, she jutted her pelvis out spasmodically. Momentarily dropping the stance, she turned to the audience and remarked, "Well, right away, I know this guy isn't doing good, or he'da bought suspend-ers!" As Carroll resumed her parodic tout stance, the camera panned out, moving from an above-the-waist shot to a full-body shot, giving the viewers a chance to appreciate the comedic contortions she used to illustrate machismo. She continued, going deeper into her parody of hip-gangster masculinity:

He says, "Kid, I got a horse for you. This horse wins, you go home with the track!" I figured that would be a nice change—I had been going home with the bus! He says, "I don't want you to spread it around. I just came from the stable." *That* he didn't have to tell me! He said, "I've been talkin' to the boys—I got a hot tip on a twenty-six-year-old Maiden. The jockey's been holdin' her back, waitin' for a price! Don't worry about a thing. . . . The race is fixed. The jockey's got a battery and a long hatpin. We give the horse a little mara-joo-ini [marijuana] and a couple of shots of Benzedrine!" I said, "That'll make her win?" He says, "Who knows, but she'll be the happiest horse in the race!"[88]

The last joke of this passage is basically an updated version of her old Carroll and Howe quip about using alcohol to get over insomnia. However, placing it in the context of crooked gambling and illegal drugs gave it a more sharply illicit connotation. She then launched into the part of her routine that received the most recognition in reviews: the "takeoff on Ted Husing announcing a horserace."[89] Assuming a low staccato monotone, she sped through a mock commentary:

Good afternoon, ladies and gentlemen. This is Ted Husing, talking from beautiful Belmont Park! It's a lovely day, and what a crowd has turned out to witness this event! Just listen to the hum of the crowd [hums melodically]. Now, the horses are being wheeled around at the starting gate. While we're waiting for them, we have a number of celebrities here. I'd like to get their opinion, see who they think is going to be the winner. Here we have a young man, Sgt. Dumbrowski, just back from three and a half years in the Pacific. Sergeant, what have you got to say?
"I want woman!"

"Thank you very much. Sergeant. I didn't know that horse was running."

And now they're all lined up at the post—eighteen horses going a mile in the sixteenth, nine left over from the last race. Number 5 is on his knees; I think he's praying. The outside horse has a leg missing, but they say he's the fastest thing on three legs. Now they're ready to go. Watch it. Get that full horse in there. AND THEY'RE OFF!

There they go. It's a good start. They all get away, with Prima Donna taking the lead around the clubhouse turn by a length and a half. Lady Flash is running second a half a length over Supermarine. On the outside, Gaybit is running fourth. [Barks] There's that dog I bet on! Around the turn they go. Into the back stretch, it's Prima Donna by two and a half. Nylon is starting to run, and Banana comes out of the bunch! At the top of the back stretch, it is Girdle going wide and dropping out! There goes Danny Jay moving up fast, taking over the lead, Prima Donna dropping back. She should drop into a sewer and get lost with my landlord together! Around the far turn they go, and Underwear is creeping up on the inside! As they turn into the stretch, it's Gaybit a longshot, leading by a half a length! Cabbage is second by a head! Crab-shooter is fading, and Detective is trailing! And now with less than one-eight of a mile to go, the favorite is beginning to move! Here comes Blue Boy! He's on the rails! Now he's back on the track! It's Blue Boy taking the lead by a head! Make it a nose. Danny Jay moving up again on the outside. And now it's Blue Boy ahead a half a length—and Danny Jay. . . . It's gonna be close! Down to the wire they come, and the winner is . . . Twilight! By six legs![90]

It is indeed a virtuosic acting feat, moving through over four hundred words and four voices in seventy seconds, all in a perfectly coordinated rhythmic signature. And the sheer ratio of jokes to time is impressive; Carroll crafts jokes by weaving together puns and wordplay involving the horses' names and racing behaviors. For instance, "Prima Donna . . . tak[es] the lead," "Nylon . . . start[s] to run," "Banana comes out from the bunch," "Cabbage" advances "by a head," and "Detective . . . trail[s]."

However, it was the subject matter of this meticulously calibrated performance that made it unique. The fact that she set her routine in the allegedly "male space" of the racetrack was unprecedented, and the fact that she was able to do so with such authority—using insider racetrack jargon such as "tout," "length and a half," and so on—even more so.

It was not just the horses that turned a corner with the racetrack routine. With this bit, Carroll made a definitive step from a comic chanteuse singing parody songs strung together by jokes to what would today be called a stand-up comic. While the more personal element of her routines was still ahead of her, Carroll had established herself in the pioneering cohort of this high-intensity new form, where success was measured on a second-to-second basis.

"Her timing is faultless," raved a critic of her appearance at the Palace Theatre (living its new life as a presentation house); "the laughs follow each other in almost unending succession."[91] She traveled across the country, playing every major presentation house on the circuit. Nesteroff asserts, "no other comic played as many presentation houses."[92]

With each crowd she worked, Carroll got faster and funnier. By 1953, she played the London equivalent of the Paramount, the two-thousand-seat Palladium. A metrically nonrigorous publication simply referred to Carroll's work as a "laugh-a-second performance."[93] The column called "After Dark" went into slightly more detail, specifying, "In the space of one minute, [Carroll] can deliver at least three major guffaws and two minor ones."[94] London's *Evening Express* was slightly less generous, estimating, "she averages a joke about every seven seconds," a figure also quoted in a column titled "Rapid Fire Wit."[95] The "Night Spot" column made such quantifiable laughter the feature of its article, titled "Six Laughs a Minute!" Mathematically deducing her humor, the columnist wrote, "She talked for thirty-two minutes, and her machine-gun wit was getting laughs every ten seconds. That makes around two hundred laughs at one go—no woman comic has ever been so funny."[96]

But there it is again—that backhanded compliment, that twist of misogyny: "No *woman* comic has ever been so funny." The motif is inescapable in Carroll's reviews. In 1947, *Variety* recognized her as "the only femme comic to hit the big time," a distinction as celebratory as it is isolating.[97] "She's one of the few femme comics who can give vigor to a funny line," raved a reviewer in 1948.[98] "Women comedians are rare and rarely good. Jean Carroll is an exception," quipped a critic soon thereafter.[99] Their praise is poison, laced with language normalizing misogynistic ideas that women cannot be funny and certainly not professionally. Even the award Carroll received from the Gagwriters Institute in 1949—Best Female Discovery—was not an uncomplicated accolade. It was indisputably a great honor to be recognized by her peer comedians. And yet even that recognition suggested something of an anomaly about her. Jean Carroll was a "Female Discovery," while the more august—and nongendered—title of "Best Comedian" went to Milton Berle.[100]

Unfortunately, this emerging sexist theme in the reception of Jean Carroll would become an enduring refrain. Whether it was on the Borscht Circuit or in the mainstream presentation houses, she was always the lone female, and her success was always qualified "for a woman." In her later years, she would speak out against this kind of marginalization, asking, "Why do people keep adding on 'for a woman' whenever they start to say something nice about one of us?"[101] But as she built her career and solidified her place in the "Younger Fraternity," she had to be creative to face her obstacles. In chapter 3, we will see how she used the baggage, preconceptions, stereotypes, and conspicuousness that came with her Jewishness and her gender to her advantage in the world of nightclubs and the dawn of the television.

3

"The First Lady of Laughs"

Jean Carroll on the Nightclub Comedy Scene

A 1950s nightclub was no place for a nice Jewish housewife. As urbane couples sneaked glances over cocktails, mobs ruled, men sneered, women judged, and male comics telling dirty jokes dominated the mic.

These dens of iniquity and wisecracks descended from the speakeasies of the Prohibition era. As Marni Davis explored in *Jews and Booze*, during Prohibition, Jewish Americans had played major roles keeping the alcohol flowing.[1] It was not a far leap into the world of speakeasies and nightclubs, or "rathskellers," where customers could enjoy "raw liquor, raw comedy, and raw companionship."[2] The more "legitimate" entertainment venue functioned as a front for the illegal operations. As a 1928 *Variety* column reported, "many of the nightclubs have bar adjuncts adjacent to or on the premises, but 'independently' operated and thus clear of the enforcement law's machinations and machinery in the event of an unsocial visit from the gendarmes."[3]

In Chicago, the famous Jewish mobster Ike Bloom owned major speakeasies like Freiburg's, the Deauxville Café, and Midnight Frolics, the latter being one of the first clubs established after World War I.[4] The Jewish gangster Joe Jacobsen (with Mike Fritzel) fronted the Mafia kingpin Al Capone controlling Chez Paree in Chicago. And in New York, the Jewish hood Louis Schwartz ran Chateau Madrid, which *Variety* called "a hotsy totsy" club where "the mob gathers and others flock."[5]

After the repeal of Prohibition in 1933, the predominance of Jewish producers and purveyors of alcohol was not as dramatic. But Jewish gangsters still remained major movers and shakers in the United States' criminal underground and burgeoning nightclub scene. Perhaps the most storied Jewish mafioso, Meyer Lansky, set up shop near Miami Beach, which the comic Alan King called "the Vegas of the 1940s" because of the boom in hotels and clubs featuring gambling, liquor, and comedy.[6] The comedy historian Kliph Nesteroff estimates that forty new hotels opened in 1940 alone.[7] In 1946, the Jewish gangster Jack Greene opened the nightclub La Conga in New York, the same year that the notorious Jewish mobster Benjamin "Bugsy" Siegel opened the Flamingo Hotel and Casino in Las Vegas.[8] Bernie Barton, another Jewish gangster—and the owner of New York's Velvet Room nightclub—referred to the Jewish mob as the "Kosher Nostra," playing off the infamous "Cosa Nostra" term for the Sicilian Mafia.[9]

By the early 1950s, when Senator Estes Kefauver held his famous hearings exposing organized crime in the United States, many American Jews were dismayed to see the highly publicized and prominent role of Jews in the "outfit." A Jewish newspaper featured the lamentation, "Only a Jew whose heart has become impervious to Jewish honor and Jewish life could have listened to the Kefauver hearings and not blanch."[10] But as some American Jews wrung their hands over the *shonda* of the Kefauver hearings, Carroll and her colleagues played the mob-run nightclubs that were quickly becoming the premier venues for stand-up comedy.

* * *

As with the presentation houses, a disproportionate number of the rising stand-up comedy stars in nightclubs were Jewish men. The comic Joe E. Lewis, born in New York to a Russian Jewish family, got connected to the mob early in his career, during Prohibition. He established a popular act with dipsomaniacal humor and one-liners like "I drink to forget I drink." In a highly storied incident of 1927, he angered the proprietor of Chicago's Green Mill club and was attacked by mob thugs, who slit his throat and left him for dead. Lewis recovered, relearned how to speak, and returned to the mob's good graces by refusing to rat out his attackers. He spent the remainder of his career as a successful fixture in nightclubs, telling jokes in between sips of whiskey.

One of Lewis's most admired colleagues was another Jewish comic, Shecky Greene, né Sheldon Greenfield. Although Shecky Greene would later become the first lounge comic of Las Vegas, in the early 1950s he was working nightclubs like the House of Hastings in Minneapolis and Chez Paree in Chicago.[11] Shecky Greene also survived an attack by the mob, which he famously joked about in the quip, "Frank Sinatra saved my life. Five guys were beating me up, and I heard Frank Sinatra say, 'That's enough.'"[12]

Henny Youngman was another Jewish comic who excelled in the mob's nightclubs, explaining, "If they like you, they'll take anything. If not, you'd get your head broken somewhere."[13] And Alan King, another pioneering Jewish stand-up comic, recalled his nightclub years as "the days when everybody [he] worked for got killed."[14]

In this mob-run milieu, Jewish men entertained crowds, often making women the butt of their jokes. "A man doesn't know true happiness until he's married," went one of Joe E. Lewis's most famous quips, "and then it's too late."[15] Henny Youngman gave one-liners like, "Why do Jewish divorces cost so much? Because they're worth it."[16] While Shecky Greene's act was best known for physical antics like climbing the curtain or taking apart the microphone, he included a few of the requisite wife jokes. His favorite went, "After he performed the wedding ceremony, the rabbi told the young, happy groom, 'Son, you're at the end of all your troubles. Good luck and God bless you.' A year later the young man revisited him and complained, 'This has been the worst year of my life! And you told me I was at the end of all my troubles.' 'That's right,' the clergyman replied. 'Only I didn't say which end.'"[17] Jerry Lewis, a goofy Jewish boy from New Jersey, joined up with the suave Dean Martin to become a powerhouse comedy duo and the crown princes of the Copacabana nightclub in New York. Lewis and Martin's buddy comedy act featured jokes interspersed with merrily sexist songs. Alan King was "an unabashed exemplar of Jewish comedy, a through-and-through New Yorker whose sensibility, delivery, and accent never migrated far from their Brooklyn roots."[18] He literally wrote the book on Jewish jokes, including such highlights as,

"Where does a Jewish husband hide money from his wife? Under the vacuum cleaner."

"What's the difference between a Catholic wife and a Jewish wife? The Catholic wife tells her husband to buy Viagra; the Jewish wife tells her husband to buy Pfizer."[19]

This colorful cast of characters (among many others) populated the mob-ruled nightclub stand-up scene that would become Jean Carroll's home in the 1950s. It may not have been the most intuitive place for a comic with a suburban Jewish housewife persona, but Jean Carroll made it work with the tools at her disposal: her skill, her body, her microphone, and her inimitable point of view.

Of course, what currently remains of Jean Carroll's "club act" is only a fraction of the comic repertoire she performed in the niteries. Because of the dearth of recordings, what happened in midcentury nightclubs often stayed in midcentury nightclubs. Because it is not customary for stand-up comedians to publish their text in the way that playwrights publish their scripts, stand-up is even more ephemeral than theater. Sadly, the nightclub forum in which Carroll was freest of social strictures is also the most elusive to scholars. Thankfully, some evidence exists in the form of critical reviews, a bootleg audio recording, and later approximations of the nightclub acts that Carroll performed on television and albums.

Turning Constraints into Comedy

Jean Carroll's transition into the nightclub scene came with plenty of rough patches. The self-declared lifelong student had a lot to learn, with hostile colleagues and audiences as her instructors. One of her earliest nightclub gigs was at the Chase Hotel in St. Louis, where she recalled that during her set, "the drummer would drop the cymbals. They did this and laughed, thinking it was the funniest thing."[20] In a 1952 article colorfully titled "Woman Comic Plays to 'Guy with a Sneer,'" Carroll shared, "If the male comics don't eat you alive, there's always a chance that the audience will."[21] In a separate interview, she added, "Both the men and the women sit there as if grimly daring you to make them laugh."[22]

Carroll's reviews from early club dates enhance this picture of a stone-faced crowd. A sympathetic critic from a Chicago nightclub observed that Carroll "had a tough time of it."[23] In 1946, the reviewer from chic New York City club La Martinique went into more detail about the obstacles she faced: "This is a tough room at all times, . . . especially tough on a distaff side comic because of the fact that customers are accustomed to male funsters. Consequently, Miss Carroll finds the going there a bit tough. Despite the fact that she's done well in large vauderies with similar material, she's in a bit of a spot here, as the verbiage isn't designed for cafes."[24]

The critic referenced an important point about the difference between the "verbiage" for vauderies versus for nightclubs (cafes). For one thing, nightclubs needed a great deal *more* verbiage. Nesteroff estimates that the average stand-up comedian in a vaudeville or presentation-house venue needed only between eight and eighteen minutes, whereas a nightclub stand-up act needed forty-five.[25] For another thing, the stand-up acts in nightclubs trafficked more in risqué jokes—usually with that distinctive midcentury blend of misogyny and objectification. Even before the dawn of "sick comics" like Lenny Bruce and Mort Sahl, nightclub audiences were looking for something a little edgier.

Ever the raconteur, Jean Carroll told a story about the formative moment in her career when she really learned how to master the nightclub crowd. She was contracted in a Las Vegas nightclub for a weeklong gig, but it was going so poorly that by the third or fourth night, she was ready to quit. In her telling, she approached the manager, whom she called Mr. X, and said,

> "I'm not doing well, it's not fair to you. It's my first appearance in a nightclub, and especially in Las Vegas. So if you don't mind, can we abrogate this contract?"

He said, "Would you do that?"

I said, "Absolutely. You're paying me to be good, and I'm not effective at all."

He said, "Oh gee, you're a great girl—Give me a few days, because I've got to get somebody else from Los Angeles."

I said, "Okay."

And that night . . . I had a few drinks . . . and I got looped.

And I walked out on the stage and I said, "Hi all you drunken bums out there! Tonight I'm one of you!"

. . . And I went on with this whole thing. And I was *funny*. I told them the whole story about coming to Vegas . . . and my impressions of the town, and the people, and they were laughing! They were really enjoying it!

After the show, Mr. X came over and he said, "That's great! You're wonderful!"

And I said, "No I'm not. I stink!"

He said, "No, you don't! *That's* what I want you to do!"

I said, "You think I'm going to get drunk every night to go out on stage just to be funny? Forget it!" But he insisted.

So I didn't do *that*. But I did change the whole tone of the thing. I just got rid of the set part of the routine and did whatever came into my head about the different people that I'd met there, and how they passed the time. . . . It was funny because they could identify with it. Any time you can get guys punching each other and saying, "Hey, that's you! That's you!" You know you've got them.

Carroll ended the story on a triumphant note, with "Mr. X" picking up her option and her becoming "the big darling" of Vegas and the night-club world.[26] But the story is perhaps best taken with a grain of salt (or even a whole rim). It is likely that the crowd-working skills that Carroll learned came not from a drunken night of comic candor but from several years of experience. Apocryphal or not, the story serves as a window into Carroll's discovery that the boozy world of nightclubs thrived on less restrained performance. Unlike the Paramount and others like it, a nightclub was a smaller, more intimate space that called for a less presentational style. So whether Carroll's Las Vegas tale is an accurate account, a composite of different experiences, or a pure fabrication, it points to the lesson that what nightclub crowds wanted was a loss of inhibition and a healthy dose of transgression.

By Carroll's debut at the Chez Paree club in 1946, she could deliver on both counts. The *Variety* critic called her a "top flight comic," noting that "the bulk of her material dips into the blue, but that's where the nitery patrons get their biggest kicks."[27] Tastefully (if frustratingly) the critic omitted any of her "blue" jokes from his review. However, a rare bootleg audio recording from Carroll's performance at a nightclub in Detroit in 1956 features some of the risqué material that she may have debuted in these earlier years. In one gag, Carroll described a suitor who asked her, "Will you have breakfast with me? Shall I call you or nudge you?" disclosing that "he was separated from his wife—she was in the living room, he was in the dining room." She also had a collection of "Old Maid" one-liners (e.g., "Did you hear about the Old Maid who died and on her gravestone was the following inscription, 'Who says you can't take it with you?'"). In a different gag, she imitated a hotel clerk, asking a guest, "Are you entertaining a woman in your room?" to the rejoinder, "Wait, I'll ask her." She even performed a fairly graphic bit involving imitations of the noises made by amorous couples that she heard through the hotel air vents.[28] Clearly, Carroll could play ball(s) with the best of them in the dirty joke arena.

However, as Carroll learned from her debut at the Copacabana in 1948, "playing blue" could be a riskier proposition for a woman stand-up than it was for a man. Appearing at New York's legendary Copacabana was a major milestone. The Latin-themed club was officially owned by the British Jew Monte Proser and managed by the American Jewish gangster Jules Podell, but it was actually run by the Italian mobster Frank Costello. The club was colorful and opulent, decorated with giant plaster palm trees and populated by "Copacabana Girls" adorned in Carmen Miranda–inspired fruit headpieces. It could fit between 670 and 1,500 audience members, who came in droves seeking its famously top-tier performers and (unexpectedly) Chinese food.[29] The club's seemingly happy mélange of ethnic influences belied its strict segregationist policy, which in its earliest years even barred Black performers.[30] But as a white woman, Jean Carroll had access to this career-making venue. And as the wife of the entertainment agent Buddy Howe, she even had an advantage; according to his obituary in *Variety*, Howe "virtually dictated which names went into the Copacabana."[31]

Carroll took every advantage offered to her, performing an expanded version of her racetrack routine and enjoying great success with the Copa crowd. The *Variety* critic called it a "socko booking," remarking, "as a monologing comedienne, she's a rarity in or out of the niteries."[32] However, even amid the critic's effusive praise, he took a moment to chastise her for unladylike conduct, admonishing, "the constant references to the Racing form, etc. more becomes a Joe E. Lewis than a femme."[33] He took no pains to hide the double standard—it was simply a truth universally acknowledged that certain material that was acceptable and praiseworthy for male comics was "unbecoming" for a woman stand-up. Nitery patrons may have gotten a kick out of transgressive humor, but it seems that a woman stand-up tested their limits.

Jean Carroll was outspoken about this double standard throughout her career, calling out the limitations on her act enforced by social norms of femininity. What she *never* spoke publicly about—but what is key to understanding why her persona was such a major intervention—is how the social norms of femininity were altered by being Jewish. Intersectional theory posits that gender norms are inextricable from racial and ethnic norms.[34] So at any given historical moment, the social norms and expectations for a white Anglo-Saxon Protestant woman will differ from those for a Jewish woman, which will differ from those for a Black woman, and so on. These norms and expectations are set by myriad cultural factors, one of which is representation in popular discourse. And in the late 1940s and 1950s, in nightclubs and beyond, much of the popular discourse around Jewish women was rooted in disparaging stereotypes.

Again, part of the cause for the widely circulating negative stereotypes of Jewish women was the Jewish men dominating the stand-up scene. Riv-Ellen Prell's study on Jewish assimilation and gender relations points to midcentury Jewish comics like Henny Youngman, the "King of the One-Liner," and Jack Carter, who explained his single status with "two words: my mother."[35] But she also charts a larger historical pattern of Jewish men projecting antisemitic tropes onto Jewish women. In the 1950s, this meant accusations of "permissiveness, indulgence, and a focus on consumption." In Prell's findings, the stereotypical Jewish mothers/wives of the 1950s were hopelessly "parochial" and "wanted too much—whether it was love, loyalty, or mink—precisely as antisemitic attitudes suggested that Jews did."[36]

Jewish women were frequently represented as unattractive, with regard to both appearance and personality. Prell excavates memoirs of the 1950s to show how a Jewish girl was "constantly conscious of physical features that made her feel different from other Americans."[37] Having one's nose "bobbed" became a painful commonality for young Jewish women who could afford cosmetic surgery.[38] Just as damning was the casual rhetoric casting Jewish women as loud, uneducated, and vulgar. In 1942, as Carroll and Howe toured the USO circuit, *She* magazine published a piece by a Jewish woman addressing her fellow Jewesses with the admonition to "stop forcing themselves upon 'more cultured' people" and urging Jews (like herself) who were "more advanced than the rest of the race" to help the others learn reserve and tact.[39] Aviva Cantor, cofounder of the Jewish feminist magazine *Lilith*, recalls growing up in the 1950s, when "the worst insult was to tell a young Jewish woman that she was talking like a Jewish fishwife."[40] Even as late as 1959, the sociologist Vance Packard published a study showing that Jewish men were excluded from social clubs partially on account of their wives, who were considered unlikely to mix well with the more refined (gentile) corporate spouses.[41] Young Jewish women in this period were fed a rhetorical diet telling them that they were ugly, excessive, and irredeemably plebeian. And all of this was part of what Jean Carroll was reacting against every time she stepped up to the microphone.

But, of course, Jean Carroll was not explicitly writing about (or perhaps even thinking about) her identity in intersectional terms. She never spoke of being a "Jewish woman"—only of being a woman. In her published writing, she focused on how being a woman restricted her in two major areas: her material and her appearance. A 1952 article titled "Jean Carroll Hits Handicap of Femininity" published Carroll critiquing the "latitude with his material" that men enjoyed:

> He can do pie-in-the-face routines and pratfalls and get big laughs, he can use risqué lines and can imitate a woman putting on a girdle. A comedienne can't. . . . If she uses "blue" lines or attempts to impersonate male characteristics, it's considered undignified. . . .
>
> A Man can jump off a stage, run into the audience, take off his jacket, roll up his sleeves, pull off his tie, mess up his hair or poke fun at the bandleader, and get a lot of laughs. A woman who does these things loses the respect of her audience.[42]

The antics that Carroll describes in this passage read like a description of Milton Berle's act, in which he not only imitated a woman putting on a girdle but did a fair bit of "cross-dressing" himself. In a separate interview, Carroll described teaming up with Berle, as well as other male comics like Bob Hope, Jimmy Durante, Jack Benny, and Joe E. Lewis, and getting a front-row seat to the "wider freedoms" that they carry. "They can imitate a woman taking a bath . . . and everyone will think it is howlingly funny," she observed. "If I imitated a man taking a bath, it would be unfeminine. People would be asking each other, "Wait, how did she find that out—was she peeking through keyholes?'"[43] Carroll's language suggests that as a woman, she had two options: either she drastically limit her repertoire to exclude the "wider freedoms" of her male colleagues, or she resign herself to "lose the respect of her audience" and be seen as "undignified" and "unfeminine."

Nevertheless, a few counterexamples were cropping up, as a handful of other women were very slowly joining Carroll on the nightclub comedy scene. In Miami, "The Mouth" Martha Raye was a fixture at the Five O'Clock Club doing slapstick humor and zany clowning. Belle Barth was playing club dates in Miami, New York, and Chicago, scandalizing crowds with her blend of bawdy parody songs and Yiddish-inflected raunchy patter. In 1950, a *Variety* critic noted that many "funmakers on the distaff side" were having success with humor that was "dependent on extreme mugging and physical gaucheries."[44] Granted, these women were primarily doing musical comedy and not stand-up, but they certainly were succeeding with outlandish routines that threw standard ideas of "femininity" to the wind in pursuit of laughter. So by the mid-'50s, Carroll had to concede that it was at least *possible* for women to get laughs with pratfalls and ribaldry, though she made it clear that this was not her métier. She was openly scornful of female comedians whom she felt indulged in "grotesque comedy," declaring, "I can't stand to see a woman lose her dignity," pointing to Martha Raye as a prime example.[45] She was also quoted giving the biting comment, "Practically everybody will laugh at a woman who lets down her dignity and makes a fool of herself in public. . . . I have an aversion to seeing a woman make a buffoon of herself on the stage."[46]

Carroll's hostility on this subject raises a fairly revealing question: Why were dignity, respect, and femininity so important to her that she would not only limit her *own* material but also criticize other women comics for not doing the same? After all, she worked in comedy—a genre not revered for its dignified, respectable, or feminine cultural cachet. It would seem logical to forgo those restrictive ideals and chase the laughs. But instead, she acknowledged the double standard but *still* conformed to the restrictive norms of midcentury American femininity.

This choice suggests that she was going after something more than laughter. Although she almost certainly would not put it in these terms, it seems that she was trying to craft a new kind of female comic persona that wove together traits deemed mutually exclusive by male stand-ups. While Alan King and his cohort advanced stories of (implicitly or explicitly Jewish) wives as vulgar harridans, Carroll embodied a genteel (if not gentile) counterpoint. She approached a microphone that was always already haunted by stereotypes of the unappealing, unruly Jewess and modeled an alternative mode of Jewish femininity. "Few men are willing to concede that a woman, especially one who is chic and well-poised, can be funny," she pronounced in Dorothy Kilgallen's famous "Voice of Broadway" column, and this is precisely what she set out to prove.[47]

Carroll's adopted moniker, "The First Lady of Laughs," speaks to this intervention—the sobriquet was coined by critics but used widely by Carroll in publicity material.[48] She did not want to be a "Bawdy Broad," like Sophie Tucker or Mae West. She did not want to be a "Dumb Dora," like Gracie Allen, or a Yiddish clown, like Fanny Brice. She wanted to be an assimilated American capital-L Lady—the picture of dignity, respectability, and femininity. *And* she wanted to get the laughs. So she stayed within a more circumscribed field of material. In one interview, she reasoned that "the restrictions weren't too bad, because actually the simple situations in life . . . are still the funniest."[49] And so shopping, parenting, and other "simple situations" of domestic suburban life—albeit from a Jewish woman's perspective—became her comedy fodder.

* * *

The other limitation that Carroll spoke of publicly was her appearance. Her attractive features, athletic physique, and fabulous wardrobe seemed to be a point of pride, silently refuting stereotypes of homely Jewish women. In keeping with her persona as a sophisticated American lady, she typically dressed in simple, elegant high fashion. Most advertisements for Carroll's nightclub shows (such as the ones in figures 3.1 and 3.2) depicted her in a body-hugging gown and elbow-length gloves, with one or two statement accessories. Her granddaughter recalled Carroll's closet filled with dresses labeled, "Expressly made for Jean Carroll by Neiman Marcus." Carroll herself offered a thriftier view, sharing, "My sister was at the time the trimmings buyer for Geoffrey Beene, and she would get me these wonderful gowns at wholesale prices!"

However, Carroll also wrote about how her good looks acted as a limitation, noting that they dictated her changing costume choices. In 1951, she was quoted lamenting that "the greatest difficulty she experiences is overcoming audience reluctance to believe that a good-looking woman in an evening dress can be a comedienne."[50] Likewise, when Carroll filled in for Dorothy Kilgallen's "Voice of Broadway" column, she wrote that her "glamorous" looks threatened to become a "distraction," as "the feminine part of the audience will be more interested in her gown and her hair-do than what's being said."[51] Far more threatening than distraction, according to Carroll, was resentment. In 1956, an interview quoted her proclaiming, "Men in the audience instinctively resent listening to anything clever by a woman, particularly if she appears poised and well-dressed. And the women resent her too, because they are afraid the men will listen to her. It's a kind of jealousy in them. They keep thinking about how nice it would be if they were up there on the stage and had all these men listening to them."[52] In these publications, Jean Carroll described her glamorous appearance as an obstacle—one that threatened her with reluctant, distracted, or resentful audiences. She made some modifications to her costume for fear of inciting jealousy, explaining, "When I started out in nightclubs, I wore cocktail dresses. And if the husband would comment, 'Hey, dig those gams,' the women didn't like me. I decided I'd cover my legs, so I went from the short cocktail dresses to the long gowns." However, she continued to see the value in a well-coiffed comic persona, adapting the ethos, "make it glamorous."[53] Carroll's appearance gained attention from critics and audiences and—perhaps even more significantly—helped to establish her revolutionary persona: an outspoken Jewish woman, a witty stand-up comic, *and* an amiable, elegant lady.

FIGURE 3.1 AND 3.2 Advertisements with full-body photographs of Jean Carroll, one captioned "hailed as woman's answer to man's superiority," n.d., saved in Jean Carroll's personal scrapbook. (Private collection of Susan Chatzky)

Few Women Click In Comedy Field

By STEVEN H. SCHEUER

Jean Carroll, America's only "stand-up" comedienne, has a definite theory on why so few gals have clicked in the comedy field. "In order to be funny, you've got to tell jokes about yourself and your family. Women are, as a rule much too self-conscious for this."

Miss Carroll, who has an exclusive TV deal with Ed Sullivan and shows up on his stage this Sunday, is obviously not self-conscious. Her routine; about her husband, daughter and herself are comedy classics. In spite of some of Jean's riotous comments about her family, she is very devoted to her husband, an exec at General Artists, and her daughter, "who just happens to be a genius."

"My husband, he's a doll," began Jean, writing a routine as she talked. "Buy a Florida hotel, he told me. Don't buy it when things are good, buy it now when it's snowing down there." Jean assured me that she would have retired years ago if it wasn't for these investments. They keep her so broke she has to work to support them. "As soon as we got that hotel, my husband suggested we hire an efficiency expert to figure out how to save money. The efficiency expert told us to fire two chambermaids who were being paid a total of $100 a week. We paid the expert his $10,000 fee and then had to rehire the maids because nobody was making the beds."

As far as her daughter is concerned, Jean is a true P-TA mother. Her youngster has an exceptional IQ and is a budding artist. "At four in the morning, she jumps out of bed and starts painting. I'm inspired, she tells me. 'So get inspired tomorrow,' I tell her. What a kid! I took her to Vegas with me once. Before I left, my husband told me to stay away from the crap table. I'm there a few days, and I'm getting a bit casino-hungry, but I couldn't shake the kid. It was about forty degrees out, but I told her to go swimming. I sneaked into the casino, and as I'm shaking the dice in walks a shivering little girl. 'Yyyyoo assanid yyyou'd sstay aaway ffrom the tntables.' I don't take her with me any more."

Miss Carroll writes all her own material, and after you talk to her for a few minutes you realize why. She's a natural wit and, although she admits she's at a disadvantage because of her sex, could probably ad lib with her male contemporaries. "I don't write the stuff I use on Ed's show. I can't write a four-and-a-half minute routine. My comedy depends on character — it has to build. If I walked out on the stage and said 'Good evening, folks. My mother's been without a husband for twelve years. No, she's not a widow, my father is hiding' it would die. But once I talk for a while it fits in."

There's No Rattle In Jean's Skeleton

By JOHN WATSON

THERE is something terribly, terribly wrong about Jean Carroll. We say this in the usual spirit of kindliness that has made our name a byword wherever bywords are spoken, and also because she ruined a lead to this piece we made up on the way to her Park ave. apartment. The imaginary lead went like this: "All right, jerk," snarled Jean Carroll, "let's get this over with."

She was smiling when we entered, smiling when we left and in between pleasant and amusing. That is what is terribly, terribly wrong. Since the invention of "Who was that lady I seen you with?" (531, B.C.) it has been incontestably established that comedians, in their private lives, are bad-tempered, venomous and churlish.

She's a Smash

And Miss Carroll is one of our foremost comediennes. The record says so. She has been a smash in almost every top club in this country and abroad. She's had her own TV show. She played a command performance in London's Palladium. Now she is appearing in Broadway's Old Roumanian Club where, on opening night, the customers kept her talking for 53 minutes and the management began to worry about overtime.

"I have a basic skeleton," she said.

"Aha," we said. "Maybe you're not beyond help, after all. Just stretch out and talk, and before you know it we'll have you in your true, surly, integrated self."

"I am very comfortable where I am," Miss Carroll said. "And my true self is not surly. The basic skeleton is that I like people."

"Abnormal and shocking," we said.

"And therefore," she went on, paying no attention, "I talk about everyday things — a woman buying a mink coat wholesale, shopping for a dress in Miami, a man at the race track, a husband when the bills come in."

"And that's all?"

"Of course. I have a couple of secrets. For instance, no matter how big or small the audience is, I talk to only one person."

"Now we're really getting somewhere," we said. "You mean this guy follows you around from place to place and has a ringside table every night. Who is he? A nom - de - plume nobleman? Clark Gable? An ousted French premier? Tell us and you'll feel normal and depressed."

He's Excepted

"I said I liked people," Miss Carroll repeated, giving us a cool, hard look, "but of course there are bound to be exceptions. In your case, for example. What I meant was that I make believe I am talking to only one person. I make it seem as if I were talking to someone in my home, and the audience feels it, too."

"What's the other secret?"

"I always turn the joke on myself." "Well," we said, "there's just one chance in a million that we can help you. Have you always liked people?" "Ever since I can remember."

We didn't want to tell her, but we will tell you. She's a hopeless case.

FUNNY GIRL . . . Jean Carroll is a toplight performer in a field usually dominated by men. She's one of the funniest on best night club comediennes in the world. [...] at the Old Roumanian.

FIGURE 3.1 AND 3.2 *Continued*

One of the best showcases of Carroll turning constraints into comedy is her "buying a dress" bit.[54] The first published record of Carroll's "routine where she is coerced into buying a gown she only stopped to look at" appeared in a review from the presentation-house circuit in 1947.[55] But shortly after, notices from nightclubs began referring to the bit as a staple of her act. The routine exemplifies her comment on the limited repertoire allowed to her: "I can be as funny as I'm able about the gullibility of women shoppers, but I don't dare make the same sort of gibes about their husbands."[56] Accordingly, Carroll sets her scene in a ladies clothing boutique, depicting an all-female cast of characters ranging from a pushy shopkeeper to the much-maligned persona, a reluctant shopper.

The televised version of the "buying a dress" routine that Carroll delivered on January 16, 1949, on Ed Sullivan's *Talk of the Town* is, of course, not identical to the versions that she was performing in nightclubs. In all likelihood, it is a highly sanitized version. But the televised footage does offer a glimpse of the basic content of the routine and how Carroll made comedy out of both unspoken stereotypes of Jewish women and mandates to traffic only in "ladylike" subjects. Her appearance on the show was meticulous, with her hair styled in shoulder-length curls pinned back with sparkling clips, her makeup heavy and precise. She began the routine by drawing attention to her fitted black drape gown:

See this dress? I didn't want it, I was only looking. So, I walked into the store—well, I didn't exactly walk in—there was a hook helping me!

And I got inside, I said to the girl, "What's the size of the dress in the window?"

She says, "It'll fit you."

I said, "Well, what is it? A 10? A 12?"

She says, "It's your size. Take it, this dress was *made* for you."

I didn't even know I was gonna be in the neighborhood, she made a dress for me!

The moment Carroll shifted from the story's narrator into the character of the shopgirl, she changed her voice and physicality. As if summoning the ghost of the Jewish woman stereotype, she transformed. As she set her jaw into a sullen expression, lowered her lids so that her eyes were nearly closed, and adopted a slower, lower voice with a stronger New York accent, the context of the garment-industry boutique became more legibly ethnic. The fact that Carroll played both the pushy (crypto-)Jewish salesperson and the relatable narrating shopper puts the difference between stereotype and "reality" into dramatic contrast. This device of one actor playing multiple characters is a staple of the theatrical tradition, and it is a very useful tactic for destabilizing stereotypes. The fluidity with which Carroll slipped from one character to the next reveals the artifice and superficiality of the stereotype. For just as quickly as she "put on" the crypto-Jewish shopkeeper character, she flung it away. The shopkeeper's scowl was replaced by the persona's bright grin, and her voice returned to its high-pitched, up-tempo cadence. Back in this "shopper" persona, she continued,

"I don't think the lines are right for me. My legs are too short."
She said, "They reach the floor, don't they?"
I said, "I really wanted something in blue."
She says [with a sidelong glance], "Jenny, look who wants blue."
I said, "What's wrong with blue?"
She says, "Blue isn't your color."
I said, "Why?"
She says, "We haven't got any."
Well, I said, "I really would like my husband to come down and look at the dress."
She says, "Jenny, look who's married!"

The shopkeeper was further villainized with every line she spoke, meeting the shopper's request to wear blue and reference to her husband with snide incredulity. And with each slight Carroll's shopper persona suffered, she became more endearing and funnier to the audience; in the televised recording, the laughs grew louder and longer. By this point in her career, Carroll was well versed in the mechanics of the status shift. Echoing Thomas Hobbes's "Superiority Theory of Humor" (which posits that audiences laugh because they feel better than the person they are laughing at) Carroll was quoted explaining, "the task is to get them to feel superior to you."[57] The audience could feel superior to both the self-important shopkeeper *and*—more sympathetically—to the contrasting character of Carroll's persona, unjustly put in a low-status position.

Riled up, the persona exclaimed to the shopkeeper, "Well, I'm sorry, the dress doesn't exactly send me!" Not to be knocked from her high-status pose, the shopkeeper returned with, "Who sent for *you*?" As the sketch continued, the shopkeeper leaned harder into the stereotype of the demanding Jewish woman:

> "Listen, we don't use pressure in this store! You don't like the dress? Try it on! Believe me, if you don't like that dress, we'll give you the store!"
>
> I figured I'd be in partners, so I tried the dress on.
>
> She said, "It's stunning. It's gorgeous. That dress is *you*."
>
> I said, "If this dress is me, I'll take *you*!"
>
> "You don't like this dress? You? [gesturing to another customer] Mrs. B—Mrs. B, I want an honest opinion. Forget that I own the store. Forget that you're my best friend. Give me an honest opinion! Look at that little doll. Go on [grimacing], force yourself. Look at that little doll!"
>
> All right, they convinced me I was a doll. I said, "How much is it?"
>
> She says, "Have you been up the next block?"
>
> I said, "No, they haven't got a hook that long."
>
> She says, "I take an oath—I'm not a well woman. I have arthritis. It doesn't matter. I'm not interested in making a sale. Because it doesn't matter. Do me a favor, buy it. Whatever you pay me, I lose money on every dress I sell."
>
> I say, "Really? How do you stay in business?"
>
> She says, "Eh, I fool around with the books."
>
> So I bought the dress!

With tactics that include gross overstatement ("This dress is you!"), guilt ("I'm not a well woman. . . . It doesn't matter"), and cunning ("I fool around with the books"), the pushy saleswoman embodied the same negative Jewish stereotypes that Jean Carroll was standing up against. But, crucially, the pushy saleswoman was not Jean Carroll's persona. The pushy saleswoman was a straw man, a superficial stereotype whose domineering, tactless self-importance made her a contrasting character to highlight the assimilated, unassuming refinement of Carroll's "true" persona: the wry observer, the amiable storyteller, the reluctant shopper. With this routine, Carroll took the ghost that haunted her microphone—the demanding Jewish wife/mother—and used it as two-dimensional foil to establish her own, far more humanized, funny Jewish lady.

After Carroll performed this set at Chicago's swanky Palmer House club, a *Variety* critic clearly articulated the disruptive potential of her chic persona, noting, "Femme is sophisticated looking, with a touch of class, and therefore it's a trifle disarming, though pleasantly, that she should speak with homey Brooklynese inflection on such mundane topics as the trials of housewifery. This incongruity of looks and personality is key to her showmanship, and she holds the crowd in her palm every inch of the way."[58] The incongruity that this critic referenced as "key to her showmanship" is also key to breaking down preconceived notions that "homey, Brooklynese" (read: "Jewish') housewives could not also be sophisticated women with "a touch of class." In other words, Carroll showed that—contrary to the stereotype of the Jewish mother/wife as parochial or vulgar—being a "sophisticated" lady and being a Brooklyn Jew were not mutually exclusive.

A series of other critics also commented on the novelty of a stand-up who was as feminine as she was funny. The reviewer Bill Smith exclaimed, "Miss Carroll is a phenomenon of showbiz. She's as feminine as any glamour gal but belts out comedy with the unabashed skill and savoir faire of a top male gag thrower."[59] Another critic suggested that her good looks enhanced her comedy writing: "Besides being at the top of her field, Jean is also a stageful of feminine pulchritude. . . . Her looks alone are reason enough why she needs no props or gimmicks, no clowning or buffoonery to command attention from the audience."[60] Rather than detract from her comic ability, Jean Carroll's beauty allowed her to traverse boundaries between "pretty" and "funny," "Jewish immigrant" and "American lady."

Jean Carroll used the female body that threatened to limit her as an asset. Her elegant clothes, meticulous makeup, and ladylike demeanor were innovative, not incidental. Unlike her predecessors like Moms Mabley or Fannie Brice—and unlike her descendants like Phyllis Diller and Joan Rivers—Jean Carroll insisted on a persona that was as glamorous as she was funny. One of her most high-profile fans, the comedian Lily Tomlin, concisely expresses the impact of this persona, calling Carroll "a whole new kind of person!"[61] Alan Zweibel, both a fan of Carroll's and a *Saturday Night Live* producer, noted, "I think it was very important that Jean Carroll looked and dressed the way she did because she looked like a woman who was not necessarily in *need* of anything—Jean Carroll had an everywoman quality about her."[62] This "everywoman" quality that Zweibel picks up on in Carroll's persona was key to her popularity, but it was hard-won. Ironically, for a Jewish immigrant like Carroll, it took years of labor, a closet full of designer clothes, cosmetic surgery, and a "cast" of well-crafted contrasting characters to become an "everywoman."

A Confidant at the Mic

Another tool that helped Jean Carroll to become the unlikely darling of the nightclub comedy world was a gadget that forever changed stand-up: the microphone. In vaudeville and the presentation houses, performers had to project their voices to be heard, and this practical need lent itself to a delivery style that was highly presentational and declamatory. In short, it is hard to shout with nuance. But with sound amplification technology, whispering, murmuring, mumbling, and other forms of intimate communication were available in performance. The public could enjoy vocal techniques that were once quite private.

The impact of the microphone was so dramatic that folklorist Ian Brodie's *A Vulgar Art* positions it as the defining factor of the stand-up genre. Well before the nightclub scene, radio comics of the 1930s and '40s took advantage of the way that microphones allowed for speech patterns that more closely resembled natural dialogue. Radio comics like George Burns, Bob Hope, and Jack Benny established a "paradigm of nonchalant patter."[63] Naturalism took hold across performance—for singers, belting gave way to crooning. For actors, understated realism was in vogue.[64] The possibilities that microphones allowed performers were heightened in the nightclubs, where audiences could respond to the more intimate delivery in real time. As Brodie concluded, "The medium of the microphone not only alters the stand-up comedy performance but also allows for new expressive forms to take place on the stage."[65] In other words, the medium shapes the message. Just as shouting to be heard lends itself to expressing "loud" emotions like frustration or excitement, whispering or murmuring lends itself to expressing more intimate emotions like vulnerability or tenderness. In stand-up comedy, the ability to speak in a softer, more intimate tone of voice lent itself to showcasing softer sides of the comic persona. Stand-up comedy began to lean more toward candor and intimate personal disclosure. The genre of stand-up was always dialogic, requiring back and forth between performer and audience. But with the microphone, that dialogue could become gossip, chitchat, or even pillow talk.

Jean Carroll was not the only stand-up using the microphone to shift into a more intimate style of delivery. The comic Alan King recalled a transformative moment in the mid-'50s when he and Jack E. Leonard went out to the 5100 Club in Madison, Wisconsin: "I watched this guy with a big nose. . . . And I swear I remember the moment that something said to me, 'this is where comedy is going.' It was Danny Thomas. Danny stopped the one-liners. Danny started telling stories about his family.

And everything he said, he swore to God. It was all a lie but he swore to God anyway."[66]

According to King, Danny Thomas—the Lebanese American stand-up better known for his TV sitcom *Make Room for Daddy*—shifted the structure of stand-up from a series of disconnected one-liners to a more cohesive anecdote. But King also picked up on the way that Thomas shifted the tone of stand-up from a presentation ("Have you heard the one about . . .") to a confession ("I swear to God . . ."). What the comic is confessing need not actually be true. But it must *seem* true. The audience must believe that what they are seeing is unvarnished, intimate, and authentic. This illusion of authenticity was an early innovation that has remained central to the genre of stand-up. Inspired by Thomas, Alan King began to rework his own nightclub routine, moving from a laundry list of gags to a more natural storytelling persona.[67]

Jean Carroll was at the vanguard of this shift, leveraging the intimacy allowed by the microphone into a form of delivery that I call *confidant comedy* because it mimics the casual, candid tone among confidants. As Carroll put it, "I try to make the audience feel that we're good friends or neighbors having a chat."[68] This new mode of delivery also may have helped disarm some of the resistance that audiences felt to a woman stand-up. By using this conversational, even gossipy, tone of a housewife chitchatting with her neighbor, Carroll reimagined the nightclub as a domestic space. Or, as she put it, "I make it seem as if I were talking to someone in my home, and the audience feels it, too."[69]

Critics also began to note this familiar, neighborly tone in Carroll's work. A review of Carroll's performance at Chicago's Palmer House Empire Room called her set "conversational" and "true-to-life," assuring that "when the ladies in the audience laugh out loud, you may be sure that Carroll has given familiar occurrences a real sugar-coating of commentary."[70] A trade magazine noted the "commercial appeal" of a persona with "personal identification so immediate."[71] Audiences were personally identifying with Carroll, not simply laughing at her. And at this point in the early development of stand-up comedy, a relatable persona was becoming just as important as solid jokes.

The intimate vocal qualities afforded to Carroll by the microphone lent themselves to more confessional subject matter, with added moments of vulnerability and seriousness balancing the punch lines. A track on her album *Girl in a Hot Steam Bath* (recorded live at a nightclub in 1960) shows a more exposed, intimate side to Carroll's persona. The revealing track, aptly titled "Girl-Talk in a Steam Bath," leans into confidant comedy. In this routine, Carroll presents herself with more candor, about both her life as a professional and the frustrations she feels about her body and self-image. Unlike the majority of Carroll's stand-up, in which she positions herself as an "average Jane" (wife, mother, shopper), this routine actually addresses her true position as a famous professional comedian. Given performers' reputation as masters of dissemblance, acknowledging her role as a performer is an ironic but effective way for Carroll to knock down pretense and get closer to her audience. Just as with the microphone, artifice creates (the illusion of) authenticity; artificially amplified voices sound *more* natural than shouts and declamations. Talking about her position as a comedy crafts(wo)man makes Jean Carroll seem *more* authentically approachable than asking the audience to believe that she is just a housewife. Equipped with a more "realistic" voice, she can present herself in a more "realistic" way. And so she begins, "You know when I walk out onstage now, the first thing I do is stand up, let everybody take a good look at me, and then I say, 'Oh my, didn't she get fat?' Psychologically, this tends to put the audience at ease, because I *am* fat." The joke is edged with irony, given Carroll's conspicuously trim figure. The crowd responds with a chuckle, which Carroll knowingly joins for several moments. Although this opener flirts with self-deprecation, Carroll is not quite dipping into the well of body shame that later female comics like Totie Fields or Joan Rivers would so frequently plumb. Instead, she wryly laughs as she refers to her body as "fat." The butt of the joke is not a fat body but a skewed body image.

Continuing in this confiding style, Carroll describes her efforts to stay thin for the public eye: "Every time I have to do a show on TV, four or five days before I have to do the show, I go on a real mad, crazy crash diet! I hate the world. I'm so irritable. I'm so nasty I snarl at the dog! Honestly, it's awful! And then after the show is over with, I can finally breathe again, you know. And then I go back to eating again." Carroll never once drops her chatty, conversational delivery, even as she ridicules the destructive measures women must take to be "camera ready." Using the natural, nonthreatening style of a lady gossiping with her friends, Carroll skewers fat-phobia.

The next passage especially showcases the more personal tone, alternating jokes with seemingly earnest statements about her own insecurities. First, she offers a couple of one-liners riffing on the excuses people give for gaining weight: "People have all these excuses for putting on a few pounds.... They've been retaining fluids, ... like martinis and beer! Or else there's another one: they have 'big bones.' ... And the bones get bigger with every meal! Well, I have no such excuses, I'm sorry to say." Carroll then shifts into a more confessional mode. Her speech becomes slower—interrupted by pauses and hesitations that sharply contrast with her usual confident machine-gun delivery. "Let's face it. I joke about it. People say to me, 'Gee, you have such a wonderful disposition, always making jokes.' Well, I'm not always making jokes. Sometimes it's a barrier. It's a defense mechanism that I develop. 'Cause I'm ... [hesitates] ... self conscious ... about being overweight." The halting cadence of Carroll's speech gives an interesting rhythmic shift, but its real impact is emotional. Carroll seems to be pausing from her sophisticated, polished persona and showing a bit of her authentic self, with its scars and fears visible and vulnerable. The more intimate vocal quality enabled by the microphone has paved the way for more intimate subject matter; instead of shopping adventures, she muses on her feelings of surveillance and shame. The audience sees something raw and real. Or so they imagine. But, the truth is, the show never stops. The moments of authenticity are as crafted as the one-liners. They are just a new part of the act.

In the final section of the bit, she hops in and out of the "joke" frame—performing sincerity for a moment to set up the "truth" that she then punctures with punch lines. For instance, after a deep breath, Carroll declares, "Actually, I'm not that fat. I still wear a size 12 dress," as if at last dropping the "show" and leveling with the audience. Then she bounces back into comedy, adding the zinger, "But I break the seams every time I get in it!" She then calls out the infantilizing undertones of fetishizing thin bodies, quipping, "My husband keeps reminding me of the times when I weighed 105 pounds. I remind him that there was a time when I weighed less—when I was born, I was 7½! [Pause] In any case, I joke about it . . . [hesitates], but I am seriously quite unhappy about the state of my figure. I'm taking pills now. They're just wonderful—they paralyze my mouth so I can't eat!" She teases the audience with candor ("I joke about it, but seriously . . .") before seeming to fall back into a wisecrack. Yet her punch lines are laced with poison—Carroll's jokes about mouth-paralyzing pills and self-starvation are clever but grim.

Through unprecedentedly personal jokes, Carroll exposes the oppressive body ideals foisted on women and women's self-destructive, gruesome pursuit of them. Carroll repeatedly plays with moments of confession, teasing the audience with a glimpse of earnestness to make the punch line surprising and potent, artful and arch. And while in a sense, the moments of authenticity may be just another tool in a comedy toolbox, they also help the audience feel an intimate connection to Carroll. Even if her confessions and insecurities help set up punch lines, they still tell the audience something profound about her struggles and vulnerabilities—something that could resonate on a personal level.

Armed with her microphone, Carroll was performing a new, more intimate kind of comedy—one interspersed with pauses, digressions, and quiet, confessional moments. Changing the style of her speech went hand in hand with changing the content—a more intimate tone led to more intimate subject matter. And by changing her performance, she was asking her audience to perform differently as well—to become not just spectators but friends and confidants. And so Jean Carroll, a funny

Jewish lady from New York, became a stand-up sensation and the chatty bosom buddy of nightclub-goers all over the country.

"The American Home Is Not a Night Club!": The Rise of Television

At the same time that nightclubs were providing an exciting night out, audiences were finding an entertaining new inducement to stay in: the television. In the period between 1948 and 1955, almost 70 percent of all American families bought a television set.[72] But as domestic television sets became popular, a moral panic set in surrounding their effects on the family. Conservative impulses regarding everything from gender norms to necklines drew headlines, as Americans took up Federal Communications Commission (FCC) chairman Wayne Coy's cry, "The American home is not a night club!"[73]

Taking the pulse of society, the FCC encouraged networks to take responsibility for the morality of their programming. By March 1952, 80 percent of TV stations and all four networks subscribed to the strict US Code of Practices for Television Broadcasters (also known as the National Association of Radio and Television Broadcasters Code or Television Code).[74] As the scholar Matthew Murray has observed, "the code likened the relationship between telecaster and viewer to one of guest and host" and therefore required even programming that was *not* specifically oriented toward children to be child-friendly. The code even included such strict mandates as, "Profanity, obscenity, smut, and vulgarity are forbidden, even when likely to be understood by only part of the audience."[75] The problem with terms like "smut" and "vulgarity" is that they leave a lot of room for interpretation, and this room allows social biases, gendered and otherwise, to creep in.

In examining the enforcement of the Television Code (and other network-specific rules governing "vulgarity"), it is clear that the double standards that Jean Carroll wrote about were an industry-wide problem. Certain male comedians were able to bend or even break the rules with impunity, while women were more strictly policed. In "Regulating Swish: Early Television Censorship," Chelsea McCracken demonstrates how Milton Berle, host of *Texaco Star Theater*, was able to flout NBC's strict rules against men performing effeminate material known as "swish" routines. These routines were strictly forbidden because they were coded representations of homosexuality—then considered "immoral" content. Berle's tendency to perform fey mannerisms and sketches in drag occasionally prompted pushback. McCracken found that after Berle played Cinderella, fifty-eight people called to complain, "taking offense at effeminacy"—compared to the fewer than ten who complained about the blackface number in the same episode.[76] However, Berle's overwhelming popularity with fans and sponsors meant that network executives gave him "special consideration," allowing him to continue ad libbing "swish" bits and playing in drag.

Other male comics were able to get away with similar transgressions of the "smut ban." For instance, *Variety* reported that Arthur Godfrey made an on-air ad lib that was so objectionable that the paper could not print it, saying only that it was off-color and "jeopardized CBS."[77] However, Arthur Godfrey had four television programs, bringing in 17 percent of CBS's total ad revenue, and so the incident passed without Godfrey losing his prominence.[78] Likewise, the *Saturday Evening Post* reported that Groucho Marx jokingly called a woman a "strip-teaser" on air, "wholly ignoring the fact that he was endangering TV investments running to millions."[79] Yet Groucho was never in danger of losing his position or forced to make a public apology for his transgressions.

The latitude allowed these male comics was not extended to female performers. Even Lucille Ball was famously not permitted to say the word "pregnant" on television, using instead the less vulgar "expecting."[80] Perhaps the most notable instance of women entertainers being subject to more rigorous scrutiny on the issue of "smut" is the so-called neckline hearings of 1952. Senator Ezekial Candler Gathings of Arkansas headed a congressional investigation into "immorality and offensive behavior in radio and television."[81] Among the issues discussed was women's display of their breasts. Covering these proceedings with its tongue firmly in its cheek, the *Saturday Evening Post* reported, "A display of cleavage, one broadcaster told the subcommittee solemnly, is sometimes quite unintended. He mentioned seeing—too late—one gown which shocked him and for which he rebuked his program director. The disastrous incident ended, he said, with a very apologetic letter from this young lady, who is extremely well known, pointing out in all honesty that the thing was completely accidental. As she left the wings to go on the stage, something slipped unbeknownst to her. And it was not a complete exposure; it was just a little on the questionable side."[82] The comparison is striking. While Milton Berle could intentionally flout the networks' codes with a swish routine or drag performance and not think twice, the "extremely well known" young lady accidentally displaying a "questionable" amount of cleavage responded with a "very apologetic letter." Even though the National Association of Radio and Television Broadcasters and network regulations were technically the same for men and women, the social norms on which these policies are based allowed male comedians to get away with bending the rules in ways that females could not. These drastically divergent enforcements show that the world of television all but formally codified the same gendered double standards that Jean Carroll spoke of in the nightclub world.

But sexism or no sexism, television was the way forward. As Jean Carroll put it, "If you don't make it with TV, there's practically no show business."[83] So not only did she try to make the nightclub stage feel like her living room, but she also ramped up efforts to join the residents of TV Land in their own living rooms. Fortunately, her husband, Buddy Howe, once again proved advantageous. He had shifted his role at General Artists Corporation to book acts for variety television.[84]

Carroll enjoyed an auspicious beginning in television. She made frequent appearances on variety shows, game shows, and talk shows across all four major networks. She did two spots on DuMont's variety show *The Cavalcade of Stars* in 1949. On CBS, in 1950, she had a highly praised guest spot on the panel show *This Is Show Business*, with a critic exclaiming, "Miss Carroll zinged over her cafe floor routine with such impact that she'll have no problem getting more TV guest shots."[85] Shortly after that, Carroll appeared on another CBS hit, *The Frank Sinatra Show*. On ABC, she made four appearances on the variety show *The Arthur Murray Party* between 1950 and 1951. And on NBC, she was featured on NBC's quiz show *Tag the Gag* and enjoyed a critically praised "guest shot" on its *Perry Como Chesterfield Show*.[86] The industry column "Nite Side" reporting on this spot predicted that it was merely a "warm-up for the comedy series Tommy Rockwell [General Artists Corporation president] has in mind," asserting, "Tommy figures she'll be one of 1950's television biggies."[87]

For a comedian in 1950, being a "television biggie" meant hosting your own variety show. In these early days, TV was packed with vaudeville-inspired variety shows using an olio format of comedy sketches and musical acts.[88] These variety shows were often anchored by a charismatic comedian like Milton Berle on *The Texaco Star Theater* at NBC or Jackie Gleason on the *Cavalcade of Stars* at the DuMont Network. There were no women comedians hosting variety shows—nor would there be until Carol Burnett historically became the first in 1967.[89] And yet, in 1950, Jean Carroll landing her own variety show did not seem too far off. In April 1951, Jean Carroll was mentioned as a potential host for a weekly variety show on CBS.[90] This was to be the first instance of a woman-led variety show in network history. A ripped complimentary ticket for what seems to be a rehearsal of this variety program, called *The Jean Carroll Show*, is carefully saved in her scrapbook, its torn bits neatly taped together.

By the end of April 1951, CBS was "handing its new comedy show starring Jean Carroll an on-the-air audition" Thursday night from 10:30 to 11:00 p.m.[91] These auditions were basically one-time shows "for the benefit of agencies and potential sponsors" to decide whether they would pick it up for a longer run. According to *Variety*, Carroll worked that variety show for all she was worth. She performed a comic domestic scene in which she "bandied words with a husband who "disappeared five years ago behind a paper"; she acted in a sketch about "a rich couple who marry off their daughter"; and she "did some challenge tap dancing with Bill Callahan," all while carrying on comedic monologues in between acts.[92]

The reviewer praised Carroll's "versatility" and "fine sense of timing in handling her lines."[93] They even nodded to her significance as a woman host, stating, "This CBS find proved a mistress of wit who could turn a phrase for maximum effect."[94] However, one thing that Jean Carroll did not do for her program was write. Despite the fact that she had always written both her stand-up material and the celebrated Carroll and Howe sketches, she was not given a writing credit on the variety show. Instead, the listed writers were Colman Jacoby and Arnie Rosen, who had gained acclaim with their work on Jackie Gleason's comedy *Cavalcade of Stars*.

The writing ultimately proved to be the show's most criticized point, with the reviewer dismissing it as "so-so," saying that the sketches reminded them "of the poorer Sid Caesar–Imogene Coca bits."[95] Perhaps due to the negative response to the writing, *The Jean Carroll Show* did not win the time slot, which ultimately went to the program *Casey, Crime Photographer*, starring Richard Carlyle. In denying Jean Carroll a writing credit on her own show, CBS foreshadowed the difficulties that were to plague Carroll's would-be sitcom.

Networks continued to dangle opportunity in front of Carroll before snatching it away in favor of male artists. In May 1951, the *New York World-Telegram and Sun* reported that "she is slated for her own half-hour show on CBS-TV this summer."[96] However, no such show seems to have aired. Two years after the failed CBS pilot, Carroll moved from CBS to NBC. *Variety* published that NBC-TV, "in its search for new faces to augment its comedy stable, has signed comedienne Jean Carroll to a five-year pact."[97] The column also mentioned that the network was "considering putting Miss Carroll in as a summer replacement for part of the Saturday night *Show of Shows*."[98] This deal also never came to fruition. Chapter 4 charts Carroll's rocky road to broadcast—by the time her show was on the air, variety TV was out, and the domestic sitcom was in. Television was less about bringing a nightclub into viewers' living rooms and more about showing families idealized images of themselves.

* * *

The late 1940s and '50s saw the people of the United States yearning for readjustment, searching for equilibrium after Prohibition and two world wars but embroiled in a new and unnerving Cold War. Americans craved outlets to let off steam, and smoky clubs filled with booze and transgressive laughter fit the bill. In these dimly lit havens of humor, Jewish comics could work out their anxieties about assimilation and gender with one-liners. Stand-ups could use the microphone to whisper anecdotes and confessions that turned audience members into confidants. And Jean Carroll could take the constraints of her position—stereotypes about Jewish women, gendered double standards, surveillance of her body, and policing of her language—and make them into comedy.

Always mindful of representing herself (and perhaps her people) with "dignity," Jean Carroll limited her material to be more ladylike than lewd. She leveraged her conventionally attractive figure and fashions to disrupt images of Jewish women as vulgar, homely, and unappealing. Her comic persona demonstrated that Jewish femininity was compatible with sophistication and even glamour. Her skill at embodying and moving fluidly between contrasting characters allowed her to expose the superficiality of stereotypes and to present a more humanized Jewess. As a result, she introduced nightclub audiences nationwide to a witty and winsome American Jewish lady—The First Lady of Laughs.

4

"Take It from Me" (and They Did)

Carroll's Battle for a Television Sitcom

Here is a scene that may or may not have happened: Jean Carroll, famed stand-up comedienne, had had enough of being disregarded on her own television show. First, the network had ignored her casting input. Then, it had refused her authority over the writing. Then, it said no to her character being a working mother. And *then* it had the audacity to allow a director with no comedy background to tell her what was and was not funny.[1]

Finally, eyes blazing and cheeks flushed, she stood in bold confrontation with the ABC executive Bob Lewine and declared, "Bob, I would appreciate it if you'd let me out of my contract, even now. I came off a very serious surgery, and I do have a heart condition. And I find this is much too much for me. So you're just going to have to let me go."[2]

Her agents and representatives were aghast. "You can't dictate to the network!" they chastised.[3] Undeterred, Carroll retorted, "The hell I can't! This is my show! My future is on the line here. I can dictate my own life, and I don't want to do this show anymore."

And so after a mere twelve episodes, *Take It from Me*, Carroll's long-awaited family sitcom, was no more. It was a crushing blow to the network, which soon repented its unappreciative ways. Lewine declared, "We'll do anything! You were right. We were wrong."[4] But it was too late. Carroll had moved on. The network, shamefaced, leaked a canard saying that her show had been canned. But Carroll knew the truth. She would always know the truth. Wistfully, years later, she murmured, "It could have been another *I Love Lucy*."[5]

* * *

Although the dialogue in this vignette was all quoted from various interviews with Jean Carroll herself, the melodramatic simplicity rings a bit fantastic. As a narrator, Carroll tended to be more fabulous than factual. But whether or not her account accurately documents the back and forth between Carroll, her agents, and the network, it does gesture toward the complex power dynamics at play behind the scenes of the happy family sitcom.

In the early 1950s United States, babies were not the only thing that were booming. Situation comedies about happy families began multiplying like rabbits on the major networks. To understand this happy family sitcom boom, it is important to look at the larger—distinctly less harmonious—sociopolitical context.

The year 1947 had been a banner year for anticommunist surveillance; Harry Truman had signed an executive order establishing the "Federal Employees Loyalty Program," creating special review boards to determine the "Americanism" of federal government employees.[6] These boards, a kind of younger sibling to the ten-year-old House Un-American Activities Committee, resulted in over twelve thousand government employees resigning and twenty-seven hundred more being dismissed over the next decade.[7] That same year, Congress enacted the Labor-Management Relations Act of 1947, ruling that union officers could not participate in National Labor Relations Board proceedings unless they filed an affidavit declaring that they were not supporters of the Communist Party.[8] Egged on by politicians like Senator Joseph McCarthy, communist anxieties only escalated over the following years, erupting in the McCarthy hearings (1950–1954) and the Korean War (1950–1953).

Ripples of the Red Scare shuddered through the entertainment industry. The pamphlet *Red Channels: The Report of Communist Influence in Radio and Television*, released in 1950, effectively blacklisted over 150 entertainment professionals with alleged ties to the Communist Party. A disproportionately large number of people on this list were Jewish, prompting scholars like Joseph Litvak to deem the "Red Scare" a "red herring" using anticommunist sentiment as a pretense to purge the media of Jews.[9] Likewise, the media historian Carol Stabile questions the true goals of the *Red Channels* pamphlet, contending that it was less about protecting the US from communist ideology than it was about waging "a repressive war over popular culture."[10]

By the time *I Love Lucy* premiered on CBS in 1951, that popular-culture war had come out strongly on the side of conservative, white, middle-class domesticity.[11] And the genre that best dispersed that doctrine was none other than the family situation comedy. In the popular-culture historian Lynn Spigel's *Make Room for TV*, she observes the trend of television shifting from variety shows (sequences of musical performances, stand-up sets, comedy sketches, etc.) to situation comedies. Spigel notes that within ten years of *I Love Lucy*'s debut, there were twice as many sitcoms as there were variety shows.[12] In 1952, ABC premiered *The Adventures of Ozzie and Harriet*, and NBC came out with *I Married Joan*, both of which preached the gospel of coupling, kids, and consumerism. These sitcoms also brought new levels of stardom to their leading ladies. And so while Jean Carroll may have once believed that a variety show was her ticket to television success, by 1952 she and her agent changed their tactic, campaigning instead for Carroll to have her own family sitcom.

While Carroll in various sources related the story of her show (prophetically titled *Take It from Me*) with an account that places her squarely in the driver's seat, examining the sitcom saga that led up to the (probably apocryphal) vignette that began this chapter illuminates that it is actually a story about the *limitations* of her power—and the limitations of the Cold War United States' acceptance of Jewish humor and nontraditional women.

The Rocky Road to Broadcast

In theory, the plethora of domestic sitcoms filling television schedules in the early 1950s was a great opportunity for women. Women were far more likely to be featured—and even centralized—in a family sitcom than they were to get the chance to host a variety show. The chaotic energy of the variety show was considered a place for, as Spigel puts it, "bad-boy Berles and soda-squirting Skeltons."[13] The family sitcom, on the other hand, was a kinder, gentler, and more acceptably "feminine" medium.

In a 1953 feature on the top comediennes on television, the *New York Times* columnist Jack Gould reasoned, "since the TV audience is the family at home, the domestic comedy, revolving around the woman of the house, is a natural formula." The article profiled a full pantheon of sitcom starlets; in addition to Jean Carroll from *Take It from Me*, there was Lucille Ball from *I Love Lucy*, Gracie Allen from *The Burns and Allen Show*, Joan Allen from *I Married Joan*, Joan Caulfield from *My Favorite Husband*, and more. Alongside the photo collage of well-manicured white ladies, the author boasted, "One of television's accomplishments has been to bring the distaff [female] clowns into virtually equal prominence with the males."[14]

However, while these women may have enjoyed "virtually equal prominence with the males" on-screen, their off-screen prominence was a very different matter. In Annie Berke's study of postwar women television writers, she finds that the more professionalized the TV industry became, the more it "sought to capitalize on female viewership while keeping executive power largely in men's hands."[15] In other words, executives wanted women writers around using their mysterious lady wiles to hawk products and programs to all the other ladies at home. But these women writers, however talented they were and however significant their contributions, were the exception and not the rule.

Moreover, to become these shining exceptions, they had to jump through some baroque hoops. For instance, Madelyn Pugh, the famed "girl writer" for *I Love Lucy*, tells the story of how one of her female colleagues had gotten a job by joining the network as a secretary, since (as a female executive had tipped her off) "CBS didn't hire women writers."[16] Even once they were hired as writers, women were still often held to the margins: Selma Diamond, a writer on Sid Caesar's *Your Show of Shows* (1950–1954), was often tasked with cleaning ashtrays, making coffee, and performing other housekeeping tasks not typically included in a writer's job description. Lucille Kallen, another woman writer on the program, described her male colleagues' attitude with the phrase, "We love you . . . [but] this is our house."[17] Even the *balebosta* herself, the Columbia-educated Gertrude Berg, who conceived of, wrote, starred in, and produced the radio-show-turned-television-program *The Goldbergs*, found that when she gave CBS an ultimatum, she was met with a cancellation.[18]

Jean Carroll's experience seems to follow this larger trend of dismissing women creatives. For as her show made its fraught journey to network television, Jean Carroll's control, vision, and influence seemed to dwindle into near nothingness.

* * *

An in-depth interview from 1952 that Carroll saved in her personal scrapbook gives a peek into the kind of "casual" sitcom that she dreamed of creating. She had just signed a contract with NBC for a Saturday-night show, and she hoped it would capture the same conversational, "confidant" quality that she was able to bring to her stand-up. As Carroll put it in the interview, "You can not only burn out your material on TV but you can also wear out your welcome—unless you do the type of thing that is so normal, so casual so everyday that people can poke each other and say, 'She's talking about you.'"[19]

Showing a prescient understanding of the medium, Carroll observed that a televised sitcom was a marathon, not a sprint. While jokes would of course be a component of the show, the element that would really generate sustained viewership was the audience's attachment to Carroll as a character. It was important that she present herself as a relatable protagonist that audiences could invest in week after week. To do that, she would have to rely not just on her wit but on her whole persona. Elaborating, Carroll explained, "I have to be wise and flip on my show, but also human. That's the way I've always tried to be. . . . I'll be strictly myself. . . . I'll have a household and a child and I'll be the kind everybody comes to with their problems. Of course I'll say some funny things. But I don't want it to be a joke show. There is not enough material in the world for jokes for shows that go on week after week."[20]

It appears, however, that Carroll and her fellow writers did not have a shared vision. In this same interview, she criticized their ability to come up with a "suitable story line" for her and disclosed that "script trouble" kept the show off the air for weeks. Although she did not get more specific in her critique of the script, she did make it clear that she had no intention of compromising her standards, declaring, "I want to know that when I do this thing, it's going to be right."[21] Evidently this script trouble was not resolved, because within a matter of months, NBC dropped her contract.

After the NBC fallout, Carroll began a roller-coaster relationship with ABC. In 1953, ABC signed up to produce a new Jean Carroll sitcom but then promptly dropped it from the schedule in favor of *Back That Fact*, a quiz show hosted by Joey Adams.[22] Although the show was soon restored to the ABC lineup, several drastic changes were made that severely undermined Carroll's voice in the project.

Much to Carroll's dismay, executives replaced Louis Nye, the seasoned comedian slated to play her husband, with Alan Carney, whose comedy experience came mainly from a duo regarded as the poor man's Abbott and Costello.[23] Carroll despised Carney, a husky Irish actor whom she called "bloody awful" and "deadly in the part."[24] According to an interview Carroll conducted years later, the producers had tried to enlist a number of other actors such as Alan Arkin and Lou Parker, but either they were already signed to a different project or they said, "I'm not going to take second billing to that broad!"[25] Carroll said that she would have preferred to cut the role of the husband entirely, portraying her character as "a working mother." But the studio would not have it. "I guess that was considered too radical for those days," she reflected.[26]

Not long after that, Carroll lost her director, Dick Linkroum. Linkroum had made his name in comedy with both variety shows like *The Alan Young Show* (1950) and sitcoms like *Let's Join Joanie* (1950) and *Heaven for Betsy* (1952). The fact that the sitcoms had both been women-led vehicles made him an exceptionally good fit for Carroll's project. However, Linkroum was snatched up to work on one of NBC's "pet daytime projects."[27] Adding insult to injury, the columnist announcing Linkroum's move to Carroll's ex-network disparagingly referred to his leaving her show as having "the chore dropped from his schedule."[28] Linkroum's replacement, Alan Dinehart, was an aspiring priest-turned-actor who performed in over twenty Broadway plays. However extensive his theatrical resume, Dinehart did not have much comedy experience. Carroll was skeptical of him, remarking, "I didn't want a guy—the director—who didn't know comedy telling me what's funny and what's not."[29]

Another incursion to Carroll's creative input came from her writers, Colman Jacoby (né Jacobs) and Arnie Rosen. Jacobs and Rosen both had strong comedy backgrounds, writing jokes for luminaries like Bob Hope and Jackie Gleason. They had worked on hit comedy variety shows like *Texaco Star Theater* and *Cavalcade of Stars*. Jean Carroll had collaborated with them on the variety-show pilot she did for CBS in 1950, and it seems to have been a positive experience (although the show was not picked up). She described them as "great," effusing, "They can do anything, once they know what it is we want them to do."[30] However, the second part of that sentence is telling—the writers may be skilled, but they can only do their work once they know "what it is we want them to do." Carroll still positioned herself (and perhaps her manager) as the one in charge.

And so when Carroll fell ill and had to go into the hospital for heart surgery, she was allegedly shocked to find that Colman and Jacoby had gone ahead and written the pilot without her. Over sixty years later, she recounted, "I had been in for surgery—serious surgery. . . . And they wrote a pilot. This was all while I was in the hospital. No input from me, no nothing!"[31] Although she saw problems with the script, there was little she could do about them, explaining, "Since I did not have approval of the writing, I was very ineffectual." Looking back in regret, she felt that it was "foolish" that she had not asked for editorial control. She described the network executives as ignorant pretenders who "walk around with pipes looking intelligent" but "wouldn't know a good joke if it bit them."[32]

The rocky road to broadcast was also taking a toll on the show financially. Carroll claimed that by the time the pilot was fully cast and ready to shoot, it was too late to show to the show's potential sponsor Procter & Gamble. And so instead of having a "wonderfully high-paying commercial show," they had a sustaining (unsponsored) show. With a storyteller's penchant for overstatement, she exclaimed, "I got more money doing an opening at a supermarket—$10,000—than I was getting per week on that show!"[33]

Whether or not it was for scheduling reasons, *Variety* affirmed that the show struggled to find a sponsor from the outset.[34] It later reported that *Take It from Me* was one of the costliest shows for ABC-TV, "running about $18,000 a week."[35] In an effort to keep costs down, Carroll said that the producers cut corners in the rehearsal process, bringing in the supporting cast only a day or two before the show aired.[36] The scant rehearsal hours were ominous to the meticulous Carroll. But due to her health issues, she complied with the lax schedule, reasoning, "I can't do many hours of rehearsal because I'm not supposed to be working at all."[37]

Ironically, a sitcom that had once sparked Carroll's declaration, "When I do this thing, it's going to be right," went on the air with a costar she loathed, a director she distrusted, a script she had no part in writing, an underrehearsed ensemble, and no sponsor. But however frustrated she may have been, Carroll was a professional. She had been a professional entertainer from childhood, a professional comedian for nearly a decade, and now she was to be a professional TV housewife. And so like any good midcentury television housewife, she shoved down her discontents, smiled, and graciously welcomed America into her happy home.

"Take It from Me": Putting Together the Pieces

Take It from Me premiered on ABC on Wednesday, November 11, 1953.[38] But since the show was aired using kinescope and no surviving recording exists, the content of that premiere episode is today a mystery. And as with any mystery, there are multiple accounts. One account lies nestled in the archive of Yale's Beinecke Rare Book Library—a script with *Take It from Me* typed across the first page and a hand-written "Nov. 11" scrawled near the upper-left-hand corner. It would be tempting to conclude that this was the pilot script. And yet a note in similar handwriting on the first page reads, "Publicity." Plus, the bottom-left-hand corner of the last page bears a neatly typed, "aek/lj 10/20/53 10:35 pm," suggesting that it may have been a publicity draft written a few weeks before the air date. Most confounding, the plot of the script barely matches the plot that critics recounted in their reviews.

The archival script opens with a shot, "Jean ironing in dinette: Robin to one side eating lunch. It's 12 noon," as Carroll looks to the "viewer" and says, "Oh, hiya." She then launches into a monologue that sounds almost identical to her stand-up:

Well, here I am working again. You know when I first got married my husband told me we'd have a full-time maid. I was so happy—until I found out he meant me!

But I don't mind. My husband says that marriage is a fifty-fifty proposition, and that's the way it is with the shirts—he wears them and dirties them; I wash them and iron them.

He's so fussy. Doesn't like to send his shirts out because of a horrible experience he had once with a Chinese laundry—they sent him a bill for two and a half dollars!

But don't get the idea my husband is cheap. Why, he throws dollar bills around as though they were printed on fly-paper!

What a dude! He's so meticulous about his clothes. They have to be done just so. The creases have to be as sharp as a razor; the lapels pressed flat; not a wrinkle anywhere—ordinarily I don't mind—but pajamas!

But he wasn't always so inconsiderate. The first week we were married he wanted to help, and while I was out he washed the windows, scrubbed the floors, polished the furniture—it was silly—we were staying at the Waldorf-Astoria.

Did you ever see slacks this size—44—I don't mind ironing them— what bothers me is lifting them.

I'll say this for my husband though. He's a careful shopper when it comes to bargains. This shirt for instance—pure silk and he only paid a dollar for it. He told me it had a slight imperfection—slight imperfection, one sleeve's missing.

Then, as the stage directions specify, Jean was to walk over to Robin, who was "absently dawdling," and transition seamlessly into mommy mode, chastising, "Robin, you better hurry up. You have only ten minutes to finish your lunch and get back to school."[39] After Robin sets off, Jean flips through the radio channels as she tidies the apartment, only to have her husband, Herbie, burst in for his briefcase and mess everything up again. As Jean "stands near the closet and shrugs in despair," she sighs, "There he goes—the case against marriage!" She consoles herself that at least he is going to take her to the movies that night. The scene then transitions to Robin's school, PS 17, where Jean bears wry witness to the kooky neighborhood mothers as they pick up their children. She periodically breaks the fourth wall for comical asides like, "You should meet her little boy. . . . What can I tell you about him. He's the only kid in the neighborhood with an autographed picture of [famed robber] Willie Sutton." The episode then pivots toward a plotline involving Herbie's miserly habit of feigning illness whenever he and Jean are about to go out on a date. Turning to the "viewer," Jean quotes his penny-pinching rationale: "Sixty cents an hour for the baby-sitter, for four hours came to 2.40. Sixty cents carfare makes it three dollars. . . . The tickets for the movie are a dollar a piece brings it to five dollars—we do it every week it comes to $250 a year; in ten years it adds up to $2,500. And to me, no picture is worth $2,500."[40]

As expected, as Jean gets ready to go to the movie, Herbie feels a "sharp pain" in his stomach. When Jean calls the doctor, the beleaguered physician cooks up a scheme to put an end to Herbie's cheapskate hypochondria by throwing "a little scare into him." He and Jean feign an intentionally loud "secret" conversation prognosticating Herbie's imminent demise. After the doctor solemnly bids Herbie, "Goodbye, Mr. Carroll," Herbie confesses to faking his illness, vowing to change his ways. Jean only laughs, exclaiming, "Oh, you big dope, there's not a thing wrong with you!" as she reveals her scheme with the doctor. Delighted, Herbie kicks up his heels, ending in a pratfall as a wry Jean enlists her daughter's help to "get Fred Astaire into bed." She turns to the audience and closes with a friendly, "Good night everybody, see you next week!"[41]

Thus ends the pilot according to the archival script. In some ways, this sounds like the show that critics described in their reviews of the November 11 episode. *TV Guide* offered a report that is nicely aligned with the script: "Cast as a so-called average housewife, complete with a bumbling, lazy, but good-natured husband and a moppet daughter, [Carroll] opens each show with a monologue. From her monologue, the show moves each week into the story. Most of the action takes place in the family apartment and its environs, including the basement laundry room, the corner drug store and her daughter's school."[42] The monologue opening and cast of characters seem consistent. However, the "environs" mentioned in this article include a "basement laundry room" and "corner drug store" that are never mentioned in the archival script. The mysterious laundry room comes up again in *Variety*'s review of the November 11 episode, which reads, "Opening stanza Wednesday (4) was nothing more than a report of her day at home, but its approach was lively and lighthearted. It followed her from breakfast with her husband, his face buried in the morning newspaper of course, through a laundry-klatch in the apartment house's community laundry room and winding up with a quiet evening at home with hubby reading the paper and daughter doing the homework."[43] Clearly, the episode that critics reviewed included a scene in which Carroll held court with her neighbors at their building's laundry room—a scene that is not included in the archival script.

Moreover, none of the published reviews made the slightest mention of the plotline involving Herbie trying to get out of date night by faking sick, only to be one-upped by Jean and the doctor catching him in a lie. That seems a strange omission and one at odds with *Variety*'s characterization of the show as "a report of [Carroll's] day at home." A final nail in the coffin is offered by Harriet Van Horne's column, which quotes an opening sequence quite different from the monologue in the script:

> "I have two wonderful children," she [Carroll] explained at the opening, "A girl of 8 and a boy 36."
>
> ". . . Be careful crossing the streets," Jean warns as he leaves for work, "Get an old lady to help you."
>
> "Some day I'm gonna forget where I live," mutters the master of the house.
>
> "I know," ripostes the little woman, "but when?"[44]

Between the case of the lost laundry room, the disappearance of the deceptive doctor, and the mystery of the opposing openers, one can deduce that the archival script is only a rough draft, substantially different in plot and dialogue from the final episode that aired on November 11, 1953. Moreover, it seems reasonable to extrapolate that the other six scripts in the archive are also drafts. Therefore, they ought not be read as definitive blueprints of episodes but instead as patchwork blends of bits that would find their way to broadcast, mixed with bits destined for the cutting-room floor.

STAR Jean Carroll (right), Alan Carney and Lynn Loring are a
harried but happy family group on ABC's "Take It From Me"

FIGURE 4.1. "Jean Carroll (*right*), Alan Carney, and Lynn Loring are a harried but happy family group on ABC's 'Take It from Me.'" Production photo, *Take It from Me*, 1953, saved in Carroll's personal scrapbook. (Private collection of Susan Chatzky)

Unhappy Marriages

When piecing together the extant scraps of *Take It from Me*, two things become clear. The first is that Jean Carroll was earning her paycheck. She was in every scene of the show, and critics across the board praised her performance. Harriet Van Horne enthused, "it's nice to have a girl of Miss Carroll's charm and zest on the home screen."[45] *Variety* gushed, "Miss Carroll carries the weight of the show on her shoulders. The half-hour is hers from start to finish and she shines all the way."[46] The *Newark Evening News* pronounced, "Jean, of course, makes the show."[47] And Jason Gould of the *New York Times* lauded, "She can put across a gag line with crispness and élan, and her sense of timing is extremely good."[48]

However, the second thing that becomes apparent is that even Carroll's well-reviewed performance was not enough to compensate for the show's larger issues. Jean Carroll's show suffered from multiple kinds of "unhappy marriages," ranging from the unhappy marriage of form—with its attempt to blend stand-up comedy and its variety-show aesthetic with the family sitcom and its more dramatic structure—to the (implicitly Jewish) cantankerous marriage of the main characters, Jean and Herbie. Although comical bickering would later make a splash on *The Honeymooners*, early television executives (and sponsors) were not receptive to this particular strain of mordant Jewish comedy.

Lady and the Tramp: Sitcom as a Marriage of Legitimate Theater and Variety Shows

Stand-up comedy is a markedly different genre from situation comedy. In stand-up, the emphasis is on the individual. There may be directors, managers, and a whole entourage of players in the background, but onstage, it is just the solo stand-up comic, rising or falling by themselves. Sitcom is the opposite—although there may be a star, they are always interacting with friends, family, coworkers, or an ensemble of some kind. Stand-up does not require a story with a beginning, middle, and end, whereas a sitcom hinges on a plot (or multiple plots). There is also the issue of pedigree; sitcoms grew out of the genteel world of theatrical dramas. Stand-up, on the other hand, came from the working-class milieu of variety shows like vaudeville and burlesque. Spigel points out different political valences, with theatrical drama having a conservative bent and variety being more ethnic, unpredictable, and anarchic. If it were a canine romantic comedy, variety would be cast as the Tramp from the wrong side of the tracks who fell for the genteel Lady, theater. But fall he did, as the demographic majority of television owners shifted from variety-loving, cosmopolitan city-dwellers to drama-loving, white, rural and suburban families. Television viewers and sponsors exerted pressure to tame and domesticate the unruly variety genre.

Take It from Me proves an excellent case study of this larger phenomenon of television comedy's uneasy transition from variety to sitcom. For to place a variety veteran and stand-up comic like Jean Carroll into the new medium of situation comedy, the writers Arnie Rosen and Coleman Jacoby devised an odd mongrel of a television show. Each episode opened with Carroll giving a stand-up-style routine, before pivoting into a scene with one of the other cast members, who would act as though they had not noticed her monologue. Then, throughout the episode, she would turn and give her point of view directly to the camera. For instance, in a script draft labeled "Take It from Me—Wednesday, January 13, 1954," Jean enters a jewelry shop to face an "icy stare" from a dowager holding a lorgnette. Off her magnified glare, Jean turns to the camera and quips, "She must be very rich. . . . She's got two monocles."[49]

The idea of interweaving stand-up comedy into a sitcom format was innovative but not unprecedented. George Burns (another variety transplant) did a similar thing on CBS's *The George Burns and Gracie Allen Show* (1950). In a review of *Take It from Me*, Roland Lindbloom of the *Newark Evening News* called out this parallel: "[Carroll] monologued the bridges between the three related sketches in a manner that reminded us of [how] of the wry George Burns talks directly to the viewers."[50] Burns's

direct address was a celebrated part of the program, with critics laud-
ing his "direct-to-the-viewer-monologs" as evidence that he is a "master
of dry wit."[51] His trademark glance to the camera while puffing a cigar
became iconic. The scholar Joann Gardner points out that Jack Benny
(also from a variety background) did a similar bit of direct address in
his sitcom, likening the device to Shakespearean asides.[52] But however
popular it had been in the past, this tactic aimed at marrying Jean Carroll's stand-up with her sitcom proved polarizing.

For some viewers, *Take It from Me* was a successful hybrid of stand-
up and sitcom. Bernie Harrison of the "Scene and Heard" column
explicitly noted, "Her stanza represents a compromise between a vaudeville monologue and the family situation comedy plot."[53] The *Variety*
critic praised Jacoby and Rosen, whom they felt "hit a paydirt format"
by setting Carroll in a sitcom "without sacrificing Miss Carroll's stand-
up patter forte."[54] *TV Guide* gave the most in-depth commentary on this
synthesis of stand-up comedy and sitcom:

> Jean Carroll . . . has developed into a unique art form her ability to stand
> up before an audience and whip out her gags in a monologue. The pro-
> ducers of her new TV show *Take It from Me* (ABC) have attempted to
> incorporate this stand-up brand of humor into a situation comedy motif
> and have generally succeeded. It's a good show, giving Miss Carroll plenty
> of opportunity to build laughs with her "asides" to the audience. . . . It's
> an obvious attempt to capitalize on TV's over-worked intimacy, but it's a
> fresh approach and she brings it off neatly.[55]

With the industry savvy expected of a trade publication, *TV Guide*
keyed into the way that Carroll's "asides" fit into the larger trend of intimacy as a fundamental value of televised entertainment.[56] By addressing
the audience directly, Carroll reenacted her role as a stand-up comedian
addressing a live audience in a nightclub or theater.

However, many critics responded negatively to the show as imbal-
anced in both ensemble and structure. Perhaps most impassioned was

TV GUIDE

LOCAL PROGRAM LISTINGS
Week of December 25-31

15¢

Reviews PROGRAM OF THE WEEK

Take It From Me

Jean Carroll and Alan Carney: women should take it from her —her wifely tricks are a treat.

STAND-UP comics of the feminine gender are few and far between in show business. One of the best is Jean Carroll, who has developed into a unique art form her ability to stand up before an audience and whip out her gags in a monologue. The producers of her new TV show, *Take It From Me,* (ABC) have attempted to incorporate this stand-up brand of humor into a situation comedy motif and have generally succeeded.

It's a good show, giving Miss Carroll plenty of opportunity to build laughs with her "asides" to the audience. Cast as a so-called average housewife, complete with a bumbling, lazy but good-natured husband and a moppet daughter, she opens each show with a monologue. It's an obvious attempt to capitalize on TV's over-worked intimacy but it's a fresh approach and she brings it off neatly. From her monologue, the show moves each week into the story.

Most of the action takes place in the family apartment and its environs, including the basement laundry room, the corner drug store and her daughter's school. While the lo-

cation is never pin-pointed, it's presumed to be Brooklyn or the Bronx. Some of the situations and dialogue have a strictly New York flavor, which raises the question of how the show is accepted in the vast expanse of the U.S.A. west of the Hudson. It's likely, though, that Miss Carroll's characterization and the antics of her housewifely cronies are universally recognizable.

Besides the star, much of the credit for the show's warm humor goes to its writers, Arnie Rosen and Coleman Jacoby. They helped push Jackie Gleason up the road to TV fame by heading the writing staff of his old Du Mont program, and they're doing just as well for Miss Carroll.

She herself is great, both in her monologues and in the action scenes. The sly ways she tricks her husband into whatever she wants should be welcome as helpful hints to housewives.

Alan Carney (no relation to Art) is a fine foil as Miss Carroll's husband, and little Lynn Loring is okay as their daughter. The supporting casts have been good.

22

FIGURE 4.2. "Review, 'Take It from Me,'" from *TV Guide*, 1953, saved in Carroll's personal scrapbook. (Private collection of Susan Chatzky)

Jason Gould, of the *New York Times*, whose scathing review, "Jean Carroll, the Impressionist, Gets a Poor Shuffle in Shopworn Situation Comedy," lambasted the show's "lamentable execution."[57] Gould specifically objected to Rosen and Jacoby's unsuccessful attempt to synthesize the sitcom and stand-up elements:

> Where "Take It From Me" falls down badly is in its construction. Basically, it emerges as a nightclub or vaudeville monologue in which Miss Carroll alone is expected to sustain a continuous stream of diverting patter on a single subject, her spouse. That's asking too much of any artist, and already the problem of repetition is acute. The second show was practically a carbon copy of the first. Ernie Rosen and Coleman Jacoby, the writers on the program, should make a fresh start. . . . They must conceive a strong situation that has a beginning and an end. Something must really happen to the family if dramatic interest is to be sustained. . . . "Take It From Me" has possibilities, but it needs a much surer theatrical hand at the helm.[58]

Using terminology like "theatrical hand" and "dramatic interest," Gould's critique suggests that what critics wanted in the early 1950s domestic sitcom was a medium that leaned more heavily toward conservative theatrical realism than toward the erratic and unpredictable variety aesthetic.

Harriet Van Horne's column struck similar notes, critiquing the show's deviation from the "standard formula for most situation comedies, . . . several tons of situation to one ounce of comedy." As if in answer to Carroll's early-expressed desire to avoid having a "joke show," Van Horne condemned the sitcom as "simply a series of jokes, an extended night club routine played out in the kitchen. It's strung on a plot with the tensile strength of one human hair. The day she runs out of gags, the show can close up shop."[59]

Other critics made similar remarks classifying *Take It from Me* as a "joke" show, with Bernie Harrison of the *Washington Times Herald* ominously declaring, "She burns up a lot of material. If her writers can keep up the breakneck pace—and that's a big if—the show might make it."[60] Likewise, a critic from the *Kansas City Star* noted, "Jean's specialty is comedy monologues and that's largely what takes place although there is a rather loose situation comedy format. . . . The success of a show of that type depends on the quality of the gags or smart-cracks or jokes."[61] The reviewer from the "Cue" column agreed: "Messrs. Rosen and Jacoby have given her a vehicle virtually free of plot." Their solution was for Carroll to take less screen time and stop directly addressing the audience, learning to "forget" the viewers when she is onstage with other players.[62] This advice also falls in line with the pro-naturalism aesthetic. Omitting the direct address would allow the program to appear less rooted in stand-up and the variety scene.

Why would the device of stand-up routine-cum-sitcom be so well received in *The George Burns and Gracie Allen Show* but so critically polarizing in *Take It from Me*? Perhaps the different reception had to do with the way that the convention was deployed. On *Burns and Allen*, there was a material separation between the naturalistic action of the sitcom (which took place on a house-and-yard set) and the space in which Burns would speak directly to the viewers (which resembled a proscenium stage with an ornate curtain). This material separation metaphorically sustained the Victorian-inspired boundary between public and private space.[63] Jean Carroll's show did no such thing. On the basis of the script drafts, it seems that Carroll would simply turn to the camera and deliver asides in medias res, more starkly undermining the naturalistic convention of the fourth wall.

Gender also may have played a role in George Burns being able to get away with what Jean Carroll could not. Perhaps the prejudice that Carroll faced as a stand-up comedian found its television analogue in prejudice against a woman bringing stand-up to the sitcom. The authors of *Women in Comedy*, Linda Martin and Kerry Segrave, suggest that Carroll's monologues "put Carroll ahead of her time": "Her image of a woman with equal power to men was too threatening to the male ego and females who swallowed such ideology. It was an image which was not acceptable to TV viewers in the early 1950's. It didn't conform to the norm of what a woman was, or how she was supposed to behave. Perhaps this had more to do with the quick demise of her show than anything else."[64] Indeed, if directly addressing the audience invoked a threatening and unruly vaudeville aesthetic, it would be distinctly more alarming when carried out by a housewife character, who was supposed to be the guardian of domestic harmony.[65] Thus, direct address—or any vaudevillian convention—was a more transgressive act when coming from Jean Carroll than from Jack Benny or George Burns.

Simply put, Cold War network television was not the ideal environment for outspoken wives. Jean Carroll's forthright chitchat with her audience may have flown in the freewheeling variety scene, but this stand-up sensibility strained against the naturalistic trappings urged by critics. While the "Lady and Tramp" combination of naturalistic theater and variety shows may have often made for a happy sitcom union, the genre's marriage in *Take It from Me* was clearly rocky.

Not-So-Happy Housewife

On top of genre incompatibility, another unhappy marriage troubling *Take It from Me* was the show's central relationship between Jean Carroll and her husband, Herbie Carroll. Carroll's fellow TV housewives redeemed the transgressions of their comic antics through presenting as "loving daughters" or "charming housewives," which, Spigel notes, "assured viewers of their essentially female nature."[66] Although domestic squabbles existed as plot points to be neatly resolved within a twenty-minute period, wives generally indulged and adored even the most bumbling husband. Jean Carroll's character, however, was not tamed in this way. Her character cracked jokes and griped about housework without the neutralizing force of a happy marriage. Instead, the *Take It from Me* script drafts are teeming with complaints and marital hostility barely cloaked in humor.

In the archival script of the pilot episode, Carroll turns frankly to her audience and delivers a wry account of her daily chores: "One o'clock and I'm exhausted. Let's see what I have to do yet. Clean up the apartment, dust the furniture, wash the dishes, do the shopping and pick up Robin at school and then come home and start making dinner—set the table—then my husband comes home and I have nothing to do for the rest of the evening but wait on him hand and foot."[67] Her candor may have been refreshing to women in the audience whose household labor was rarely acknowledged, but it was a far cry from the dreamy vision of domestic bliss that sold sponsors' products.[68] It was also a far cry from Carroll's chipper stand-up persona. American audiences had fallen in love with the comedienne in couture gowns who quipped that when she asked her husband to vacation somewhere she had never been before, he said, "Try the kitchen!" This sitcom version of Carroll was more mundane and less cheerful, regarding her household tasks as tedious, endless drudgery.

The deglamorization of Carroll's character was exacerbated by what she called the "biting humor" of Jean and Herbie's marriage.[69] Within the first scene of the archival pilot script, Jean gripes to the audience, "I don't mind that the romance went out of my marriage. . . . I just wish it had taken him along."[70] Episode 2 depicts a marriage-writer character opining, "The average married man is boring, tactless, uninteresting, and unromantic," prompting Carroll's character to spend the rest of the episode living in a fantasy about what it would be like to be married to someone else instead of Herbie. In a typical "happy family" sitcom, this episode might end with her fantasy giving way to a touching realization that her reality (warts and all) is even sweeter. However, this script simply ends with Jean screaming as her husband enters and her fantasy bubble is burst.[71]

The grim gags just keep coming in the January 13 episode as Jean declares, "Today's my anniversary. It was just 11 years ago that I stood before the judge and he sentenced . . . er, pronounced us man and wife."[72] In a particularly dark joke from the November 11 episode,

Herbie reminds Jean that she promised not to argue with him in front of their daughter, so she instructs her daughter to leave the room—and get a sharp knife from the kitchen.[73] And in the November 18 episode, Herbie asks Jean point blank, "You're happy, aren't you?" to which she answers simply, "No," and later fantasizes about divorcing or killing him.[74]

Of course, a script draft is only a worm's-eye view of the actual program that aired. Even if the script had not been significantly altered before broadcast (which it almost certainly was), the actor's inflections, chemistry, and performance can drastically change the tone of the lines. But it would take far more than a tonal shift to make the Carrolls look like an argument for marriage.

The real Jean Carroll was dismayed by the program's mordant depiction of married life. About a month after the pilot of *Take It from Me* aired, Jean Carroll was published in the *Pennsylvania Tribune* declaring, "If a woman spoke to her husband like that all the time in real life, she wouldn't have a husband." She disclosed in the interview that she was in the midst of meetings, "conferences, conferences, and more conferences," on the show's problematic marriage, explaining, "The question is am I looking to remain caustic and keep making with the poison about my husband's stinginess, fatness, and sloppiness. I've been against that from the start. . . . I don't want people to start to hate me. They'll look at me and think I'm some bitter old shrew."[75]

On the surface, Carroll's objection to her character "making with the poison" may seem ironic, given that so much of her wildly successful stand-up routine consisted of "husband jokes." But with astute media savvy, she realized that the shift from stand-up to sitcom meant that the audience went from getting a secondhand account of marital discontent to becoming eyewitnesses. As Carroll put it, "It's all right in a theatre or a nightclub, where you're talking about somebody who isn't there, but when you're making cracks about somebody who's right next to you— that's murder." She hoped that her revamped character would be "more humble, less sarcastic."[76]

Another way that Carroll hoped to brighten up the family dynamic was by shifting the character of the daughter, Robin. "She shouldn't be so wise," Carroll insisted, "She should be naive, and think her father's a great guy."[77] In other words, little Robin Carroll should mirror her mother, tempering jokes with comforting displays of patriarchal devotion. This, after all, was the key to a happy sitcom family.

Too Jewish for TV?

Leo Tolstoy famously wrote, "Happy families are all alike; every unhappy family is unhappy in its own way."[78] The way in which the Carrolls were unhappy had a subtle *Yiddishe tam* (Jewish flavor) to it. It was not the bold, unmistakable savor of Jewishness that characterized a show like *The Goldbergs*, which began running as a televised sitcom on CBS in 1949. In *The Goldbergs*, Jewishness was built into the premise of the show. The tensions between Jake and Molly's Old World immigrant ways and their more assimilated children provided both comedy and—key to sponsors—opportunities to preach values of consumerism, as Molly learned lessons like the obligation to "live above [the family's] means—the American way."[79] In order for *The Goldbergs* to fulfill its project of showing that Jewish immigrants were "just like everybody else," it had to foreground the family's Jewish immigrant identity. *Take It from Me*, however, never incorporated Jean Carroll's Jewishness into the show. It was a neat inverse: on *The Goldbergs*, the US-born Gertrude Berg played an immigrant; on *Take It from Me*, the immigrant Jean Carroll played a US-born woman. Jewish assimilation on *The Goldbergs* was often a plot point, but in *Take It from Me*, it was a presupposition. Yet it was an unsuccessful presupposition. For even without ever saying the word "Jewish," without referencing Jewish customs or practices, and with an entire episode detailing the family's Christmas festivities, there was *still* an unmistakable *Yiddishe tam* to Jean and the Carrolls.

Part of this telltale Jewish flavor came from the writers' room. Like many television writers of this period, Carroll's writers, Jacoby and

Rosen, were Jewish New Yorkers. Rosen had been born in New York City in 1921.[80] Jacobs moved to New York at age sixteen, after being raised in a Pennsylvania orphanage called the Jewish Home for Babies and Children.[81] Scant biographical information is available about precisely how the two young men cut their teeth in show business, but an examination of the performance landscape of New York as they came of age in the 1930s and 1940s can provide some clues. On the Lower East Side, a handful of Yiddish theaters—left over from the Yiddish theater boom at the turn of the century—remained popular. Throughout the 1930s, the ARTEF Arbeter Teater Farband (Workers Theater Association) was staging provocative communist-influenced political theater.[82] The Yiddish Art Theatre, founded by Maurice Schwartz in 1918, was taking on everything from folk comedies like *The Wise Men of Chelm* (1933) to literary adaptations such as *Song of the Dnieper* (1946).[83] As the Jewish theater scholar Debra Caplan has proven, there was substantial cross-pollination between the Yiddish theater community and the mainstream comedy world. Midcentury comedy icons including Lucille Ball, Groucho Marx, and Neil Simon were closely connected to Yiddish theater artists such as Alexandre Astro and Wolf Barzel.[84]

This period also saw American Jews' renewed interest in one of the old masters of Yiddish comedy, Sholem Aleichem. Aleichem's comedy was bitingly satirical, often referred to as "laughter through tears."[85] The scholar of Jewish comedy Jeremy Dauber describes Aleichem as part of a tradition of Jewish humor that "isn't always funn-ee," going "less for the laugh than the wry nod, the gentle smile, or even the horrified gasp."[86] This tradition is perhaps best characterized by Irving Howe, who noted, "Strictly speaking, Jewish humor is not humorous. Rather it is disturbing and upsetting, the phrases dipped in tragedy."[87] Aleichem, who was born in a Russian shtetl in 1859, had written primarily about the poverty and religious persecution of the Russian Jewish community of the late 1800s. However, his work resonated among Jews in the United States in the years during and after World War II, as they grappled with the brutal violence occurring in Europe.[88]

Given Aleichem's prominence in the Jewish arts community in the period during and after World War II, it is perhaps not surprising to see traces of his influence in the work of Rosen and Jacoby. For example, Sholom Aleichem's Tevye character would often engage in funny one-sided conversations with God, using a humorously familiar tone and even giving God diminutive nicknames. The *New York Times* columnist David Everett noted that the Sergeant Bilko character on *The Phil Silvers Show* (known in syndication as *Sergeant Bilko*), which Colman and Jacoby wrote on from 1955 to 1959, did the same thing. Bilko's comical apostrophe was "continuing [Tevye's] dialogue with God. Not exactly a devout dialogue, perhaps, but a dialogue nonetheless."[89] One could even see Jean Carroll's direct address to her audience as part of this lineage, though her one-sided conversations are even less reverent than Sergeant Bilko's.

Another example of the lingering influence of Sholem Aleichem is his darkly humorous depictions of marriage.[90] The premise of sparring spouses served Rosen and Jacoby well in 1951, when the duo wrote "Bread," for the DuMont sketch show *Cavalcade of Stars*. This historic sketch introduced the world to the squabblings of Ralph and Alice Kramden, the couple who would later become famous on the television show *The Honeymooners*.[91] And it seems that Colman and Jacoby drew on the same comically combative relationship dynamic for Jean and Herbie Carroll.

Certainly, Jewish comedians do not have a monopoly on depictions of miserable marriages. Nor would audiences necessarily "read" these couples' high-strung hostility as Jewish. But, as the performance theorist José Muñoz argues, heightened emotion of any kind is often read as antithetical to the "affective performance of normative whiteness," which he describes as "minimalist to the point of emotional impoverishment."[92] Picking up on this thread, the performance studies scholar Henry Bial identifies a recurring "rhetoric of ethnicity as excess."[93] Behavior that is too loud, too unruly, too discordant is often "coded" as ethnic. In contrast to the stereotypical white Anglo-Saxon Protestant ideal of harmonious marital tranquility, these confrontational couples and their high-spirited rows gave an impression of ethnic otherness.

If the *Yiddishe tam* was not strong enough in the embattled relationship between Jean and Herbie, there were plenty of other ways that it came through in *Take It from Me*. One of the characters introduced in the script draft for December 9, 1953, is Madam Olga, an opportunistic headmistress at a local talent school. The colorful character assures Carroll that her daughter "sings like a bird," and when a confused Carroll corrects that Robin is studying dance, the unflappable Madam Olga counters, "So she dances like a bird—you mothers are too technical." Carroll's aside to the audience describes Madam Olga as "a Russian refugee . . . teaching children in Russia for years until she was almost liquidated by that dread organization—the Moscow PTA."[94] This line stops short of literally labeling Madame Olga Jewish, but her "Russian refugee" status does much the same thing, as at the time of this episode's projected airing, the "dread organization" of the Soviet government had been conducting drastic "purges" against Jews. These tragic and well-publicized human rights infractions contributed to President Dwight Eisenhower's enacting the Refugee Relief Act of 1953, a "humanitarian act" welcoming over two hundred thousand refugees.[95]

Madam Olga's thick Russian dialect provides comedy while further "outing" her as Jewish with giveaway Yiddishisms. A signal instance of this lapse into Yiddish comes in a scene where Madam Olga's pupils perform their recital. The headmistress proudly introduces "Little Geraldine MacBride, who will recite a poem" that Madam Olga "personally ha[s] taught her," only to be "embarrassed" when the child declaims (dialect scripted),

Voss de night before Christmas,
ven all thrru da hous,
not vun creature vas stirring
not even vun mouse.
Da shtockings vas hung byvda fireside mit care.[96]

The incongruity of the (presumably Scottish) MacBride child speaking with a Russian accent is a reliable bit of "ethnic shtick," and Madam Olga's use of "mit"—a German word, rather than her native Russian—gives her away as a speaker of Yiddish, the Jewish language that blends German, Russian, Polish, Hebrew, and Romanian. While it is uncertain whether the character of Madam Olga made it to the airwaves or remained on the cutting-room floor, her presence would have been a strong signal of Yiddishkeit.

* * *

A final—and somewhat counterintuitive—indicator of Jewishness in *Take It from Me* is the show's special "Christmas" episode, scheduled to air December 16. This episode is part of a much larger trend of Jewish artists creating Christmas media culture. This phenomenon is most famously demonstrated in the extensive discography of Christmas carols written by Jewish composers in the years between 1930 and 1960. For instance, 1946's "The Christmas Song"—better known as "Chestnuts Roasting on an Open Fire"—was written by Jewish composer Mel Tormé. Irving (né Israel) Berlin wrote "White Christmas" the following year. The St. Nicholas Music Company, which produced such classics as "Rockin' around the Christmas Tree," "A Holly, Jolly Christmas," "Silver and Gold," and "Rudolph the Red Nosed Reindeer," was formed in 1949 by the Jewish composer Johnny Marks. And as Jean Carroll's show hit ABC, the Jewish composers Joan Javits and Phil Springer found a hit with "Santa Baby." The author of *The Encyclopedia of Jewish American Popular Culture*, Kenneth Kantor, explains that this surge of Christmas compositions was a way for Jews to acculturate into American Christian culture, remarking, "These songs made Christmas a kind of national celebration, almost a patriotic celebration."[97]

However, the Christmas episode of *Take It from Me* from December 16 is riddled with moments of comical failure—bungled attempts at proper "Christmasing" that belie the Jewishness the writers try so hard to obscure. In this episode, the Carroll family attempts to celebrate

Christmas with all the appropriate (jingle)bells and whistles but are thwarted at every turn. First, a no-show Santa at the children's Christmas party leads to Jean filling in. Although she protests, "Whoever heard of a woman playing Santa Claus?" it is to no avail. Out she comes, in an "oversized suit with pillow stuck under coat. . . . When she pats stomach, the pillow slips out. . . . She shoves it back."⁹⁸ Despite her best efforts, the children are skeptical of Carroll's Santa charade. The running gag of Carroll's failure to "pass" for Santa offers an interesting metaphor for the show writers' attempt to "pass" into the WASPY American mainstream. Like Carroll, they keep giving themselves away.

The next segment of the episode finds Herbie reading Robin the "actual text of Dickens' Christmas Carol about twenty seconds" and urging her to go to sleep as she pleads to stay up and see Santa Claus. Once she is finally asleep, Herbie and Jean try to set up a magnificent Christmas display. However, Herbie's first faux pas comes when he gives a miserly tip to the boy delivering the Christmas tree. Then, hapless Herbie tries to nail the tree to the floor, only to injure his hand. On top of that, he attaches the "Christmas bulbs" to a worn-out extension cord, prompting Jean to get electrocuted when she plugs them in. The bungled bedecking continues as Herbie's attempt to hang the lighted Christmas wreath outside results in him slipping and "hanging from the window holding on with the window-sill under his arm-pits."⁹⁹ Eventually, the Christmas bulbs explode, waking Robin. Using the classic comedy-sketch structure of "a simple yet impossible task," this portion of the episode turns Jean and Herbie's simple attempt to deck their halls into a quagmire.¹⁰⁰ As Herbie and Jean stumble through the parade of pratfalls, this image of people at odds with their environment again offers a potential metaphor for Jews at Yuletide.

In the final act, things take a turn for the better—the script specifies a brief interval in which "Christmasy Type Music" plays and "the old tree is replaced with a beautiful decked out one. . . . Also the gifts have been placed on the floor."¹⁰¹ Little Robin looks at the plenitude in wonder, asking, "Is this what you call Xmas spirit?" As the exultant Robin opens her gifts, the family is interrupted by "Mrs. Johnson's niece." As the character, named only BABY in the script, stares in awe at the gifts, Jean asks if she would like a Christmas present. BABY points to a large teddy bear—the present that Robin loved most—and exclaims, "I want that." Then, the stage directions note, "There is a very definite pause and then Robin very slowly hands the teddy bear to the kid who hugs it happily." Jean turns to her daughter and proclaims, "Honey, *that* was what you call Christmas spirit." Then, all four of them end the episode by singing "Silent Night" while the curtain falls and Carroll bids the viewers a merry Christmas.[102]

This conclusion restores the blundering Carroll family. Although they cannot pull off a Santa cameo or hang a wreath, they comply with the most important Cold War Christmas custom: generous and enthusiastic consumerism. Fittingly, it is Robin—the next-generation American—who redeems the family with her intuitive understanding of the "Christmas spirit." Again, the nature of this "Christmas spirit" is connected to material goods and is broadly charitable, rather than specifically ecumenical. The closest that the episode comes to referencing Christianity, church, or the birth of Jesus Christ is the few bars of "Silent Night" as the curtain falls. The Christmas of *Take It from Me*, like the Christmas of "White Christmas," is not about Jesus Christ per se. Rather, it is about acculturation—especially through purchasing habits. As the sociologist James Barnett noted in his 1954 study, "The American Christmas is no longer devoted exclusively to celebrating the Nativity. . . . This makes it possible for non-Christians to participate in its folk and secular aspects even if they do not accept its religious significance."[103] In creating a Christmas episode, the *Take It from Me* writers, Jacoby and Rosen, were participating in a long-standing Jewish tradition of displaying successful Americanization. Or at least, they were trying. Unfortunately, it seems that the show was still too "New York" (Jewish) for television.

* * *

Whether it was the mordant marriage so redolent of shtetl comedy, the slips into Yiddishisms, or the blundering display of Christmas zeal, *Take It from Me* was reading as Jewish even without using the J-word. *TV Guide*'s review of *Take It from Me* heavily suggests that the show was legibly Jewish. Describing the show's environment, the critic said that while the show's location is "never pin-pointed, it's presumed to be Brooklyn or the Bronx." They emphasized that "the situations and dialogue have a strictly New York flavor, which raises the question of how the show is accepted in the vast expanse of the USA west of the Hudson."[104] Although the word "Jewish" was not explicitly uttered, the critic's use of "New York" is a fairly transparent euphemism.

The *TV Guide* critic was not wrong to be concerned about the show's acceptance "west of the Hudson." The year 1951 saw the establishment of a coaxial cable, which allowed the feeds of New York–based live programming to be picked up nationwide. And in 1952, the year before *Take It from Me* aired, the FCC allowed the licensing of new television stations, further broadening TV audiences.[105] Therefore, the television audience that had begun as predominantly East Coast, urban, and relatively well versed in Jewish culture was now dominated by a more ethnically homogeneous population, for which references to immigrant families—Jewish or otherwise—would be unfamiliar and unrelatable. In 1952, Irwin Shane, the executive director of New York's Television Workshop, famously warned fellow producers, "A comedy show built entirely upon Broadway humor (or frequent references to the borscht circuit, the Brooklyn Dodgers, the Palace Theatre, or even famous New York Nightclubs) will find an indifferent audience in Kokomo, Indiana, and in the hundreds of Kokomos around the country. To assure an out-of-town audience, the show's content must be broad in its appeal."[106]

This pressure for broad appeal contributed to what Vincent Brook calls "an industrywide trend toward elimination of the urban, ethnic working-class sitcom that had flourished in early TV."[107] The Italian American family sitcom *Life with Luigi* was canceled in 1952. *Amos 'n' Andy*, about a pair of Black men making their lives in Harlem, was pulled from the air in 1953.[108] *Mama*, a sitcom about a Norwegian American immigrant family, met its end in 1956, the same year that *The Goldbergs* left the air—despite the show having undergone a thorough "Americanization." And so the 1954 cancellation of *Take It from Me* seems less like an isolated incident than it does another instance of television sitcoms shutting down programming with too strong an ethnic flavor.

Returning to Irving Howe's definition of Jewish humor, he notes that it is full of "acute social observation" because its characteristic strategy is "an irony which measured the distance between pretension and actuality."[109] As relative outsiders, American Jews in the 1950s were poised to see the distance between the idyllic cult of domesticity and the actual experience of living in the Cold War United States. Their observations—be they about the combative relationships between husbands and wives, the omnipresence of immigrants, or the impossibility of hanging Christmas lights—interrupted the vision of the United States that networks needed to sell toasters.

* * *

Whatever Jean Carroll might have fantasized, ABC was not, in fact, laid low by the loss of Carroll's show. After the network, as one article graphically put it, "swung the axe down" on *Take It from Me*, it quickly replaced the show with a "government-distributed film series on the armed services called 'The Big Picture.'"[110] Although rumblings regarding the potential resurrection of a Jean Carroll sitcom at ABC or Kline Studios continued to run in *Variety* for another year, neither of these projects ever came to fruition.[111] A few years later, in 1958, ABC premiered *The Donna Reed Show*, about the adoring and adorable Stone family. That same year, ABC acquired *Leave It to Beaver*, which depicted the wholesome antics of the Cleaver clan. These cheerfully patriotic, white Anglo-Saxon Protestant families delivered to America everything that ABC's sponsors desired.

Perhaps more surprisingly, Jean Carroll was also not laid low by the loss of *Take It from Me*. Throughout the entire, frustrating process, she had shown remarkable equanimity. When faced with the onslaught of criticism following the debut of *Take It from Me*—criticism that she had presciently anticipated in her statements against "joke shows" in 1952—Carroll kept a relatively calm public face. An interview with the *Dayton News* shows her joking about the massive criticism that comes with a television audience, recounting comical anecdotes about friends and relatives calling her up to "dissect the scripts" or offer "constructive criticism like, "You look cross-eyed in one of the scenes," concluding, "Everybody who looks at a TV show is a critic. People go to movies and stage shows and maybe they don't like them. But they have sensible reasons. They don't just pick up on the fact that maybe the leading man needed a haircut or that the seam of one of the heroine's stockings was slightly out of line."[112]

Carroll was able to dismiss critiques of her show as petty quibbling, rather than the reason for its cancellation. For whatever *Variety* said, Carroll always insisted on the version of the story in which *she* was the one who ended the show. In a speech she gave at the Friars Club nearly fifty years later, she made a point of correcting the papers, exclaiming, "In the write-up, they made it sound like I had been canned. I wasn't canned. I refused to do it anymore."[113] Armed with this narrative, Carroll refused to slink off with her tail between her legs. Instead, she redoubled her appearances on *The Ed Sullivan Show* and continued to appear live at clubs and theaters in the US and the UK. No longer part of a television family, Carroll embraced the freedoms of returning to her role as an autonomous stand-up comedian.

Sullivan Spots and Party Records

Playing Jewish without Saying "Jewish"

In 1955, on an average Sunday night, forty-seven million people were doing the exact same thing: watching *The Ed Sullivan Show*.[1] The hour-long variety show captivated American audiences for twenty-two years, exposing them to a staggering ten thousand acts ranging from the opera singer Maria Callas to a roller-skating chimpanzee. For comedians, Ed Sullivan was the kingmaker, boosting the careers of comics from Milton Berle and Henny Youngman to George Carlin and Phyllis Diller. While other televised variety shows, such as Milton Berle's *Texaco Star Theater* and Sid Caesar's *Your Show of Shows* fizzled when television moved beyond the East Coast, Ed Sullivan was what the historian Gerald Nachman calls a "TV anomaly, . . . a New York creature who played beautifully in Kokomo."[2] Or, as Joan Rivers put it, "Johnny Carson gave you the cities. Ed Sullivan gave you the country."[3] Fortunately for Jean Carroll, the man who gave you the country had been a fan of hers since her vaudeville days. So when Jean Carroll's sitcom ended in 1954, the then-five-time veteran of *The Ed Sullivan Show* returned to TV with old pal Ed. By 1956, she signed an exclusive contract. Altogether, she appeared on *The Ed Sullivan Show* twenty-nine times, making her one of his top ten most frequent guests.[4]

It was an almost ideal scenario. The show filmed in New York, close to Carroll's home. It was prestigious, it was well-paying (according to Carroll, she received "$10,000 a crack"), and it did not demand a lot of rehearsal time.[5] However, Ed Sullivan was a difficult person to work with. For one thing, he was a notorious micromanager, which did not sit well with Carroll's desire to control her own work. According to her interviews, he was stricter even than the Television Code, the set of rules enforced beginning in 1952 by the National Association of Radio and Television Broadcasters, which demanded that even programming not specifically oriented toward children must be child-friendly.[6]

Sullivan flexed his power by playing fast and loose with the performers' time slots. Carroll complained, with her flair for hyperbole, "He'd find somebody in the lobby that could sing two choruses, he'd put them on, and he'd come back and say to me, 'Cut four minutes from your routine.'"[7] When she protested his cuts, explaining, "Sometimes it takes a minute or two to develop a character before it can even be funny," he shut her down with, "You don't know what to eliminate."[8] Sullivan also irritated performers with what the journalist Gerald Nachman calls his "one more time fixation"—if he found a bit of theirs that he enjoyed, he would make them perform it even when it got repetitive. He once pushed Carroll to repeat the "buying a dress" routine that she had done on his show only a few weeks before, insisting, "I'm the boss, I pay you!" She complied and then faced "all kinds of criticism because [she] was doing the same old routine."[9] Ed Sullivan's temper was the stuff of legend. He famously banned Jackie Mason from his show for years after mistakenly thinking that Mason had made a rude gesture at him. And once, when Jean Carroll referenced "a pretty young girl driving a Cadillac" in her act, it made Sullivan—whose show was sponsored by Cadillac's competitor Lincoln—furious. "He could have strangled me!" she recounted. "He lit into me and insisted I did it deliberately."[10] It took two years before he booked Carroll again. For her part, she was baffled by how he "achieved the position he achieved in show business," declaring, "He was a real enigma."[11]

The difficulties of the enigmatic kingmaker notwithstanding, appearing on *The Ed Sullivan Show* was not a bad way to rebound from the disappointments of *Take It from Me*. Decades later, Carroll reflected, "If you have the tapes, you'll see it. . . . It was my comeback."[12]

In Carroll's nearly thirty appearances on *The Ed Sullivan Show*, she was performing for virtually the entire country. And as Carroll had learned all too well from her failed sitcom, Jews performing for a nationwide audience had to be very careful about how they represented themselves. What Jean Carroll did on the *Sullivan* stage shaped the way that the United States saw Jewish women—and the way that Jewish women saw themselves. The ways that she modulated her performances on this show offer an interesting reflection of the complex negotiation of assimilation and difference that American Jews were enacting after World War II.

In 2007, when a filmmaker asked Jean Carroll whether her Jewishness had influenced her comedy, her answer was as flustered as it was emphatic. She stuttered, "No. No, nothing. Absolutely nothing to do with it. Nothing to do with it because I spent so much time with people who were not Jewish. I spent a lot of time with people who were not Jewish. One of my best friends was a priest, Father Kelly. . . . I spent time with him."[13] Carroll rambled on about Father Kelly's diocese and several more priests whom she counted among her friends—all peculiar evidence of her main point that being Jewish had "absolutely nothing to do with" her comedy. But—as is so often the case when people use the "some of my best friends are . . ." defense—she undermined the very point she was trying to make.

Her skittishness surrounding Jewishness is understandable. In the mid-1950s, Carroll and other Jewish performers were facing very mixed signals regarding American attitudes toward Jews. In the years between 1937 and 1962, the social scientist Charles Stember ran a longitudinal study, *Jews in the Minds of America,* and his public opinion polls on attitudes toward American Jewry were fairly unsettling. There were high levels of antisemitism in the US throughout the World War II years, which did not disappear after the war ended.[14] Instead, Stember found a fraught relationship between overt antisemitism and underlying sentiment. Having just fought a war with Germans espousing blatant antisemitism, Americans were reluctant to admit to officially holding prejudice against Jewish people. And yet, on the other hand, "anti-Semitism continued to lead a vigorous life in the unofficial minds of many Americans."[15]

However loath Jean Carroll was to acknowledge the influence that Jewishness had on her work, its influence is undeniable when watching her on *The Ed Sullivan Show*. The *way* that Jewishness influenced her work changed dramatically over the four decades of the show's existence. In Carroll's *Sullivan* spots in the mid- to late 1950s, for example, her Jewishness prompted her to stress the assimilated, deethnicized elements of her persona, using only subtle, coded references to Jewishness. Conversely, in appearances in the mid-1960s, as the civil rights movement inspired other ethnic groups to celebrate their own differences, Carroll's Jewishness influenced her comedy through more overt displays of Yiddishkeit. But amid the changing historical contexts, what was consistently evident in Carroll's appearances on *Sullivan* is precisely the thing she tried so hard to deny to the filmmaker: Jewishness had influenced her comedy.

1954–1961: Double-Coded Jewishness

American Jews in the years after World War II were, in some ways, enjoying a whole new level of privilege. Veterans' legislation like the GI Bill of 1944 and the 1944 Serviceman's Readjustment Act meant that Jewish GIs had access to preferential hiring, affordable college education, and cheap home mortgages. Triumphant sociological texts like Oscar Handlin's *Adventures in Freedom: 300 Years of Jewish Life in America* (1954) and Nathan Glazer's "Social Characteristics of American Jews, 1654–1954" documented American Jews of the 1950s outearning and outrepresenting their non-Jewish peers in the professional sphere. Yet despite this social uplift, American Jews were still reckoning with the aftermath of the Holocaust. It was yet another in a series of traumatizing historical moments in which Jews' sense of acceptance and security was shattered by antisemitism on a genocidal scale. If Jews in Germany—who had been among some of the most assimilated and prominent citizens in the country—had been so quickly destroyed, that did not bode well for Jews anywhere. With "Jewish enough for Hitler" as a metric, many American

Jews felt a new sense that their Jewishness was a matter of descent, not consent.[16] And with that involuntary Jewishness came a great deal of anxiety and insecurity.

Anxiety about one's status in the United States is especially clear in the ways that Jewish artists of this period addressed Jewishness in mainstream performances—or the ways they chose *not* to address it. Often, Jewish artists never uttered the "J-word," nor did they reference Jewish holidays or customs. Instead, their references to Jewish life were indirect or implicit, perhaps only legible to other Jewish audience members. The Jewish performance scholar Henry Bial has introduced the idea of "double coding," in which the same performance can speak differently to a Jewish audience than it does to a general or "gentile" audience. For example, Bial examines Arthur Miller's 1949 hit play *Death of a Salesman*, noting, "The Yiddish-inflected English of Willy Loman can be seen as . . . gesturing towards his own Jewish heritage for those who recognize, consciously or subconsciously, the underlying Yiddish grammar, while not calling attention to the characters' Jewishness in a way that might alienate a gentile audience."[17] Double-coded performance was a crucial strategy for Jewish artists to address their own cultural particularity without sacrificing universal appeal. The aural and visual performance codes that Bial discusses—"underlying Yiddish grammar," as well as "accents, rhythms of speech, and emotional affect"—are key to reading Jean Carroll's appearances on *The Ed Sullivan Show*.[18] To create authentically personal, original comedy, she was continually drawing from Jewish experiences, without ever labeling them as such. Put simply, she exemplified the art of playing Jewish without saying Jewish.

The Secret's in the Syntax: A Jokebook of Yiddish Linguistic Devices

The form of "playing Jewish" that is probably easiest to identify is the syntax. Nu? You probably knew that already. Syntax shmyntax, some may say, but insignificant it is not. Many Jewish comedians wanted that

Jewish audience members should pick up on the syntax they used as an implicit code of Jewishness.

As this little bit of performative writing attempts to illustrate, the Yiddish language can be felt in grammatical constructions even in the absence of actual Yiddish vocabulary. In 1968, Leo Rosten published the comical but informative *The Joys of Yiddish,* in which he offered a parodic taxonomy of these rhythmically distinctive grammatical constructions, which he named "Yiddish Linguistic Devices."[19] These devices are amply exemplified in Jean Carroll's appearances on *The Ed Sullivan Show* in the mid-'50s to early '60s. To wit, the following are a number of Rosten's Yiddish Linguistic Devices, illustrated by Jean Carroll, care of Ed Sullivan:

- "Mordant syntax," in which a complimentary adjective begins the sentence and is then bitingly canceled out by its negative application to the sentence's subject. E.g., "I got a husband—handsome, he isn't!"[20]
- Reversed word order to convey scorn. E.g., (Carroll recounting a doctor's visit) "Four quarts of my blood they took!"[21]
- "Politeness is expedited by truncated verbs and eliminated prepositions." E.g., (instead of "Look at this coat") "Look-a-coat!"[22]
- "Derisive dismissal disguised as innocent interrogation." E.g., "There was one fella, he stayed at the Royalty Plaza, he was there for six weeks. His wife came down to join him, she walked into the room, she said, 'My goodness, Joey, you're so pale, what's the matter?' He says, 'Thirty dollars a day I should leave the room?'"[23]
- A question is used to answer a question to convey indignation. E.g., I turned to my oldest brother, Al. . . . I said "Al, can Mama live with you?"
  He said, "What kind of question is that?"
  "*You* have to ask me, after *all* Mama's done for us? You have to ask *me*?"
  . . . "Where will I put her?"[24]

Indeed, the phraseology that Rosten terms "Yiddish Linguistic Devices" is abundant in Jean Carroll's comedy routines on the mainstream stage of the *The Ed Sullivan Show*. And though non-Jewish audience members without familiarity with Yiddish speech patterns might not pick up on Carroll's participation in this linguistic signature, those in-group members would be able to discern her as a "member of the tribe."

* * *

Jean Carroll was never just targeting a Jewish audience. She was after that brass ring of "universality." And so on *The Ed Sullivan Show* in the mid-1950s through the early 1960s, Carroll was ever mindful of her mainstream (read: white Anglo-Saxon Protestant, heterosexual) audience. She eschewed obvious references to Jewishness. Her persona was assimilated, glamorous, and—perhaps most American of all—deeply invested in ascending to the upper middle class.

One of Carroll's most memorable appearances from this period featured a sequence of "moving monologues," bits she created about moving from one residence to another. While ostensibly about her personal experience with her husband, these routines tapped into the widespread experience of postwar Jews of a phenomenon that some sociologists refer to as "becoming white."[25] Simply put, "becoming white" is used to refer to the process of merging identities and interests with a privileged class, often at the expense of a working class, disproportionately including people of color. This socioeconomic uplift was met with profound ambivalence on the part of the many Jews making that transition. While doubtlessly enjoying the privileges of wealth and "whiteness," many Jewish people felt a fraught kind of ambivalence about leaving behind the more "authentic" Jewishness of the working class. The historian Matthew Frye Jacobson terms this anxiety "the assimilation blues."[26]

Carroll captures this dynamic in miniature through her comic narratives about moving. As she breezes through anecdotes about dragging her reluctant husband through a series of residences, she consistently positions herself as the enthusiastic driver of action and her husband as the reluctant passenger. Jewish men comedians of this era gave their own take on the apotheosis of suburbia and the nuclear family, cracking jokes at the expense of their wives. Alan King released an entire record titled *On Suburbia* (1960), much of which came from material King developed on *Sullivan* throughout the 1950s. His segments comically characterized his wife as a psychological terrorist, with wisecracks like, "I've been reading about brainwashing and psychological warfare. If the scientists want to come to my house for two weeks, my wife will show you how to pick a brain apart, destroy a human being without even try-ing."[27] The wife character in Henny Youngman's segments wreaked simi-lar havoc—he described coming home one night to find, "There's the car, in the dining room! I said to her, 'How did you get the car in there?' She said, 'It was easy; I took a left turn when I got out of the kitchen!'"[28] And a beleaguered Sam Levenson entreated the audience, "I admit my wife is outspoken, but by whom?"[29]

Comics like Levenson, King, and Youngman, as well as other *Sullivan* mainstays like Myron Cohen and Jack Carter, seemed to feel particular anxiety about the "until death do us part" element of their marriages, often riffing on the theme of marriage and mortality. In one segment, Alan King quipped, "Women live longer than men. There's a reason for it: they're not married to women."[30] In a different segment, he declared, "For my wife to live in the style that she's accustomed to after I'm gone, when they dig my grave, they're going to have to strike oil!"[31] Jack Carter came on the *Sullivan* show to tell the tale of a weeping woman he met on the street. "I felt such compassion," he began. "I went up to her and said, 'What's the matter lady?' She said, 'Oh, my husband, oh, I'm gonna miss him!' . . . I said, 'When did he die?' She said, 'He starts tomorrow.'"[32] The homicidal housewife theme continued in a spot Henny Youngman did on *Sullivan*, describing a child asking, "Mommy, why are you taking out $100,000 worth of insurance on me?" to her loving retort, "Shut up and eat your cranberries!"[33] Even the gentle dialect comic Myron Cohen got in on the act, doing a spot on *Sullivan* about a wife who asked that her portrait painter add extravagant jewelry to her image. When the painter asked about this curious addition, she explained (in thick Yiddish ac-cent), "My husband happens to be a louse. And ven I die, I'm sure he's going to get married again. I vant his next vife should drop dead looking for the jewelry."[34] This kind of "morbid marriage" comedy suggests that behind the postage-stamp yards and cookie-cutter houses of suburbia waged a battle of the sexes—a battle to the death.

In a way, Jean Carroll's comedy is quite aligned with that of her male colleagues. She, too, found rich comic fodder in beatniks, suburbia, and what Sam Levenson termed "the kindergarchy," society built around child rearing. But she offers a totally different perspective as a woman. In the men's gags, wives played the role of the fool (at best) or the villain (at worst), while the men played the wry, relatable commentator. Jean Carroll's comedy is from the wife's point of view; the husband is the comic relief, while her perspective is framed as "the norm." The experience of suburbanization—seen from the man's perspective as a devouring wife's obsession with consumption and shopping—becomes reimagined from Jean Carroll's perspective as an assimilatory and progressive move, in which the wife's embrace of Jews' shifting status is hindered by her regressive husband's ambivalence.

For instance, on Carroll's September 23, 1956, appearance on *The Ed Sullivan Show*, she did a bit about her move from a tenement-style apartment building to a Park Avenue co-op, in which she acts out working with an interior decorator to shed her old (lower-class) possessions in favor of her new upper-middle-class lifestyle. In the bit, Carroll stands center stage, dressed in a low-cut, sleeveless lace gown with a pencil skirt that highlights her slender frame. Earrings and a bracelet sparkled subtly, and she holds a pair of neat white gloves. Her perfectly arranged updo, neatly plucked brow, and heavy makeup complete the picture of a glamorous, modern, white American lady. She rushes on, clasps Sullivan by the hands, smiles down at the audience as she finds her mark, and begins joking about her formerly dismal living conditions:

I've just been going through something all you women will understand. I've been moving from one apartment to the other. You see, before I got married, my husband promised me that I'd have a place of my own, even it if it was just a hole in the wall. And that's where I've been living—a hole in the wall. But really, we had to get out because it was a sublease, and the mice wanted it back. I'll tell you, you never saw such a building in your life! They had what you'd call a "finished basement." You go down there, you're finished! All the tenants, they do their laundry down there. It's easy, 'cause there's four feet of water, see? I don't mind the water, but—ooh—those alligators! But my husband! He loves this neighborhood! He says, "Where else could you get six rooms for thirty dollars a month?" This he likes! I tell you something, such a neighborhood! My husband, he likes it. He says, "It's quiet at night!" It is quiet—all you hear is a few screams for help. You know, in some neighborhoods, in some buildings, if you want heat, all you do is knock on the radiator with a wrench. Here, you knock on the landlord's head! But you know, I got lucky! I got a lucky break, because, as I said to my husband, "The building has been condemned, and we've got to move!"

Unlike women in stand-up by male comics, who exist merely as references and joke targets, Carroll is a whole person with a whole point of view; her voice and perspective engender the audience's sympathetic view of her former apartment as a "hole in the wall," rife with the dangers of floods, alligators, cold, mice, and whatever is prompting those "screams for help" in the night. Her husband's love of the neighborhood, while perhaps connected to Jewish immigrants' desire to maintain their roots in an immigrant community, is here represented as a miserliness that is both unreasonable and comically foolish. Nevertheless, his stagnation means that they must remain there until the situation reaches a crisis point, prompting Carroll to refer to her building being condemned as "a lucky break." Carroll further emphasizes her husband's role as a force of stagnation as they battle over furnishings:

He said, "All right, we'll take all our old furniture."
I said, "No, nothing doing!"

He said, "Look, honey, I want you to take *everything* of value with us."

So . . . I filled up the shopping bag and we moved. I'll tell you where we moved. You know it's hard to get an apartment to rent. We bought one! You know those co-ops? You know co-operatives? In case you don't know what that is, I'll tell you: if you've got $5,000 to throw away, they cooperate. It's a very swanky building on Park Avenue. . . . You even have to gift-wrap your garbage, or they won't take it!

In this bit, Carroll foregrounds the tension between her husband, who wants to bring all of their old furniture, and her aspirational upper-middle-class persona, who deems only a shopping bag's worth of items to be "of value." Her husband's penchant for low-cost conservation, held up against her desire for new products, mirrors the trend that Paula Hyman uncovered in her research, in which women assimilate more quickly than men largely through consumer behavior.[35]

The other tension that Carroll introduces is between her persona and her "swanky" new neighborhood, which demands gift-wrapped garbage and "$5,000" to "cooperate." Here, she nimbly exemplifies the off-putting experience of being confronted with largess unknown to most Jews of the prewar period. Her incredulity at the cost of her new class is heightened as the bit continues:

I decided, "This one, I'm gonna do right!" I had the whole place painted. The guy handed me a bill: $900 to paint the living room wall.

I said, "Nine hundred bucks for a wall?!"

He said, "Lady, I gave it two coats."

I said, "What were they, mink?"

Her word choice of "I'm gonna do right" is telling, for it suggests a moral value in this consumption—her spending is a way to "do right" by her new environment, to assimilate into her new status without marking herself and her husband as "Other" with their inferior furniture and unmanicured walls. Of course, assimilation also prompts marital tensions, evident in the next passage, which highlights the husband-as-hindrance:

> [The decorator] looked around and he said, "Now everything you brought with you from the *old* apartment has got to go. Especially that [pointing accusatorily]! That is in very bad taste!"
>
> I said, "Mr. Thorpe, *that* happens to be my husband!"
>
> He said [sympathetically], "Ohhh, yes dear! Well, that horrible *green* face *does* play havoc with our color scheme, doesn't it!"
>
> But anyhow, you know these decorators, they have ideas. He had a wonderful idea for a den for my husband. No big deal, just a water trough and some straw on the floor!

Carroll's depiction of the decorator dismissing her husband along with her old furniture stages a widespread anxiety among Jewish men. As Riv-Ellen Prell has shown, Jewish husbands in the mid-twentieth century felt growing insecurity about their ability as providers and projected that insecurity onto their wives, presenting them as nagging, demanding, and dismissive.[36] In this bit, Carroll uses the avatar of the "interior designer" to dismiss her husband as "green" (also a slur for new immigrants), "in very bad taste," and animal-like, while her persona occupies the comparatively progressive role of the assimilatory consumer. She concludes her bit with some well-trod stereotypes of Jewish men as misers:

> My husband got into the whole spirit of the thing. I wanted a coffee table, so he decided he would make it. He went out and he got a big slab of marble. But he got a real bargain! Underneath, it said, "Rest in Peace."
>
> I said, "Honey, I don't want that!"
>
> He said, "Jeanie, be practical. We can take this with us *any place we go!*"

With bits like this, Carroll turned her husband's stubborn stasis and obsessive bargain-hunting into a joke with every bit of the acerbity that Henny Youngman and his male colleagues were mocking their wives' consumption. Carroll's "moving monologue," which comically contrasts her enthusiastic mobility with her husband's stagnation, is an apt forum for Carroll to dramatize a larger trend, in which, as Joseph Roth put it, "the assimilation of a people always begins with the women."[37]

Carroll's other "moving monologue" about heading to the suburbs also cryptically depicts a wider sociological trend of Jewish economic uplift, foregrounding her own perspective as the sympathetic voice of reason surrounded by comically heightened interlocutors. The "moving to the suburbs" routine developed alongside the real-life phenomenon of Jewish suburbanization, as the housing subsidies provided by the GI Bill prompted the Jewish population in the suburbs to more than double, "in contrast with the total suburban population, which increased only 29 percent."[38]

In Carroll's appearance on *The Ed Sullivan Show* on April 5, 1959, she begins her routine with an exchange between her persona and an overly candid girlfriend character:

> I met this girlfriend of mine—well, she's not really a friend. . . . We know a lot about each other. She used to live in New York, but, *you* know, now she lives in the suburbs. You know, *big deal*!
>
> She met me on the street. She said, "Jean, I have to talk to you about your rotten kid. You know something, it's *your* fault that she's a rotten kid."
>
> I said, "Why, what have I done? Am I a rotten mother?"
>
> She said, ". . . You're trying to raise this child in New York, and you know that nobody grows up in New York! Today people just don't grow up in New York! Who ever heard of raising a kid growing up in New York?"
>
> Well, that mixed me up, because I've seen a lot of grown-ups in New York. But I figured it out: They grow up in Westchester. They run in for a few days to confuse me!

This part of the monologue—with its references to Westchester and suburban living—is coded to reflect the Jewish experience. By 1957, Jews accounted for almost 16 percent of the total population of Westchester County.[39] But more universally, it foregrounds Carroll's particular experience as a woman sympathetically trying to do her best by her family amid a torrent of judgment. Creating the character of a "girlfriend who's not really a friend," Carroll is able to critique both the universal frustration of judgmental mothers and also the Jewish upper middle class's mass exodus from New York City to the suburbs. Her next passage continues to mix broad suburban satire with Jewish codes:

> She said, "Now listen, move to the country!"
>
> Well, I thought she meant the Old Country! . . . Well, I moved to the country, and of course, you know, everything is organizations; everything is done in groups!
>
> Two women meet on the street:
>
> "Oh Agnes, I'm going to have a baby!"
>
> "Isn't that wonderful. So am I! Who else can we get?"
>
> So I became active, I joined the organizations, it was wonderful. PTA, PTA, PTA! I spent so much time attending PTA, my kid became a delinquent!

Again, while seemingly trafficking in staples of "universal" America, Carroll's stand-up is actually rife with coded Jewishness. First, the persona's reference to "the Old Country" coyly alludes to Carroll's family background as eastern European immigrants. Second, her allusion to the PTA speaks directly to a trend of Jewish women in the midcentury US becoming more involved in community organizations, producing a shift in power that troubled their husbands. Carroll's jibe about being so involved with PTA that her daughter became a delinquent reveals a skeptical attitude toward this culture of organizational involvement. But equally notable, Carroll's way of conjuring characters within her stand-up—in this passage, it is "Agnes" and her friend championing cohort pregnancy—positions her as the contrasting voice of reason, a savvy wiseacre who both embodies suburban life and comments on its peculiarities. Carroll's foil characters, be they her stagnant husband or her suburbanized friends, allow her to present *herself* as a more reasonable, sympathetic, and relatable human being.

Stereotypes as Codes

Another code that Carroll employed to particular effect was the use of popular Jewish stereotypes to gesture toward a Jewish American experience—without explicitly referencing them as such. One such stereotype is that of the Jewish mother, while another is that of the passive Jewish husband.

In Irving Howe's classic study of Jewish immigrants, he characterized the Jewish mother as "a brassy scourge, with her grating bark, or soul-destroying whine . . . and unfocused aggression."[40] Martha Ravits argues that this cartoonishly dissatisfied stereotype reveals the resentment her children felt toward her embodied reminder of their immigrant roots. Rather than embrace their mother and the cultural particularity she signified, many assimilationist Jewish children "devalued and stigmatized [her] as a regressive force."[41] By the 1950s, the Jewish mother already had an extensive genealogy in performance, ranging from Sophie Tucker's self-sacrificing Yiddishe Mama to Clifford Odets's domineering Bessie to the countless mothers satirized by Carroll's male stand-up colleagues.

By invoking the Jewish mother stereotype, Carroll was able to mark herself as a Jew—and trade in Jewish humor—without explicitly Jewd-entifying.[42] Signal among her characteristic traits is the Jewish mother's ties to food—preparing it and forcing it on the people around her. This compulsive feeding provided fertile ground for Jean Carroll's coded comedy in the 1950s. For example, in a *Sullivan* appearance in 1950, Carroll uses a timely coded reference to embody the Jewish mother stereotype of a coercively nurturing matriarch, suggesting that the dimple in her daughter's cheek is not actually a dimple but an indent from her fingers constantly pinching the child's face. To illustrate, Carroll mimes grabbing her cheek, screaming, "Eat!" Eat!"[43] In another appearance several years later, Carroll again draws on the stereotype of the dominating Jewish mother, this time positioning herself as the daughter. Again, the matron's overzealous feeding habits replace any explicit affirmation of her Jewish ethnicity: "Mama is the type . . . she likes to cook. She runs around, chases people around with food. The minute she comes in the house, she takes over the kitchen. Honest! Unless you eat like you're going to the chair, she's not happy! I took her to a museum once. She saw a skeleton, felt sorry for him, took him home to fatten him up."[44] The pause that Carroll gives after referencing her mother's "type" allows audiences to "fill in the blanks." Her eyes shifting mischievously to the side, Carroll lets the word "type" linger, waiting for a few pregnant beats before filling in the innocuous, "she likes to cook." This code of a force-feeding mother establishes a Jewish perspective, allowing her Jewish audience members to identify her as an in-group member and laugh at their perhaps shared reference point. Similarly, other ethnic groups in which women were stereotyped in similar ways (e.g., Polish, African American, Italian) can "fill in the blank" with their own relevant "type."

Likewise, when the increased incidence of Jewish women having plastic surgery to meet mainstream American norms of beauty prompted a stereotype of the superficial Jewish woman, Carroll took it, too, up for comic fodder.[45] In a 1959 appearance on *Sullivan*, Carroll complains about her "teenage shlump" daughter's irritating need to feel unique, mimicking her whine, "I don't want to be like the other girls," before tossing back the cutting reply, "All right, so we won't bob your nose!"[46] This arch quip on the preponderance of "bobbed noses" (e.g., noses subject to cosmetic rhinoplasty) calls out a trend in a way that audience members could read as either a wry commentary on Jewish assimilation or a general disparagement of cosmetic surgery, depending on their position.

Existing alongside negative stereotypes of domineering, domestically averse Jewish women was the stereotype of the passive, weak, Jewish man. This comical target was a staple of Carroll's act, and according to testimonials of some of her most famous female fans, it was a gratifying form of empowerment at men's expense. Like the stereotypes of Jewish women, the stereotype of the passive Jewish man comes from a tangle of historical and sociological factors. Daniel Boyarin historicizes the stereotypical depiction of Jewish men as passive in *Unheroic Conduct*, where he argues that the passive Jewish man stereotype has its origins in the unconventional masculine ideals of early modern eastern Europe: *edelkayt*, the ideal of a "gentle, timid, and studious male."[47] This ideal, Boyarin explains, emerged because "those who stood outside or were marginalized by society provided a countertype that reflected, as in a convex mirror, the reverse of the social norm."[48] Therefore, rather than exist purely in the antisemitic imagination, this stereotype existed as an intergroup ideal. Ruth Wisse also charts the depiction of Jewish men as innocent, weak beings in her examination of the schlemiel in literature from the 1800s in eastern Europe to the 1950s in the United States. She argues that this timidity was a strategic posture: "his absolute defenselessness the only guaranteed defense against the brutalizing power of might."[49]

From a more sociological view, the professions in which Jewish men were most frequently employed in the United States were trade based, not land based. Stephen Steinberg points out that while European immigrant groups were often put into industrialized modern sectors, immigrants of color were put into land-based labor like farming and coal mining. German Jewish immigrants had a particular competitive advantage because they came from urban settings and therefore had a skill set oriented toward industry (e.g., reading, accounting).[50] However, the scarcity of Jewish men in land-based professions also came with a sense of urbanity that registered to some observers as effete.

Much of Carroll's material on the men in her life nodded toward their Jewishness by invoking the Jewish male stereotype of passivity and impotence. For example, Carroll does a bit about her brother Al, remarking, "Al is sort of a timid fella. When you ask him a question, he answers in a high voice. . . . It's his wife."[51] The joke attacks Al's masculinity on two fronts: first by suggesting that his voice is "high" or effeminate and then by revealing that Al does not speak at all but sits passively and is spoken for by his wife. Carroll also does a generous amount of material about a fictionalized version of her husband, whom she describes this way: "so quiet I'm collecting his life insurance." Another of her husband zingers attacks his passivity, quipping, "He's a real do-it-yourself guy—anything I ask him, he says, 'Do it yourself!'" One of Carroll's most popular attacks on her husband's passivity reminisces about their honeymoon, as Carroll rhapsodizes,

> We had reserved a honeymoon suite in a very nice hotel. And after the wedding, I went up to my room, he was in his room. And I got into this negligee, beautiful, chiffon. I wanted to look as pretty as I could possibly look. And I brushed my hair, and I put mules on my feet, and I thought, "Well, better get in that room tonight unless you want to annul the marriage!" And so I started back in, and when I saw him, I stopped dead. He never looked more virile, more masculine in his life. Handsome! His hair was slicked down. He had a pipe in his mouth, a maroon smoking jacket on, and bedroom slippers and white silk pajamas. Oh, he looked so nice, I hated to wake him![52]

In this bit, Carroll emphasizes her own preparations for a sexual encounter with her bridegroom, only to find him in the utter state of passivity—asleep. Yet his slumber is decked out in the accoutrement of seduction: a "smoking jacket," "bedroom slippers," "white silk pajamas." This image of the highly adorned, sexually unavailable, utterly passive man is a precise inversion of the negative stereotype of Jewish women circulating at that time—what would later be called the Jewish American Princess.[53] Carroll reinforces this image of what might be called the Jewish American Prince in a zinger aimed at her husband's disinterest in recreational sports: "Here's a guy—never had any outside interests. He doesn't bowl. He doesn't golf. He doesn't fish. Well, he did have an outside interest once, but I caught him and he had to stop seeing her."[54] Although the punch line references infidelity (potentially disrupting the stereotype of sexual passivity), the setup allows Carroll a jab at her husband's passive lack of athleticism. Not only does Carroll draw on popular stereotypes of Jewish men as effete, weak, and passive, but she also takes the early stereotype of the proto–Jewish American Princess and shifts the target from wives to husbands.

Likewise, Carroll takes on the other reigning stereotype of Jewish women—that of the domineering, suffocating Jewish mother—and revises it into a critique of sons who are overly dependent on their mothers. Specifically, she casts her husband as an ultimate "mama's boy," whose adoration for his mother relegates his wife to second place in his affections. This relationship dynamic is key in a joke she tried out on a *Sullivan* appearance in 1959: "The night before [her husband] left, he was so sad. He sat there with tears in his eyes. He was saying, 'Honey, I'm gonna miss you so! I'm gonna miss your cooking.' He was talking to his mother on the phone!"[55] Characteristic of the period, the joke turns on misdirection, the expectation of marital sweetness comically reversed into oedipal dysfunction.

Carroll's invocation of Jewish stereotypes as codes allowed her to achieve that 1950s aspiration of speaking to a Jewish experience among an in-group audience, while also creating a white (and red and blue) persona for the mainstream crowds.

* * *

As the late 1950s gave way to the 1960s, *The Ed Sullivan Show* was not the only platform on which Jean Carroll was making national headlines. In 1960, Columbia Records released Jean Carroll's "party album" *Girl in a Hot Steam Bath*. Party records were a midcentury phenomenon of nationally released comedy albums, usually recorded live at nightclubs and presentation houses. These records bridged the experience of consuming comedy live in a club with the convenience of consuming it in a home setting. Hit party records of the period included *Improvisations to Music* by Mike Nichols and Elayne May (1958), *Inside Shelly Berman* (1959), and *Sick Humor* by Lenny Bruce (1960). Jean Carroll's party record is an extraordinary artifact because it time-stamps some of her greatest hits as they were recorded in 1960. Bits that she had done on *The Ed Sullivan Show* years earlier had been polished and revised—developing in concert with the changing times. And the times, they were a-changin'.

A positive shift was taking place regarding the social status of Jewishness—and ethnicity more broadly—in the United States. The effects of victorious grassroots African American civil rights efforts like the Montgomery Bus Boycott of the mid-1950s and the Greensboro sit-in of 1960 rippled through the country, inspiring some Jewish people to join the movement and many to reclaim their own cultural particularity. Matthew Frye Jacobson writes on the relationship between the civil rights movement and "the ethnic revival of the 1960s," noting that "after decades of striving to conform to the Anglo-Saxon standard, descendants of earlier European immigrants quit the melting pot. Italianness, Jewishness, Greekness, and Irishness had become badges of pride, not of shame."[56] This voluntary exit from the melting pot is evident when examining four iterations of Jean Carroll's famous "buying a fur coat" routine—three of them on *Sullivan* and one on her concurrent party record.

"Buying a Fur Coat" Four Times

Looking at four different performances of the same routine over time highlights how as Jewishness shifted from a taboo to a talked-about subject, the supporting characters in Carroll's stand-up shifted from a coded to a downright cartoonish representation of Jewishness.

In 1949, on the January 16 episode of *The Ed Sullivan Show*—then called *Toast of the Town*—Carroll introduced the television audience to what would become one of her most beloved routines: a story about buying a fur coat. After being introduced as "a particular treat this holiday season," Carroll sashays onto the stage, decked out in a plumed hat and a fur coat. "Like my *chapeau*?" she asks coquettishly, emphasizing her French affectations and fashionable ensemble before drawing the audience's attention to the pièce de résistance with, "I gotta tell you about this coat!" The first section of the bit invokes the stereotypically materialistic, nagging wife: "You see, this year, my husband gave me this! It was a surprise. He didn't know I was getting it. It's very expensive! It cost him three ulcers. I'll tell you how I got the coat, you see: I nagged him!" In the next section, Carroll begins to approach a more specifically Jewish stereotype: the tribal tendencies of "middle-man minorities" to support their own networks rather than go through more established mainstream consumer venues.[57]

> He knew a fella that had a friend that knows a guy downtown in skins.... [The audience laughs.] Now, you must be very careful with furs because it's a blind article—that's what the furriers tell you. So . . . through an emissary and a carrier pigeon, we set up an appointment with this fella! And this hadda be done with the utmost in secrecy, at three in the morning on a foggy night. . . . [The audience laughs.] Now, the reason is, to protect the furrier—no one should find out he's selling retail! So we get there, eight in the morning—there's fourteen other people sitting waiting.

Here, Carroll parodies what would be for some audience members a recognizable phenomenon of the tenuous connections that become salient networks in immigrant communities ("He knew a fella that had a friend that knows a guy") and the lengths that community members will go ("emissary," "carrier pigeon," etc.) to support one another and save money. Even without the recognizability factor, Carroll still offers humor in this passage with the absurd subterfuge of the purchase.

The next beat of the piece moves to Carroll's interactions with the furrier, who in this first iteration is presented as a standard, if not entirely scrupulous, American salesman with no discernible dialect or body language.

> We walk in. The furrier says, "Well! What can I show ya?"
> "Well," I said, "I want a coat."

He said, "What kind?"

I said, "Well, I don't know how to describe it exactly, but I want a coat. My friends should take one look and drop dead."

He says, "You came to the right place! More women die from coats here than anywhere else."

He disappears in an iron door. He's gone for six months! Comes back.

I said, "You could have gone to Alaska!"

He says, "Where do you think I got the frozen ear?"

He says, "But I brought you a garment!" [She takes off her fur coat.] "I brought you a fur coat." [She holds it out to display.] "This coat, the finest; the most wonderful merchandise." [She throws it to the floor.] "Lookacoat!" [The audience laughs.]

Here, the furrier is presented without the ethnic markers that would later come to dominate his character. In fact, the contrast between the furrier's otherwise-vernacular speech and the Yiddish-inflected absence of prepositions in "Lookacoat" seems to be a major source of laughter. In the next beat, Carroll's persona and the furrier continue their comical clash:

I always wondered why they threw these things on the floor. Now I know. That's so when they tell you the price, you'll have something soft to faint on!

He says, "There is a garment—you could go from here to the corner, you wouldn't see another one like it! This coat is practical. This coat will wear like iron! This coat will live longer than you!"

Well, I figured by the looks of it, it already had!

He said, "A coat like this, you can sit in it, ride in it, walk in it. You can go anyplace in it! You'll get tired of it. You'll bring it in. I should remodel it! *This* coat—believe me—there is a coat! Feel the thickness! Go on, feel the thickness!"

I felt it. No wonder it was thick! The furrier was inside, sewing in the lining!

In the next section, Carroll gently alludes to the stereotype of the crafty Jewish merchant, with the furrier's false protestations against haggling:

> I said, "All right, it's a beautiful coat. How much is it?"
>
> He said, "How much is it? I'll tell you one price. Don't waste my time. An absolute price, rock bottom—no bargaining! I don't want anybody to know what I'm charging you. I don't want my partner to find out. I don't even want the minks to find out! For you . . . $6,000."
>
> I said [shrieking], "6,000?"
>
> He said, "Shhh!! Don't holler! I'm not going to let a few dollars stand in the way! Being you were recommended, . . . $3,000." [The audience laughs.] And he says, "Believe me—I'm losing money on it!"
>
> Well, I was stuck! How can I pass up anything a man's losing money on?

Suggesting the furrier's dissembling ways, he initially claims to offer a "rock bottom" price but soon reveals his own prevarication by halving the price when faced with losing the sale. The final section of the "buying a fur coat" bit concludes with the merchant sneakily reversing all his grandiose claims about the coat's strength and versatility:

> I gave him the money. I go to pick up the coat.
>
> He says, "Uh-uh! Don't pick up the mink coat with the hands! This is a very, very perishable garment! A coat like this, the way you're handling it, wouldn't last six months! You have to be very careful. These things fall apart! Don't ever let the sun hit this coat, and don't let it ever get wet! And a coat like this, you don't sit in it, you don't ride in it, you don't walk in it! A coat like this, you don't even wear!"
>
> I said, "Wait a minute! I pay you $3,000, you tell me I can't sit in it, I can't ride in it, I can't walk in it—what good is the coat to me?"
>
> He says, "To you? No good! But you'd be surprised how it dresses up a closet!"

The routine was met with resounding applause, and Sullivan seemed extremely pleased, calling Carroll back onstage for an encore bow. Compared to later versions of the "buying a fur coat" routine, this bit is remarkably and intentionally devoid of ethnic humor.

Carroll later shared that in the early years of Sullivan's show, there were a number of officials who weighed in on how to keep the show as mainstream as possible: "On his [Ed Sullivan's] show, you had the rabbi, the priest, the school teacher, the principal from school. And Ed. And at the dress rehearsal, they said, 'Out this is out, delete, delete, delete.' And I'd say, 'Why?' 'Well, because the Catholics won't like that.' 'What about that?' 'The Jews won't like that.'"[58]

But when Carroll performed the routine again on *The Ed Sullivan Show*, nearly ten years later, on November 30, 1958, it was substantially changed, in ways that more directly invoked Jewish stereotypes. First, the character of Carroll's narrating persona becomes more aggressive, and the character of the furrier acquires a faintly eastern European accent and a penchant for Russian words. Carroll's persona's increased assertiveness is clear in the bit's new opening, as she struts onto the *Sullivan* stage with a gleaming mink wrapped around her shoulders. Unlike the routine's earlier version, in which she coquettishly modeled the coat to the audience, the 1958 version sees her unceremoniously slipping it off and throwing it on the ground as soon as she hits her mark, brushing herself off with a casual, "Well, hiya. . . . Don't get nervous. That's the way the furrier showed it to me!" With her cavalier handling of this expensive item, she is able to depict a kind of ambivalence regarding the ultimate status symbol for women. This ambivalence is also evident in the word choice she uses to describe the fur-clad women she describes seeing in high-class restaurants, gushing, "I never saw so many well-kept and beautifully groomed women in my whole life!" Rather than describe the women using praise like "elegant" or "glamorous," Carroll chooses to refer to them as being "kept" and "groomed." Using the register of pets, Carroll implicitly likens the fur-clad women to their animal counterparts. Then, while the Carroll of 1949 disclosed that she got the coat by "nagging" her husband, the 1958 version takes a more aggressive tact, threatening,

> There was no argument, because I said it simply. I said, "Either a mink or a separation."
>
> And my husband, he's very practical. He said, "You'd look silly wearing a separation—Get the mink!"

Carroll then adds a new transition section invoking the familiar stereotype of Jewish men as miserly, specifically through an aversion to buying retail: "I had seen a beautiful mink coat on Fifth Avenue, and I was gonna get it. But my husband found out it was *retail*. [She narrows her eyes as the audience laughs knowingly.] Now, he's the kind of guy who can't *bear* to see you get stuck retail. [She purses her lips to the audience's laughter.]" The piece then proceeds into the husband's familiar wrangling of the immigrant network. But what is telling about this new transition is that the biggest laugh lines are the silences—those wordless moments in which Carroll looks meaningfully at the audience, asking them to fill in the blanks. In fact, the laugh that occurs after she pronounces the word "retail" is the longest one of the entire set. Although impossible to ascertain, it does seem as though the audience's laughter reveals their recognition of a stereotypically Jewish zeal for a deal.

The next major change that Carroll makes to lean into more ethnic humor is her pushing the furrier in the direction of the stereotypical eastern European merchant. This shift is clearest in her addition of the piece's new signature line, "Feel the pough!" (pronounced *puch*):

> He says, "Try those skins! In your *life*, you never felt skins like these!" He says, "Feel the pough!"
>
> I said, "Feel the who?"
>
> He said, "Don't feel the who. Feel the pough!"

I mean, when I went to college, I didn't major in pough-feeling.[59] So I stood there looking stupid.

He says, "Why don't you feel the pough?"

I said, "I'll tell you the truth: if I knew where to find it, I'd feel it!"

He said, "My dear girl, pough is thickness. It's only thickness."

. . . I said, "I'll tell you the truth: I can't stand the coat, but I fell in love with the pough!"

Although the furrier's accent is barely perceptible in most of his lines, when ordering Carroll's narrating persona to "Lookacoat!" and "Feel the pough," his voice takes on a distinctively eastern European dialect. Each time Carroll pronounces the word, accenting the guttural *ch* noise at the end of "pough," the audience titters, perhaps as amused by the Yiddish sound of the word as by its unclear meaning. The coding of the character as Jewish is heightened at the part where the furrier is coming up with a price, which Carroll introduces using the new line, "Did you ever see a wholesaler figure a price?" Carroll takes on the *physicality* of the whole-saler, putting herself through a contorted series of chin rubbing, cheek squeezing, and, most prominently, no fewer than six "Jewish shrugs."[60] Overcome by the furrier's devolving from language into shrugs, Carroll's frustrated persona demands, "Listen, before the coat goes out of style, how much do you want?"

Again, the piece moves through the furrier's feigned opposition to haggling, the persona's shocked reply, and the furrier's prompt back-tracking. However, the newer version has a substantially reworked ending. While the 1949 version closed with the furrier stressing the delicacy of the coat—ending on the button, "it dresses up a closet!"— the 1958 version takes out this entire section. Instead, after Carroll's persona screams at the price, the furrier flinches and replies, "If I don't put the coat in a *box*, . . . I could do a little better," promptly knocking $5,000 off the price. This edited version, which heightens the absurdity of the furrier's haggling, became the new closer. Thus, Carroll's major changes between 1949 and 1958 included making her persona more aggressive, heightening her husband's hatred of retail, and giving the furrier an eastern European patois, all of which more overtly invoke Jewish stereotypes.

By the recording of "Buying a Fur Coat" on Carroll's live album, *Girl in a Hot Steam Bath*, released in 1960, the furrier had become full-fledged dialect humor, a larger-than-life stereotype against whom Carroll's persona could act as straight man (or woman). It is important to note the different media, both because Carroll is freed of some of the restrictions of the *Sullivan* show and because she is performing to an audience that largely cannot see her. Thus, some of the visual codes that she used in 1958 to invoke Jewish stereotypes have to be communicated verbally here.

One of the clearest pieces of evidence of the less stringent restrictions of the record medium (as compared to network television) occurs in the ultimatum that Carroll's persona issues to her husband. While the 1958 version threatened, "Either a mink or a separation," the more risqué 1960 version goes, "It's mink coat or twin beds." But the most telling modification of the routine is Carroll's invocation of the larger-than-life stereotypical Jewish merchant through the furrier. On the album, the moment the furrier shows the merchandise, he adopts the strong eastern European dialect that often codes for "Jewish."

> He takes the coat and throws it on the floor. And when it's on the floor he says [in heavy eastern European accent], "Look-a-coat! Look . . . a . . . coat!"
>
> If he holds it up, you can't "look-a-coat"? Only on the floor you can "look-a-coat"? If you want to try it on, you lay down, you creep into it.
>
> So I [mocking his accent] "looked-a-coat!"

The neatly layered moment in which Carroll, as her narrating persona, imitates Carroll as the furrier highlights the way in which her persona is positioned as the "normal" Americanized speaker, vis-à-vis the cartoonish man. This contrast is also clear in the next section, as the furrier's eastern European origins go from implied to explicit:

"This coat, you can live in it. Sit in it. Feel the pough!"

. . . I didn't want to feel it, because I thought "pough" was not a nice word. . . . But you see, I didn't want this fellow to think that he was dealing with an absolute greenhorn. . . . So I stood there trying to look intelligent.

He said, "What are you standing there looking so stupid?"

I said, "I'll tell you the truth, if I knew where to find it, I'd feel it."

. . . He said, "'Pough' is a word used by furriers. It's used in the trade. It's a Russian word. It's just a trade expression. . . . It's thickness. That's all it is, thickness. Now, feel the pough."

And I was relieved!

This passage's "outing" of the furrier as Russian, along with her desire not to seem like a "greenhorn," gestures to the world of Jewish immigrants in a barely coded way. The dialect humor ramps up to its highest degree on the record as the furrier begins haggling over the price of the coat. "Have you ever seen a furrier . . . [audience laughs] in skins . . . [audience laughs] on Thirtieth Street . . . [audience laughs] doing what is quaintly known as [in cartoonish Yiddish accent] 'figgehrin' a pehrice'? He is 'figgehrin' a pehrice.' . . . He holds his hands over his eyes, like the whole thing is giving him [in Yiddish accent] 'Sush a chead-ache!' [Next, she mumbles a faux niggun (Yiddish song)] 'Daya . . . daya, ne . . .'"

Knowing that on the album, audio would be all she had to convey the character of the furrier, Carroll went in big with dialect humor and verbal descriptions of the furrier's contortions, describing how he "holds his hands over his eyes" like he has a headache. As the piece ends, Carroll tweaks the closing joke so that now the reasoning that the furrier gives for knocking thousands of dollars from the price is that he will not put "a string on the box." With his heavily accented equivocation, the furrier character exemplifies the stereotypical shifty Jewish merchant. One effect of creating this larger-than-life Jewish caricature is to make Carroll's persona seem more "Americanized" by comparison. This comparison also contrasts the "Old World," lower-class, still-accented immigrant generation with the more upwardly mobile, Americanized, second generation.[61]

Carroll is also able to turn the tables on her male colleagues for their constant use of Jewish woman stereotypes by invoking an equally absurd stereotype of a Jewish man. Furthermore, by mocking Jewish stereotypes, she shows herself "in" on the joke. She is able to take the stereotype of the consuming Jewish mother/wife's passion for shopping and the Jewish merchant's heavily accented fumbling and use them as fodder to exhibit her wit, mimicry, and comparative assimilation.

When Carroll performed the "buying a fur coat" routine for her third and final time on *The Ed Sullivan Show*, it was December 27, 1964, and both Carroll's persona and the furrier were firmly embodying recognizably Jewish stereotypes. Carroll's narrating persona, partially due to her older, more matronly form, was far more in line with stereotypes of pushy, dissatisfied housewives. Perhaps inspired by the growing popularity of up-and-coming women comics like Phyllis Diller and Joan Rivers, Carroll's 1964 persona spits sassy one-liners that had previously not been part of the routine. For instance, the following sequence, in which Carroll's persona first encounters the furrier, takes on a new edge riddled with sarcasm:

> The furrier is a very intelligent fella. He says, "What do you want?"
> I said, "Well, I didn't come to get the weather report. I want a mink coat!"
> He said, "What kind?"
> I said, "What do I know from mink coats?"
> Then he gives me a look and says, "Don't go away!"
> I said, "Don't worry about it. If the building burns, I go with it, I guarantee ya."

Where once Carroll's persona demurely answered the furrier's questions, by 1964, she replies to each of the furrier's questions with a sassy rejoinder. Later in the routine, her snappy repartee takes an explicitly Jewish bent with a line that references halachic practices like separating dairy from meat:

I didn't want this furrier to think that he was dealing with someone who didn't know anything! I know about furs! I have a girlfriend who goes around blowing on fur coats in stores. My mother does the same thing in the market. She blows on all the chickens in the butcher shop before telling the butcher, "We'll eat dairy." Anyhow, I decided I'd show him something, so I blew on the fur.

He said, "What are you blowing on? It's not a plate of soup!"

Carroll's clearly Jewish persona reflects a larger trend in which Jewishness—and ethnicity more broadly—became celebrated as an integral part of American identity. However, this increased Jewdentification could veer dangerously toward promoting negative stereotypes. Indeed, this negative stereotype is ultimately where the furrier character ends up. By 1964, Carroll's depiction of the furrier is really a caricature; his accent would be extreme even by Myron Cohen's standards, his voice riddled with *krechts* (the break in the voice associated with Yiddish music) and his duplicity foregrounded in both feigned hearing loss and haggling. All of the following traits are evident in the new variant of the bargaining beat:

I said, "How much do you want for this coat?"

Now, up to now, this man has had no trouble hearing me. [The furrier hunches over, rubbing his chin contemplatively with his pointer finger.] Have you ever seen a wholesaler in skins "figgering out a peh-rice," a bargain?

He says, "Eeehh . . . this coat . . ."? Looking at it like he's never seen it in his life! Like he doesn't know how it got there! "This coat eh-heeeeeh" [high-pitched hemming and hawing]. He's getting a message from the minks up here, ya see! "This coat, for you—" [Furrier holds one finger up in front of his face, putting it down and then up again.] "This coat . . ." [Furrier turns over his shoulders sneakily as if afraid of being overheard.] "I'll make you a price I myself shouldn't hear . . . Shhhhh!" [Furrier gives a dramatic finger-to-lips gesture.]

I said, "How much do you want for the coat?"

He says, "Aright, I'm figgering a peh-rice. This coat, you can have—*mit* de box, *mit* de lining, *mit* trowing in every-ting!—you can have it for . . . [six shrugs] . . . altogether—"

I said, "Listen, before the coat goes out of style, how much money do you want for this coat?"

He said, "Look, don't give me aggravation! [shrugs] I'm figgering!"

The bargaining section, once a relatively small beat in the overall routine, has expanded over time to accommodate the growing Jewish merchant caricature into which the furrier has developed. Carroll's persona's wry commentary to the audience, observing the furrier's feigned hearing loss, astonishment at the coat, and overwrought, hyperaccented "figgering," peppered with Yiddish words, comes together to form a fairly unmistakable invocation of the Jewish merchant stereotype.

While Carroll's shifting the "buying a fur coat" routine from code to caricature suggests that she felt more comfortable trafficking in Jewish stereotypes in 1964 than in 1949, it also speaks to a growing normalization of these stereotypes. Carroll, at any rate, was willing to invoke this merchant stereotype, partially in order to make her persona seem more successfully Americanized by contrast. A Freudian reading might connect the furrier's depiction as an Old World tradesman to Carroll's father, a Russian immigrant and baker. In order to emphasize her persona's status as an American consumer, Carroll was willing to make the Jewish tradesmen of the previous generation into a laughable caricature.

1961: Jewdentification on *Sullivan*

On June 18, 1961, on the special episode celebrating thirteen seasons of *The Ed Sullivan Show*, Carroll had what could be considered a "coming out" moment on *Sullivan*. Carroll's Jewdentification on the thirteenth-anniversary show is comically apt, given the significance of thirteen as the age when Jewish children receive a Bar, Bat, or B-Mitzvah welcoming them as an adult member of the synagogue. It also marked a turning point for the show itself, as leadership had recently shifted from longtime producer Marlo Lewis to the younger, more liberal Bob Precht. According to the author Jerry Bowles, Precht was adamant about pushing the show toward a younger audience, and a more multicultural style could very well have been part of that campaign.[62] For the thirteenth-anniversary special, Precht arranged for both the usual slate of guest stars and news makers *and* what *Variety* termed "a full-fledged special tune" performed by Jean Carroll, Dorothy Louden, and Marion Marlowe.[63] The stated purpose of the modified rendition of "Cryin' All the Way to the Bank" was to pay tribute to Sullivan's success, in spite of his initially poor critical reception. However, its execution models Jean Carroll's turn from tentative, coded Jewishness to exaggerated Yiddishkeit.

The musical number, which opens the show, is a study in comical contrast, playing off the classic comedy "rule of threes," with Jean Carroll as the disruptive "third." The announcer, Art Hannes, begins the show introducing "three lovely ladies—a million-dollar trio!" He then names "Mrs. Dorothy Louden, Marion Marlowe," and, lastly, "Jean Carroll!" The three women stride onto the stage holding newspapers in front of their faces, as the band strikes a brassy entrance tune. The camera first rests in wide angle on the three women, only their hips, legs, and high-heeled feet visible behind the newspapers, before zooming left to the thirty-five-year-old singer Dorothy Louden. In close-up, the camera shows her pull the newspaper away to reveal a pretty, pouting face, as Louden exclaims, "Critics are nasty old men!" Raising her newspaper, Louden remarks, "It said here in 1948," before bursting melodiously into the verse, "Ed Sullivan . . . he doesn't sing / he doesn't dance / his talents are so weak! From what we see / we guarantee / he'll never last a week!" "Now," she questions the audience, "who else would say that but a nasty old man?"

The camera then shifts to a close-up of Marion Marlowe, the strikingly beautiful thirty-two-year-old chanteuse, as she proclaims, "But

FIGURE 5.1. Jean Carroll holding *Der Forverts* on *The Ed Sullivan Show*, June 18, 1961. (SOFA Entertainment)

by 1961, things had gotten better." Shifting from speech to song, Marlowe continues, "It says here, 'Ed Sullivan . . . impossible, deplorable / he bores us all to tears! We ought to know / we haven't missed his show for thirteen years!'" Abruptly, the camera moves to the then-fifty-year-old Jean Carroll, standing in the center, as she, without fanfare, pulls from her face a copy of *Der Forverts*, written entirely in the Yiddish alphabet (known as the "aleph-beys," this alphabet is almost indistinguishable from the Hebrew alphabet).

"Ce zogt do," she begins, not stopping to translate into English ("It says here"). Carroll pauses only for the audience's giant laugh to subside. Somewhere in the crowd, there is an audible shriek of laughter, to which Carroll responds with a smirk and a knowing raise of her eyebrows. She continues, "By Westra Goldfarb?!" her voice breaking with incredulity at the notable Jewishness of the critic's name before she speak-sings against the distinctive klezmeric strains of a violin, "Sullivan, I've watched your show for thirteen years. My sentiment I can sum up. I can tell it to you all in one sentence, Sullivan: Zoldu shtinken from dein kopf!" Again, Carroll does not translate the Yiddish insult into its English counterpart

("You stink from your head") but launches into yet another Jewish joke, remarking, "I got that from a writer in Tel Aviv!"

Within the first minute and a half, the musical number establishes what is to be the running joke of the bit: the melodic loveliness of Louden and Marlowe countered with the strident "ethnic" screeching of Carroll. Thus, in a bit that ostensibly mocks Sullivan, the true "butt" of the joke is Jean Carroll, positioned as the comical Jewish outlier of the "million-dollar trio." It is a startling reversal of her usual commitment to a persona of assimilated, attractive "dignity." However, Carroll manages to play against the stereotypical text using those knowing glances and an almost parodic over-the-top quality. The next stanza showcases Carroll's substantial vocal chops a bit more, as each woman sings a line about Sullivan's acid critiques, culminating in a three-part harmony on the line, "He never got a single good review." As the song shifts into a swinging jazz tune, the camera rests again on a wide shot of the three women from head to calf, emphasizing their individual apparel. On the left, the tall, slender Marion Marlowe is garbed in a full A-line skirt with a statement belt emphasizing her small waist. On the right, Dorothy Louden has a form-fitting gown covered in sequins. Standing in between these two willowy women in a conservative monochromatic dress, even the well-proportioned Jean Carroll looks strangely squat and heavyset by contrast. Her well-maintained looks, though remarkable for a woman of fifty, seem matronly when bookended by women twenty years her junior. While the contrast is not stark enough to confidently interpret it as a visual joke, it is notable that Carroll, whose figure and beauty had so famously transcended stereotypes of dowdy Jewish women in the previous decade, would now be positioned in that very role, relative to the younger starlets.

The three women sing in equal measure, with the camera zooming in on each as she delivers her solo verse cataloging Sullivan's many accomplishments. But as the song comes to an end and Louden and Marlowe both deliver graceful bows, Carroll raises her hand in protest. "Wait a minute, Wait a minute!" she cries, leaning back and shaking her hands.

FIGURE 5.2. Jean Carroll stops Dorothy Louden and Marion Marlowe from bowing on *The Ed Sullivan Show*, June 18, 1961. (SOFA Entertainment)

"No no no! *No*! Please! No applause yet!" she goes on—heavily emphasizing the Brooklyn-accented second syllable of "applause." Embodying the stereotype of the domineering Jewish woman, Carroll begins barking directions at both the audience and the other members of her trio: "No applause yet, not yet. I'll *tell* you when. And *don't* start bowing. We have more to this number!"

Off the women's prettily puzzled expressions, Carroll exclaims, "If you'd show up to rehearsals, you'd know I have a very dramatic part to say. I'd like to say it, please, if you don't mind. Just because you're taller than me, don't get smart!" The acknowledgment of physical disparity in Carroll's reference to Loudon and Marlowe being "taller" again reveals that keen self-awareness of her position in the sketch, communicating that she is not simply uncritically parroting a matronly stereotype. There is a winking, exaggerated quality to her outburst, as she guilts and bosses her costars like a larger-than-life Yente Telebende.[64] When Dorothy Louden peevishly snips, "Well, if you want to be pushy," Carroll responds with a full-throated, "I do! I do! I want to be pushy!" nudging the other two women to face the curtain while she addresses the crowd.

"My dramatic part!" Carroll declaims with a flourish of her arms as the klezmer violin pipes up again. "Ah yes . . . they said it couldn't be done." She then breaks into a deafening screech. Sticking her neck out and gesticulating wildly, she screams, "Who the heck are *they* to say what could be done?!" The other two women give clownish startle reactions before visibly throwing their hands up and walking offstage, shocked by their fellow woman's shameful flouting of demure femininity. Unfazed, Carroll continues her melodramatic monologue: "Them with their cotton-picking mouths. Sure, they're talking about Ed Sullivan, the man they don't know! Ed Sullivan, the host of the *Sullivan Show*! But there's another man. And you don't know Sullivan the way I know him [giving a grimace]. Are you lucky! This is an *unusual* man! A man of integrity of character, great strength. I'd like to tell you more about him, but I'm so choked up." At this point, as the curtain opens, Carroll announces, "Let the cast of thousands tell you about this man," and she gestures toward the ensemble that launches the show into its next segment.

And so, in spite of Carroll's role as the comically ethnic "other" in the sketch, she is its central figure, both literally and figuratively. While the other two women are presented as performing "properly," they are also not given as much stage time, as many lines, or the distinction of transitioning from the opening number to the rest of the show. This centrality, then, is Carroll's reward for foregrounding her Jewishness in a way that she had not done before. And while she typically did not experiment with such an extreme embodiment of the stereotypically domineering Jewish woman as she did on that thirteenth anniversary special, her brief flirtation with caricature did show the potential rewards for reinscribing popular stereotypes.

Thus, while Carroll did not replicate her embodiment of a cartoonish Jewish mother, her post-1961 *Sullivan* appearances did reliably reference Jewish customs or phrases. For instance, Carroll's monologue on the May 8, 1966, episode demonstrates the kind of explicitly Jewish references that would have raised eyebrows ten years before: "You know today, parents can hardly wait for their children to grow up. It's a fact!

Years ago, you gave a child time to grow up. Today, a kid is born, and the *day* the little boy is born, the father runs out and brings a present to his son in the hospital: his Bar Mitzvah suit. [The audience laughs.] You think that's funny? You don't know how funny. It's *ridiculous*. The kid is Irish! [The audience laughs.] But he does come from a mixed marriage—a mother and father!" Carroll's reference to a Bar Mitzvah presupposes both that the audience will recognize this reference to a Jewish custom and that they will tolerate the normalization of Jewishness that it implies. In fact, Carroll foregrounds this normalization, jokingly hinting that Jewish customs like Bar Mitzvahs have become de rigueur even for non-Jewish families. She then alludes to perhaps the biggest "problem" facing the Jewish community in the mid-1960s: mixed marriages. A constant topic both on- and offstage, marriage between Jews and non-Jews was perhaps most ominously catastrophized in Thomas Morgan's article "The Vanishing American Jew," which provided statistics forecasting the increased incidence of interfaith marriage as the harbinger to American Jewry's disappearance. Jean Carroll's joke about a "mixed marriage" being between "a mother and a father" turns on the fraught issue of Jewish assimilation by marriage. However ambivalent Jewish audience members may have felt about this assimilation, it does seem to have given Jean Carroll confidence to Jewdentify to the masses.

In fact, this episode closes with a curiously coded reference to ethnic pride, as Carroll delivers a joke that turns on the subversion of expectations. She begins by discussing progressive education, a favorite target of her acerbic wit: "Today, educators have a new approach to everything in life—they're realistic! You know, they say, 'Concerning the facts of life, be honest with your children. Give them an honest answer when they get curious about the facts of life!' If your boy, sixteen years old, walks in to you and says, 'Daddy, where do I come from?' don't give him any evasive answer! Stand up! Square your shoulders! Look him right in the eye and say, 'Son, you come from Brooklyn!'" The response to this joke is revealing: First, it elicits a gentle wave of laughter from the audience. Then, after a few seconds, this laughter is joined by a few scattered noises of applause, which quickly turn into a full round of applause lasting six seconds long. While it is impossible to confirm, a reading of this response using Bial's idea of double coding might suggest that that first gentle wave of laughter acknowledges Carroll's neat misdirection, pivoting "Where do I come from?" away from sex and toward geography. However, upon reflection, the audience may have grokked the deeper shift that she makes in this joke, transforming "the facts of life" from reproduction to acculturation. In this new context, her exhortation to "Square your shoulders" and proclaim proudly, "Son, you come from [the famously ethnic] Brooklyn," takes on a new sense of pride in immigrant roots—the kind that might well provoke an impassioned round of applause from a 1966 audience. While it still maintains some vestigial guardedness of her more coded Jewish humor, this multilayered joke also betokens a growing pride in ethnic origins.

"Not a Jewish Comedian"?

An unusual but revealing testament to Carroll's unconventional embodiment of Jewish femininity is the way that contemporary critics who are reluctant to label her a "Jewish comic" nonetheless admit to recognizing her Jewishness. For instance, in 2006, Alan Zweibel, the producer of a number of comedy shows including *The Garry Shandling Show* and *Saturday Night Live*, opined, "I wouldn't necessarily categorize her as a Jewish comedian. I suspect she was Jewish, and I love her even more for that, because she's one of the tribe. But at the same time, I don't think she was *particularly* Jewish. Totie Fields—you knew immediately was Jewish, okay? Certain people, that was a part of what they tapped into, and what their persona was based on. Jean Carroll, Yes, she was Jewish, but at the same time, her experiences were universal."[65] Zweibel begins with the assertion that Jean Carroll would not fall into his category of Jewish comedians and then immediately acknowledges his "suspicion" that she was Jewish. This side-by-side mention of Carroll's in-group status as "one of the tribe" but out-group status as a

"Jewish comedian" prompts Zweibel to justify why the former would not entail the latter—namely, that Carroll was not "particularly Jewish," in her "attitude," the way that "Totie Fields"—a later comedian known for her zaftig appearance and self-deprecatory jokes—was. The contrast with Fields is telling: as a woman whose jokes conjure images of her flesh packed into too-small clothes like a "Jewish waffle, with a square of fat sticking out," Fields made her body the object of cheerful derision in a way that Jean Carroll generally did not.[66] Fields also employed a more pronounced New York accent and matronly demeanor, aligning her more easily with a stereotypical midcentury notion of a Jewish woman than the comparably svelte, conventionally attractive persona that Carroll inhabited for the majority of her career. Zweibel's characterization of Carroll as "Jewish" but "universal" suggests that while her Jewishness is pronounced enough to be legible to him—a fellow in-group member—it was somehow *less* Jewish than the femininity embodied by a more matronly, marginalized Jewish woman. However, the crucial Jewish attributes of Carroll's comedy that Zweibel underestimates (and perhaps what caused him to "suspect she was Jewish" in the first place) are her coded references, her playful invocations of Jewish gender stereotypes, and her aspiration—shared by other immigrant populations—to acculturate into upper-middle-class mainstream America.

The author Jane Wollman Rusoff voiced a similar sentiment, identifying Carroll as a "*landsman*" while simultaneously dismissing her Jewishness. Describing the first time that she saw Carroll on *The Ed Sullivan Show*, Rusoff reflected,

> I was a little girl. . . . It was *wonderful*! She was funny, she was good looking, she was smart, and she was a *woman*! Standing there, being funny and telling jokes.
>
> At that time, funny women on the television landscape were doing wacky things—mugging, and making faces and being funny physically—and she wasn't!

She just talked, and made observations, and her monologues were hysterical!

It was odd, it was novel, it was unique to see this in early television. I'm talking about the late '40s, early '50s—when we watched television, it was brand-new.

I lived in a Jewish neighborhood in New York, and if there was someone on screen that was Jewish, people would say, "She's Jewish!" "He's Jewish!"

You know . . . it was like, a *landsman*![67] But when Jean came on, even though it was pretty obvious—I mean, *we* knew she was Jewish—but *that* wasn't the point with her. It was a *woman*. And a woman being funny— and she was so confident. And she had this fantastic charisma that was captivating! A wonderful smile with white teeth, and her eyes sparkled. And that was my first glimpse.[68]

Like Zweibel, Rusoff seems to take it for granted that for in-group audience members, it was "pretty obvious" that Jean Carroll was Jewish. Foundational to Rusoff's wonder-struck rhapsodies about Carroll's "fantastic charisma," "wonderful smile with white teeth," is the recognition that this "captivating," "confident" woman *was* a "*landsman*." This assertion of in-group knowledge again points to the fact that there *was* something distinctly Jewish about Carroll's comedy. Even without explicit references to Jewish practices, Carroll was unmistakably speaking from the experience of a Jewish woman, albeit one who eschewed Yiddishkeit in favor of American glamor.

Shaina Hammerman offers crucial insight here by applying Naomi Seidman's "parenthetical Jewishness" to comedy and asserting, "Jewish men make Jewish jokes. Jewish women make women jokes." Drawing on evidence provided by both contemporary and historical Jewish women comedians, Hammerman shows how "gender and sexuality keeps trumping Jewishness for women."[69] However, she cautions against the wholesale dismissal of Jewishness in the humor and personae of women comedians, arguing that even though they may be less likely to explicitly reference Jewish customs or practices in their content, "their feminism, even when not placed within a Jewish context, may be inextricable from their Jewishness."[70] In this, she echoes arguments made by Sarah Blacher Cohen and Joyce Antler, both of whom have linked the feminist impulses necessary for comedy to female expressions of Jewishness.[71] In other words, there is something essentially, but not exclusively, Jewish about the subversive impulse for women to step out of their socially prescribed roles and stand up at the comedy microphone.

Given Jean Carroll's exchange with the PBS filmmaker, in which she so passionately disavowed Jewish influence, she may have been pleased to hear Rusoff minimizing her Jewishness as "not the point" and instead choosing to foreground the novelty of Carroll's gender. But ultimately, Jean Carroll's femininity was inseparable from her Jewishness—indeed, her rejection of traditional representations of Jewish women as gawky, vulgar, or otherwise "funny physically" was part of what made Rusoff and others find her so "odd," "novel," and "unique" as a comedian.

* * *

Who Jean Carroll decided to be on *The Ed Sullivan Show* was no small matter. Her appearances were delivered to and decoded by millions of Americans watching from their living rooms, shaping their understanding of who she was and—by extension—who Jewish women were. Somewhere in Michigan, a young Lily Tomlin was watching and mimicking Carroll's *Sullivan* spots, swapping her mother's nightgown for Jean Carroll's cocktail dress and telling "husband jokes" to her parents while dreaming of being a comic.[72] Somewhere in Brooklyn, Joy Behar was staring at Carroll on *Sullivan*, convinced that she herself must be Jewish, because Jean Carroll reminded her of a better-dressed version of her relatives.[73] Nearby, a young Jane Wollman saw a *landsman* like she had never seen before. And a child who would later be known as Joan Rivers was watching, memorizing Carroll's jokes and forming her understanding of what a Jewish woman looked like.[74] And they were only a select few of the millions of viewers tuning in.

Some viewers may have recognized Jean Carroll as a Jew, and some may not have. But for those who did read the codes, they saw a different kind of Jewish woman: glamorous and emphatically American. Glimmers of this new Jewess appeared in 1937, when Dinah Shore won a coveted spot as a cheerleader at Vanderbilt University.[75] They glittered once more in 1945, when Bess Meyerson won the Miss America Pageant, becoming the first Jewish woman to take up that banner of idealized patriotism and femininity. The glimmers appeared again in 1950, when Judy Tuvim (who had long since changed her name to Judy Holliday) won the Academy Award and Golden Globe for Best Actress. Again they sparkled in 1959, when the first-generation Jewish American Ruth Handler reimagined her teenage daughter Barbara as a blond, plastic "Barbie" doll.[76] Jean Carroll's spots on *Sullivan* brought to the uncharted realm of stand-up comedy some more glimmers of that same elusive ideal—the fully Americanized Jewess.

This assimilationist fantasy is not without its problems. Most obviously, when Jewish artists make extreme efforts to perform whiteness, these dynamics play into a system of white supremacy in media that devalues and marginalizes people of color. That difficult truth is crucial to understanding Jean Carroll—and the larger tradition of Jewish performance in the postwar years. Arthur Miller, Jean Carroll, Dinah Shore, Bess Meyerson, Judy Holliday, Ruth Handler, and the many other Jewish public figures emphasizing their "universal Americanness" were actually appealing to a quite narrow kind of Americanness: white, heterosexual, cis-gender, upper middle class, and able-bodied.

The viciousness of these limitations comes full circle in Jean Carroll's own exclusion from the canon of "Jewish comics." With some notable exceptions toward the end of her career, Jean Carroll spent most of her life refusing to be seen as a stereotypical Jewish woman. And because her persona does not align with dominant ideas of a "Jewish comic," she is often removed from histories of Jewish comedy—even histories of Jewish women's comedy. But Jean Carroll was making history at the microphone of *The Ed Sullivan Show*, expanding viewers' images of what Jewish women comedians (and Jewish women) could be. Jean Carroll took this promising, problematic ideal of the wealthy, glamorous, American Jewess and placed it where no one else thought it belonged: stand-up comedy. And she did it with everybody watching.

6

Not without My "Rotten Kid"

Caretaker versus Comedian

"Having a child is the greatest blessing in the world," Jean Carroll declared on *The Ed Sullivan Show* in 1950.

> As a matter of fact, when I see children in an audience, I get such a feeling! I love kids; I used to go to school with them! But children sometimes can be very testing. I heard one woman say when her little boy was three months old, she could have eaten him up, and now she wishes she had! . . . I have a little girl, a rotten kid! . . . I remember the big day in my life. I had my baby. I was so happy! I couldn't *wait* to send her to camp. But I waited until she was old enough; she could meet other children, she could adjust. . . . She was a year and a half. It cost me four thousand bucks. She learned how to make a wallet![1]

As millions of people watched from their glowing TV screens, one in particular would stare, rapt, at the television, counting down the minutes until the show was over.[2] Her name was Helen Roberta Howe, but she was better known to fans nationwide as "that rotten kid." Having her mother be a famous stand-up comedian was a mixed bag for Helen. She enjoyed growing up on the road, staying in hotels and hiding under the craps table while her mother played. "I was like Eloise. . . . I had the best life in the world!" she effused in an interview.[3] But those trips also involved long stretches of solitude, while Carroll was performing or writing, and Helen was left to her own devices. In that same interview, she recalled being a nine-year-old in Atlantic City, wandering around the Steel Pier while her mother did "five or six shows a day." "That was a little dull for me," she reflected.[4]

Worst of all were her mother's fans. Not only did they interrupt her family when they tried to share a meal out, but if they saw Helen at a show, they would constantly bring up her mother's routines about the "rotten kid." Helen vividly recalled,

> They would look at me with this sort of glow in their eyes and they would get really fervent and say something about me being a rotten kid. Now, if that were true, . . . if she really did spend her life calling me a rotten kid and mean it, that isn't exactly a privilege, do you know what I mean? *If* that were the truth—and I knew it wasn't—then . . . that's . . . that's basically exploitive. And they would essentially tell me that I was the luckiest little girl in the world because I was being exploited for their entertainment. I didn't feel exploited by my mother, but I felt exploited by them. . . . I really hated the fans, I did. That's not fair, but at that age, you know . . .[5]

Helen could discern what the audience could not: rotten kid was fictional; she was real. The rotten kid was birthed from her mother's typewriter; she was birthed from her mother's body. The rotten kid was an entirely different being from Helen, and Jean Carroll the comedian was an entirely different being from Jean Carroll, her mother. Moreover, the comedian and the mother were often at odds with each other, competing for time and prioritization in a society designed to accommodate only one.

Many of the same fans who so irritated Helen found in her mother a spokesperson for their own frustrations—a straight shooter who spoke about motherhood with a frankness that was truthful but taboo. In a media landscape where Dr. Spock was gospel and sweet Molly Goldberg was the reigning Jewish mama, it was a relief to find someone like Jean Carroll, who was willing to burst the fictive bubble of maternal bliss. In the words of one fan, "Jean Carroll talked about motherhood in a way that *no one else* did."[6]

Talking about Motherhood "in a Way That No One Else Did"

Motherhood was a hot topic in the mid-twentieth century. In 1943, the Jewish author David Levy published *Maternal Overprotection*, which accused women of making "maternity into a disease."[7] That same year, Philip Wylie published his best-seller *Generation of Vipers*, in which he railed against "Momism," accusing mothers of using excessive displays of sentiment and affection to foster "sickly dependencies" among their sons.[8] The kinder, gentler voice of Dr. Spock joined the conversation in 1946 with *The Common Sense Book of Baby and Childcare*, urging mothers to lean into their impulses for "natural loving care." A plethora of advice was heaped on mothers, much of it coming from men.

Popular entertainment was also filled with mothers—cooking pot roasts and kissing their husbands on the cheek and being adorably adoring. The Tony Award–winning Broadway production of Arthur Miller's *All My Sons* in 1947 featured the matriarch Kate Keller, a woman whom the playwright describes as defined by "an overwhelming capacity for love."[9] The radio program (later turned television sitcom) *Father Knows Best* (1949–1954) featured Margaret Anderson, the paragon of patience. For a more *Yiddishe tam* (Jewish flavor), one could turn to *The Goldbergs* (radio 1929–1946), where Gertrude Berg was creating the lovable Jewish mama Molly Goldberg. Joyce Antler credits Berg with "combin[ing] the Yiddishe mama's sentimentalized saintliness with the power and energy of her real-life counterparts, [emerging] as a beloved 'surrogate mother' to millions of Americans."[10]

It was at this cultural moment, in 1945, when Jean Carroll gave birth to her daughter, Helen. Almost immediately, she began discussing motherhood in her stand-up. But she was an unmistakably new voice, entirely different both from the pathologically overprotective nightmare of Momism and also from the sweetly solicitous Molly Goldberg. Standing in stark contrast to the adoring/smothering mother, Carroll's persona discussed motherhood with snark and notes of desperation, jabbing at "her rotten kid" and the child-centric suburban culture. This irreverence was particularly shocking coming from a Jewish mother, given the long-standing stereotype of Jewish mothers devoting themselves—wholly, worshipfully, and vocally—to their children.[11] Carroll's comedy about the frustrations of motherhood both disrupted stereotypes of the Jewish mother *and* allowed her a platform to give voice to so many women's unspoken critiques and commentary on issues like trends in child rearing, progressive education, and the growing generation gap.

On the April 5, 1959, episode of *The Ed Sullivan Show*, Carroll did a selection of her most famous "rotten kid" bits.[12] Taking on the child-care guru Dr. Spock's injunction for "firm but gentle" child rearing, Carroll exclaimed, "Today, you know, if you want to hit a kid, he's a monster. You gotta *read a book* first, find out if the guy gives you permission to hit him! And if you *can* hit this kid, you think you can reach him? Never! [Widens her stride, extends her arms protectively] There's a grandmother standing there! 'Don't hit that boy. Hit *me!*'"[13] On one level, these jokes address the universally acknowledged truth of grandparental indulgence. However, a more specifically Jewish reading is also available. The way that Carroll describes the "interfering" grandmother—adoring, protective, standing with arms outstretched as she howls self-sacrificing declarations—very clearly recalls the stereotypical Jewish mama. Carroll's second-generation persona, however, stands in sharp contrast. She is irreverent, candid, and secure enough in her place in the US to poke at its sacred domestic ideals.

While magazines such as *Ladies' Home Journal*, *Good Housekeeping*, and *Redbook* advocated self-actualization of children, Carroll unceremoniously mocks the literature of the day, exclaiming, "Today, they read in *Child Psychology*, 'you should never frustrate a child, a child must have something it can learn to lavish love and affection on. Like a hamster.' God forbid it should learn to love the mother or father, that's beside the point. A hamster!"[14] Her comic persona unapologetically flies in the face of prescribed child-rearing methods. For instance, women's magazines urged mothers, "Always be in firm control of all situations involving their children. Parents should not let children manipulate them. . . .

Rather, the parent should show the child who is the 'boss.'"[15] This loving but firm ideal creates the comic foil for Carroll's own hapless persona, in a bit about her daughter wanting a pet dog: "I haven't got enough trouble raising this kid. I need a dog in the house? But I don't want to say no to her, 'cause she hits. But you know, you reach a saturation point and put your foot down. And I put my foot down . . . and she stepped on it . . . and I got her the dog!"[16] In this joke, it is not her maternal instinct or adoring indulgence for her daughter that prompts her to grant her request for a dog; it is merely the self-preservation of a desperate woman avoiding her "rotten kid's" violent tantrums.

Carroll again offers up her own self-serving impulses as comic fodder in her special Mother's Day appearance on *The Ed Sullivan Show*: "Parents haven't got what to eat, they give the kid a car. The answer is always the same: 'I want my child to have what I never had.' You've heard that, haven't you? Well, I'm different! I don't want my kid to have anything I never had! I just want her to return what belongs to me!"[17] Again, Carroll contrasts the stereotypical image of the self-sacrificing Jewish mother (and, more broadly, self-sacrificing immigrant parents) with her own comically self-serving persona.

Another target of Carroll's new Jewish mother persona was her daughter's progressive education. The progressive education movement became popular in the United States in the mid-twentieth century, championed by advocates like Caroline Pratt, author of *I Learn from Children* (1948). With declarations like, "The child, unhampered, does not waste time," Pratt and other progressive educators urged schools to deemphasize the textbook and extrinsic motivators from teachers and other authority figures.[18] Instead, they espoused letting children take the lead in their education, emphasizing the educational value of self-directed play. This child-centered philosophy came under attack in the conservative Cold War period. And nowhere was that critique rendered more archly than by Jean Carroll, whom one newspaper described as "taking up cudgels against such latter-day perversities as progressive education" with jokes like, "One woman, she had a son going to a 'progressive school.' He didn't take up penmanship. He didn't like it. So they gave him a course in forgery."[19]

Far from the adoring mothers who sit poolside in Florida and boast that their kids are talking by the age of thirty, Carroll's persona talks with refreshing frankness about her travails in motherhood. Her complaints not only disrupt stereotypes of doting, protective Jewish mothers but also allow for timely jokes highlighting the disparity between the Cold War generation and the more liberal young people of the 1960s. Responding to the middle-class lifestyles of their parents, many young people in the 1960s were drawn to the Beat Generation, a literary movement championing values of spiritualism over materialism, as well as sexual liberation. These young people were called—with some disparagement from the older generation—"beatniks." Ever timely, on July 24, 1960, Jean Carroll did almost an entire set on *Sullivan* complaining about her "beatnik" daughter:

> You've heard me talk about my daughter, my rotten kid. I really do have a problem: she's a beatnik. [Responding to the audience's laughter] Oh, please, this isn't funny! At first, I tried to fight her, but I've given up! I don't mind anymore that she wears the sneakers and the funny blue jeans and the sloppy sweaters, but why a beard? And it's not just their manner of dress today. Who can understand them? They have kind of a hep talk, you know? Like, everything's a cat! I'm a cat, her father's a cat, her grandmother's a cat, even our dog is a cat! The only thing that isn't a cat in our house is our cat—he's a kook!

After mocking the beatnik garb and patois, Carroll moves onto a specific attack of her daughter's suitor, whom she depicts using the stereotypical register of a beatnik as a long-haired, unemployed, parasite:

> Every mother plans and dreams of the day when her daughter will bring home a nice presentable young man, who makes a nice living, to support you and your husband! But my daughter . . . she's got herself a poet!

A character with a *pony tail.* Very nice fella, but I said, "Honey, how is he going to support you?" She said, "He has an income from the government." He has: he's on unemployment insurance! She brought him home! This poor fella! I don't know when he ate last! We invited him home for dinner; he ate like he was going to the chair! This guy! My heart went out to him! I've seen people eat with their hands before—but not soup! He looked like a vacuum cleaner with teeth! We had fruit after supper. The orange peels? He ate 'em! The almonds? He ate 'em with the shells on! We had wax fruit. He said they were delicious! As he was leaving, he walked out, he was chewing on a big bone. I almost dropped dead. My husband's shoe was on the other end! After he left, my daughter came up to me. She said, "Well, Mommy, what do you think? What do you think of him?" I said, "Honey, he's perfect! But not for you—for the daughter of a garbage collector!"

In this piece, Carroll performs a neat reversal of the stereotype of the force-feeding Jewish mother. In this scenario, her persona is not trying to push food on an unwilling mouth—instead, she is actively horrified by an insatiable one. Her stereotype-breaking Jewish mother stands potently contrasted with the stereotypical beatnik loafer, whose "pony tail," dependence on "unemployment insurance," and abysmal table manners render him fit only for "the daughter of a garbage collector." Jean Carroll's persona may have been Jewish and a mother, but her wry, unabashedly self-serving, skeptical perspective made her a whole new kind of Jewish mother.

Caretaker/Comedian: Stories from the Road

While Carroll found motherhood to be a rich source of comedy, it was also a major obstacle to having a career as a comedian. In spite of ongoing attempts to reconcile her role as a mother with that of a comic, Carroll faced repeated roadblocks from an environment in which women were socialized to make their families their first and only priority.

The stand-up circuit was not designed with children in mind. For that matter, motherhood was not designed with stand-up comedy in mind. So when Jean Carroll became a mother, she was already in an incongruous situation, a baby on her arm as she journeyed to unfamiliar towns, often staying in seedy motels populated by characters one could diplomatically call "remarkable."

Looking back on her career, Carroll offered story after story of the misadventures of motherhood as a stand-up comedian. There was one gig when Carroll entrusted one-year-old Helen to her niece, who promptly set the baby in her crib and sneaked backstage to watch the performance. When Carroll went to check on Helen before going onstage, she found her "covered with black ants." With her baby covered in bugs, Carroll took the stage, recalling, "I'm out there, and I wasn't good. I really wasn't. . . . I doubt that any comic, doing a routine act, could have been a success there. Given those conditions."[20] What is key about "those conditions" is that they are specific to a comic who was also a caretaker. While many male stand-up comedians were also parents, they typically did not take on the role of a primary caretaker such that they would ever find themselves dividing their attention between the audience and an ant-covered baby.[21]

In another story of early motherhood on the road, Carroll described when infant Helen got sick, potentially from ingesting some of the water from the motel pool. She recalled, "I went to [the manager] and I said, 'Can you tell me anything about a doctor in town? Is there a pediatrician? Is there anything?' He wouldn't lift a finger. He wouldn't even make a phone call. 'I don't know.' I said, 'You don't *know* if there's a doctor in town?'"[22] Because of her work, Carroll found herself in an unfamiliar town with a sick baby and no one to turn to for help except an intransigent manager. Although told with the fond energy of reminiscences, these stories point to a grim truth: as long as Carroll brought Helen on the road, she was potentially endangering her.

By 1950, when Helen was five years old, a press clipping from Carroll's scrapbook reveals that Carroll was so divided by her coexisting roles as caretaker and comedian that she was "counting on quitting the footlights for good come Christmas to devote herself to husband Buddy Howe, the theatrical agent, their five-year-old daughter Robin, and homelife in general." However, this intended turn to domesticity came precisely at the time when Carroll's comedy career was gaining momentum, with the paper referencing "a starring engagement at the Latin Quarter starting in October, a new television show to begin later this winter, and a series of comedy films for the Columbia Studios."[23] Carroll's husband-manager urged her to take advantage of this momentum, both because she "owe[d] it to [her] public" and because she was making "pots of money."[24] Therefore, Carroll continued to juggle her multiple roles, in spite of the strain.

The Scrapbook Story of Mother and Daughter

Both Carroll's and Tunick's accounts depict a mother-daughter relationship in which deep love and attachment were intertwined with the stressful surveillance and separation anxieties of the entertainment industry. From early in Helen's childhood, Carroll made an effort to bring her along into the spotlight. At the tender age of five, Helen appeared alongside her mother on the Jack Barry program *Juvenile Celebs*.[25] Eleven years later, Carroll would try to get adolescent Helen cast as her on-screen daughter in a new family sitcom. And throughout her daughter's life, Carroll made a point of mentioning her in publicity features and interviews. However, when speaking of her daughter, Carroll rarely used her legal name. To the rest of the world, she was Helen Howe, but for Jean Carroll, she was always "Robin." Carroll had created the pet name when her daughter was young, saying that she reminded her of "a bird, bringing beauty and sunshine and happiness into [her] life": "From the day she was born, she was like a robin, full of beautiful sounds, sent to me by God."[26]

Carroll's personal scrapbook reads like a testament to her intense, sometimes fraught efforts to interweave her family life and career. For this carefully curated collection of press clippings shows a remarkable emphasis on Helen. In a sample of approximately one hundred clippings, Carroll's daughter is referenced twenty-nine times and referred to by the name "Robin" an additional thirteen times. The narrative of Carroll's career, seen through the lens of her scrapbook, becomes a kind of worm's-eye-view biography of Helen. Peering out from her mother's profiles in a sentence here and there, Helen grows from a "five year old child" to a fourteen-year-old "lovely flower unfolding" to the "artistic daughter Robin, now married."[27] In most of these mainstream publications, Carroll's constant references to Robin seem to be attempts to assure the public of the harmonious coexistence of Carroll's comedy and family life.

The Jean Carroll who exists in these "family" profiles shows remarkable agility, nimbly hopping from comedian to parent. In the *Milwaukee Journal* profile by John Mosedale, she immediately transitions from "proud mama" mode, showing off Robin's paintings and praising her as "a wonderful, sensitive child," to "stand-up comic" mode, using her daughter as comic fodder: "I asked her the other day, 'Robin, why do you talk so much?' . . . She talked herself pale once. I said to her, 'Honey, you have to stop long enough to take a breath.' She even talks under water. I ask her a question when she's on the diving board and she doesn't stop or wait to come up—strings of bubbles appear."[28] Mosedale acknowledges the shift into stand-up, remarking, "This, of course, is the Carroll material on which are built the monologues that have won her fans at home." But he still comes away commending both her talent as a comedian and her housekeeping of "Hollywood's idea of what a Park Avenue Apartment looks like."[29]

Another profile begins by identifying Carroll as "one of the country's top comediennes," explaining, "on stage or TV, being funny is her business," before neatly pivoting to a contrasting assertion: "But to Jean, the business of motherhood is a serious thing." In her quotations, Carroll employs a jovial "kids-say-the-darnedest-things" playfulness, quoting her daughter's naïve questions ("What does it mean when Lassie is in heat?"). But within the very same paragraph, she moves to earnest parenting philosophy, asserting, "Questions like these . . . give me a chance to spark discussions that invariably bear fruit. I get a better insight into the depth of Robin's mind, and it gives me a perfect opening to get across my own ideas and beliefs. The better we know our children—and the better they know us—the cleverer and tranquiller our relationship is bound to be."[30]

The photograph accompanying this profile is an apt summary of the dual roles of comedian and caretaker that Carroll represents (figure 6.1). Featured in the center of the background is a print of Carroll's headshot, hanging prominently on the wall in an opulent frame. In the foreground, Carroll and her daughter pose with Lassie, their collie. Carroll is dressed in a high-collared plaid shirt, with one hand holding a cup of tea and the other being licked by the dog. Her daughter sits by her side, hair neatly plaited. Both are smiling widely. The juxtaposition of Jean Carrolls is striking. In the background is the impeccably coiffed and revealingly dressed glamour girl, alone and aloof, her gaze peering coyly off to the right. In the foreground is the flannel-clad mother, Lassie and Robin by her side, her bright smile directed frankly to the left. The photograph, holding the two Carrolls side by side but separated by frames, visualizes the very objective of "domestic profiles" like these: the coexistence of Carroll's role as a performer and mother.

The *New York Daily News* released a similar profile a few years later, declaring, "Jean's just as talented in the role of mother as she is comedienne." A section of the article is subtitled "Mother and Daughter," reading, "While it's true the comedienne enjoys star billing on TV, at home her role is definitely that of co-star to her lovely, attractive daughter Robin. Not once during our interview did Miss Carroll upstage her or treat her like an intruder. Theirs, as any stranger could quickly detect, is a genuine, warm relationship based on mutual understanding and honesty."[31] The register of this piece is distinctively "show biz"—positioning Carroll's motherhood as a "role" and contrasting her "star billing on TV" with her "co-star" status with her daughter at home. The writer implies

FIGURE 6.1. Photograph of Jean Carroll and Helen Howe, with Lassie in the foreground and Carroll's framed headshot in the background, 1956, saved in Carroll's personal scrapbook. (Private collection of Susan Chatzky)

some degree of surprise that Carroll does not try to "upstage" Robin, concluding that the Howes were a "contrary situation" to the "unhappy second banana role usually allotted the children of theatrical parents."[32] Like the profiles in the *Providence Evening Bulletin* and the *Milwaukee Journal Green Sheet*, this *New York Daily News* feature participates in a long tradition of the press emphasizing women celebrities' family lives, to soften the stigma attached to being a working woman. These articles reassure Jean Carroll's fan base that the famous comedian was not shirking her duties as a devoted mother.

"Not without My Daughter"

Several of the articles that Carroll scrapbooked reflect the professional sacrifices that she made on her daughter's behalf. For instance, when Helen was eight years old, she got the measles and needed her mother to take care of her. Of course, many children get the measles, but few can then read in the newspaper about how their measles disrupted an international comedy tour. In an article bemoaning the fact that Carroll would no longer be touring the British provinces, Carroll explained to the reporter, "They're trying to talk me into staying, . . . but I talked myself out of it."[33] When the choice arose between performing for her fans and caring for her daughter, Carroll chose the latter. But, it is worth noting, she also made sure to publicize that choice. The sacrifices that Jean Carroll made for her family were both profound and public.

Carroll's narrative of sacrifice for her family was not lost on Helen, and it may have been part of the wedge that arose between them as Helen approached adolescence. In an interview at her mother's Friars Club retrospective, Helen recalled expressing frustrations with her mother's career: "I remember, as a kid, 11, 12 years old, maybe, now and then making some cracks like, 'Nobody else's mother worked.' . . . I think I did say something one time about, you know, 'Why can't you stay home and bake cookies like everybody else's mother?' Because I really didn't get it. Why she 'had' to work."[34]

Perhaps to Helen's dismay, her crack about staying home and baking cookies made it into several newspapers, including an article in which Carroll gave a paragraph-long defense of herself: "Her 13-year-old daughter has a good sense of humor, [Carroll] says, especially when she suggests that Mom quit the stage and bake cookies for her. 'At times like that I remind her that she sees more of me than many children see of their mothers, that she eats dinners out with us, and spends weekend and vacation trips with her parents, unlike her friends.'"[35]

The overarching tone of articles like this one reveals their more anxious dimension, as Carroll defensively compares herself favorably to her daughter's friends' parents. Carroll's defensive stance became even more pronounced in a lengthy feature detailing her many shifts between retirement and career plans. A profile in the *Kleiner TV Notebook* reveals a complex mixture of self-aggrandizement and defensiveness:

[Jean Carroll will] accept no big tours and won't consider the offers of a TV show of her own.

"It's because of my daughter," she says. "Robin is 14. Well, really, I guess it's not because of her, but because of me. I don't want to miss any of this—she's like a lovely flower, unfolding." It wasn't too long ago that Robin came home from school one day with a problem. "Something had happened in school," Jean says. "Robin said to me, 'I don't think I have a normal home life.' She was thinking about the times I was away from home. So I said, 'Don't other girls' parents go on vacation?' I'm up at seven with her, and at night, I get her dinner—I like to cook—and I'm her friend. I take her to school, go to the PTA meetings and all. So I said to her, 'How am I remiss?' She had no answer. You know, parents who don't work at all often spend less time with their kids than I do with my daughter—than most show business parents do with their children." She wasn't a comedienne then. She was deadly serious.[36]

This profile emphatically points out that Carroll's choice to depart from show business was not a matter of decreased demand, for she still "turns down more work than she accepts."[37] Rather, it was a testament to her prioritization of family over show business (and the implied mutual exclusivity of the two). The fact that Carroll depicts Helen's complaints, foregrounding them as the main "conflict" of the story, suggests that she wants to highlight the difficulty of being both a parent and a performer. And the fact that Carroll spends twice as long countering her daughter's complaint with a description of her own intense involvement (cooking, chauffeuring, and meeting with the PTA) before comparing herself favorably to "most show business parents" suggests her need to defend herself to the public, protesting (a bit too much, methinks) that her career has not come at the expense of her motherhood. Still, the columnist sees the roles in tension, evident in the wording of his final statement—that when Jean Carroll spoke of her commitment to motherhood, "She wasn't a comedienne then. She was deadly serious." The play on words betokens a larger worldview, in which the playful role of comedienne is at odds with the serious role of mother. Overall, the pieces capture Carroll's fraught emotions surrounding her need to juggle a career and motherhood.

Trying to Get "the Lovely Flower Unfolding" on Camera

In the early 1960s, after years of Jean Carroll's (perhaps halfhearted) attempts to leave show business to spend more time with her daughter, she finally switched tactics. If she could not bring Mohammed (herself) to the mountain (her family), she would bring the mountain to Mohammed. That is, she would bring "Robin" on set—and even on camera—with her. Unfortunately, Helen had no interest in pursuing show business.[38]

The resulting anxiety-laden dynamic was painfully on display in an episode of *The Gary Moore Show* on January 3, 1961. Carroll did a stand-up set, followed by Moore calling her back as part of a commercial for Polaroid Electric Eye Camera. As the spokesman concluded his pitch with the request, "Jean, may I take your picture?" Carroll sashayed on-stage, effusing, "Oh, I'd love it, but look, I've been talking to you about my beatnik daughter so much. Do you mind if I bring her on, show what a lovely girl she is?" The spokesman agreed: "Oh, sure, come on. We'd love to meet her." Carroll reached her arm backstage, beckoning Helen, who entered in a fitted suit with a peplum waist, her hair pulled neatly back. Helen's smile looked a bit forced, but she stood obediently, leaning her head against her mother's. As the camera flashed, Carroll put one hand protectively around Helen's shoulders, the other at her waist, pulling her close. Carroll's position, face turned to the camera but arms gripping her daughter, seemed a neat encapsulation of her predicament.[39]

ATV Sitcom

The recurrent tug-of-war between motherhood and show business came to a head when Carroll was offered a high-profile sitcom overseas. The ATV (Associated Television) network, based in London, aired programming in England, Canada, and Australia and was eager to book Carroll for a twenty-six-episode family sitcom.[40] Carroll had gained recent accolades in England with performances at the London Palladium and long-term (four-week) engagements at the Savoy, prompting the sitcom offer with the hefty and well-publicized fee of £50,000. Carefully pasted into Carroll's scrapbook are a series of articles emphasizing this exceptional sum, one headlined, "Dream Contract," and another—illustrated with a cartoon of Carroll draped in a mink stole and opulent hat—proclaiming, "Talkative Miss Carroll has a £50,000 problem" (figure. 6.2).[41]

The problem, it seems, was the same as it had always been: how Carroll could pursue show business while also being the kind of caretaker that she wanted to be. The article attributed her indecision over the television series to three causes: "(a) I am not desperate for money (b) I don't like leaving my 16-year-old daughter alone in New York and (c) I am frankly beginning to get very tired of hearing myself talk."[42] Her allusion to her daughter, couched inconspicuously between a reference to her successful husband's career and her quip about growing tired of hearing herself talk, became more of a focal point of Carroll's

FIGURE 6.2. Caricature of Jean Carroll in British periodical, n.d., saved in Carroll's personal scrapbook. (Private collection of Susan Chatzky)

argument in other articles documenting her fraught process of decision-making. "It's most important that I should be with her now. She's leaving adolescence for womanhood," Carroll declared in a separate interview. Carroll explained that Helen bore the brunt of her absence when she was gone: "We don't have a housekeeper or anything like that. When I'm away, Helen looks after everything." She concluded, "This TV series means big money, but if I can't do it with Helen by my side, then I shan't do it in Britain."[43] Again, Carroll is not an unimpeachable narrator.

Compounding her professed concern about Helen's increased household responsibilities in her absence was the issue of Helen's health. According to Helen's daughter Susan, Helen struggled with addiction from a young age.[44] Carroll, however, judiciously avoided any mention of her daughter's health complications.

The "Dream Contract" clipping gives a bit more information on what Carroll meant when she said that she would not do the show without Helen "by her side." First, she asked ATV to schedule the filming of the series around Helen's school calendar. A British publication wrote, "She wants the series to be made in the summer so that her 16-year-old daughter, at present at school in America, can be here with her during vacation."[45] The same article included a bit of commentary in which Carroll seemed intent on softening the perceived "demand," insisting, "I have not presented them with an ultimatum or anything like that. I have just asked if it could be arranged for the shows to be done while Helen can be here."[46] Evidently, Carroll's summer-schedule demand was met, for an article in the *Reporter Dispatch* revealed that filming was scheduled to start in June 1961. This article reveals another of Carroll's attempts to integrate her daughter into her career: casting her actual daughter as her sitcom daughter:

> "My 16-year-old daughter Robin will do the series with me," Jean commented. "Since I'm going to use a teen-ager in the series, why shouldn't I use my daughter? She claims she has no talent, but if she can act natural and take direction, she'll be fine. I've been working with her and with a little prodding and a little aggravation she'll do all right. I told her if she feels like reacting differently than the script calls for to go right ahead— put the burden on me. I'll have an answer. If worse comes to worse, I'll hit her. I always have an answer."[47]

In this context, Carroll's statement "I always have an answer" seems to work on multiple levels, ostensibly referring to her ability to turn her show-business neophyte daughter into a working actor but perhaps also referring to her ability to figure out the "answer" to her chronic problem of balancing family and career. Yet the resistance suggested in Robin's claim that she "has no talent" suggests that the "answer" that her mother found may have been a one-sided solution.

Ultimately, the ATV sitcom did not happen. Carroll's carefully preserved clippings, with headlines like "£50,000 TV Offer, but Jean Thinks of Daughter" and "With Jean, It's the Family First, Show Biz Second," suggest that the television show was halted in its tracks by her decision to prioritize her family.[48] In one of the articles, Carroll explicitly stated, "You know, I'm too much in love with my family to keep going away from my home. My husband and 16-year-old daughter are dead-heat for first place and I just don't want to travel around anymore. The only dates I want are those on home ground—and not more than a mile away from where I live. Yes, I still love show business, but I love my family more."[49] This declaration, "I love show business, but I love my family more," reveals how the two were—had long been—at odds with each other. The fact that Carroll saved these particular articles, arranging them into a narrative of family-based self-sacrifice, suggests that the choice to prioritize family over show business is how she chose to craft her own professional and personal story. From her early days dividing her attention between a crib backstage and the microphone onstage to her later ones trying to shoehorn an unwilling daughter into the television spotlight, Carroll had been fighting a losing battle against gender norms that idealized motherhood as an all-consuming vocation.

The Complicated Relationship of Mr. and Mrs. Howe

Even *before* adding motherhood into the equation, Carroll was already violating midcentury American gender norms by being a married woman with a career. While women's labor-force participation increased from 18 to 25 percent between 1890 and 1940, the mythologized ideal depicted women primarily as caretakers for their children and—equally important—for their husbands.[50] One of Carroll's jokes got very near the truth when she quipped, "I have two wonderful children, . . . a girl of 8 and a boy of 36."[51] Child care and husband care were equally crucial for the ideal woman of the mid-1900s. And so, just as Carroll's role as a mother was complicated by her work, so was her role as a wife.

In 1954, Carroll was exhausted by the struggle. She later described a moment of crisis when she approached Bob Lewine, the head of ABC, and proclaimed, "I want out of show business! I don't want it—I've had enough! It's not like I'm looking for a career. My career is my marriage—that's my career!"[52] This declaration of marriage *as* career suggests that it demanded the same level of attention and effort as her work as a comedian. But it also speaks to the ways in which Carroll's career and marriage had been bound from the start.

In some ways, Buddy Howe was his wife's biggest fan. One could even think of him as "Mr. Jean Carroll"—the managerial force behind America's "First Lady of Laughs." It was at his urging that Carroll became a solo act in the first place. In the days when they were a double act, he convinced her that she was the more talented one of the two of them, and he had been holding her back as a costar, urging her to keep performing while he was drafted into military service. After he returned from the army and became a talent agent, he took her on as a client and represented her for over twenty years. His position as a booker of talent for the hottest nightclubs and variety shows ensured that Carroll would always have a high-profile gig when she needed one.[53] Later in life, when Carroll felt strained by the efforts to balance comedy and caretaking, Howe continued urging her on. Carroll shared that when she wanted to retire, he said, "I won't permit it. You owe it to your public." Of course, she also recognized his financial stake in her success. Still, Carroll firmly believed that her husband's economic and professional interest in her career was undergirded by a passionate belief in her talent, declaring, "My husband thought I was the greatest talent that ever lived."[54]

The couple's professional relationship was a symbiotic one, for just as Howe devoted his labor and resources to representing Carroll, her talent and social capital helped to advance his career. Her growing network of comedy colleagues became valuable clients for Howe as he moved from being a nightclub booking agent to president of General Artists Coordination (GAC) and then to vice chairman of International Creative Management, one of the world's largest talent agencies, which represented such luminaries as Barbra Streisand and George Carlin.[55] Another prestigious title held by Howe was his seventeen-year tenure as dean of the Friars Club, a philanthropic and social men's club for comedians. His granddaughter Susan Chatzky contends that Howe's relationship to the Friars Club was purchased by Carroll's professional and social capital: "[It was] very much because of my grandmother and her relations with other comedians, . . . which is kind of funny, because it was a men's club."[56]

Indeed, Buddy Howe benefited from his wife's nonnormative career, and he supported her achievements onstage and on-screen, unusual though they were for one of her sex. However, her career also put a strain on their marriage. According to their family members, Howe wanted Carroll's deviation from gender norms to stop short of the domestic sphere. Their daughter, Helen, reasoned that her father was a product of the era's gender norms, threatened by his wife's professional and personal independence: "My father . . . he was probably a fairly typical man of his time. You know, his wife was supposed to kowtow to him, Ha, and I mean, that wasn't happening, and so I think he was mystified by her and . . . always loved her but just didn't know what to do with her because you couldn't control her. . . . *He* couldn't control her."[57] Helen's older daughter, Susan, confirms Carroll's unconventionally powerful role in their family, remarking, "I grew up with a grandmother who was the major breadwinner. She made more money than he did, and she had a lot of power in the relationship, a lot of power in the house, and a lot of power over our family."[58] In this remark, Chatzky unwittingly paraphrases the dynamic that Carroll had observed in her childhood home, in which if you were the breadwinner, you made the rules. Yet while Carroll had been able to supplant her father as head of the family without misgivings, it became a different matter when her husband was involved.

Carroll's characterization of her marriage suggests both attachment and a struggle for control and power: "He was my soul mate, . . . but he was a control freak. I couldn't stand his constantly criticizing me."[59] The domestic power struggle was an ongoing source of strife in their marriage, with their daughter quipping, "Rocky would be generous."[60]

Rumors of infidelity circled abundantly around the marriage, on both sides. Buddy Howe's granddaughter alleged that he was repeatedly unfaithful to his wife.[61] And both the *Daily News* and the *Daily Mirror* reported an alleged affair that Carroll had with Robert McHale, an engineer who had helped remodel her summer home in Wurtsboro, New York. According to Carroll, McHale's wife, Dorothy, had invented the affair—and a sordid story of Carroll attacking her with a handbag—as a way to blackmail Carroll for $25,000. Dorothy McHale sued Carroll, and the case went to trial but was thrown out by a jury, leading Carroll to comment, "The whole thing was fantastic. I knew I'd be vindicated."[62] However, the episode did lead to a rare public acknowledgment in 1954 in which Carroll "admitted that she has been separated since early 1951 from her husband."[63] According to Helen, that separation lasted approximately six years.[64] A friend of Carroll's attested that even during the separation, Carroll and Howe continued to collaborate and even had dinner together each night.[65] Their professional relationship was always a major force in their marriage, and like a magnet, sometimes it pulled them together and other times it drove them apart.

Happily Ever After (?) at Rainbow's End

As Jean Carroll's mother and sister fell ill, she felt the tension between caretaking and comedy more acutely than ever. She described traveling constantly between hospitals and comedy clubs:

> My mother was in Physician's Hospital in Queens, so I would go to the hospital in Queens, and from there take the shuttle to Boston, where my sister was in the Lahey Clinic. That was my life.

And although I was appearing at the Copa and places like that, I was always listening for someone to say, "Jean, you're wanted on the phone," [saying] that my sister had died. And it was awful. I couldn't concentrate on it. I didn't enjoy it. And I didn't think it was being fair to the guy paying me, or to the customers.[66]

Even Carroll's verbiage suggests that at this point, show business was more a job than a calling. She used the transactional term "the customers," as opposed to a relational term like "fans" or "my public." In a separate interview, Carroll confessed to the emotional toll her dual labors took, recalling, "You're cried out. Then you walk on stage and your eyes look like two big red onions. All that's going on and you have to be funny."[67] The classic trope of "the weeping clown" had become her unmanageable reality.

And so, in the late 1960s, after four decades of Carroll struggling to reconcile her roles as caretaker and comedian, she finally managed to have something resembling retirement. Although she would occasionally do a performance in the Catskills or another nearby venue, she was primarily focused on her family.[68] The *New York Post* announced that Carroll "retired from a prospering career as a comedienne in the 1950s, having chosen family, fresh air, and golf instead." She, her husband, and Helen moved from their Manhattan apartment to a "rambling ranch house" in Wurtsboro named Rainbow's End. It was an apt name for Carroll's beloved home, where she held family reunions for years to come. She described it as "tranquil and serene, . . . opulent without being ostentatious, it's the pot of gold at the end of the rainbow."[69] Like its mythical namesake, it was her place of long-sought reward.

In some ways, Rainbow's End was the happy ending to Jean Carroll's story of long-standing struggle. She was able to devote herself to her family in a way that hewed closely to midcentury ideals of womanhood. No longer one of her husband's clients, she could become his biggest cheerleader, while still being a source of social and cultural capital. The historian Christiane Taylor Diehl has written of the midcentury valorization of the corporate wife. These winsome wives served as fonts of free public relations for companies, for "engaging in community activities enhanced their firms' public images." More importantly, the charity work performed by corporate wives "created networks with potential customers, suppliers, and even officials who had regulatory powers over their firms."[70]

Carroll took on her role as corporate wife with aplomb, getting involved in fundraising efforts with Hadassah and the National Tay-Sachs and Allied Diseases Association. She was even named "Tay Sachs Woman of the Year" in 1964, during which she headed "a new Speakers Bureau which will bring the Tay Sachs story to many organizations in the metropolitan area."[71] She enjoyed her role playing the Lady Bountiful and doting wife, interspersed with afternoons spent "golfing, gardening, swimming, and walking."[72]

With each year spent focused on her family, Jean Carroll's name appeared less and less in industry periodicals and national papers and more frequently in local papers announcing charitable events. By 1972, Carroll's name was so unfamiliar to *Variety* audiences that it was seldom seen without the accompanying "Mrs. Buddy Howe."[73] The juxtaposition of these two names, "Jean Carroll" and "Mrs. Buddy Howe," highlights the peculiar double life of the professional woman: the mutual exclusivity of Jean Carroll, comedienne, and Mrs. Buddy Howe, attentive corporate wife to the vice chairman at ICM. Carroll's colleagues Milton Berle, Henny Youngman, and of course, Buddy Howe did not have such bifurcation demanded of them. Although *Variety* only began recognizing her dual existence with the appellation "Jean Carroll–Mrs. Buddy Howe" after her retirement, the truth is that she had been struggling with that challenge for many years.

Carroll's retirement was an active one—she approached full-time domestic life with the same level of dedication and vigor with which she had pursued professional life. Her role as matriarch extended beyond simply caring for her husband and daughter. Her granddaughter reflected, "Someone once said something about, 'It's a shame your grandmother gave up her career for a husband.' But she *didn't* give up her career for her husband! . . . My grandmother also had an elderly mother she was taking care of. She had a sister who was a single mom; she helped raise that kid. I think she was just very immersed in her family. She was a full-time parent and grandparent and friend and aunt and sister and daughter—all at the same time. . . . She had a big, rich, full life."[74]

Jean Carroll's scrapbook documents her family with the same conscientiousness that she documented her career. Toward the end of her scrapbook, the pages hold not reviews or features on Carroll but ephemera about her family members: an invitation to a party thrown in Buddy Howe's honor, a photograph in the local paper showing a smiling granddaughter petting a horse, a program from a dance recital featuring her daughter, Helen, and granddaughter Andrea.[75] Moving from clippings from *Variety* to clippings of the Howe household, the implicit message of the scrapbook pages is that family was replacing show business as Carroll's career. In a way, family had been her driving passion all along—from the time that she began performing to support her mother and siblings. And in that sense, Carroll's story ends happily ever after.

An Ongoing Struggle

But no happily ever after is without complications. To some people, Carroll's choice to pivot from comedy to caretaking in her golden years erased the decades that she devoted to the industry. Among some of Carroll's fellow comedians—show business "old-timers" like Georgie Jessel or even later comics like Joan Rivers—there was a mentality that show business must be your first love and top priority. Viewing show business as simply a job, to build an income and then retire from, was sacrilege. "The Great Entertainer" Al Jolson used to boast, "I got so much money that fourteen guys couldn't spend it, but I'd rather die than quit show business."[76] "Very few people in show business ever really retire," explained the comedy legend George Burns, rhapsodizing,

"Show business is some wonderful lover. Once you feel that embrace, ... it's a relationship in which there's never been a divorce."[77] Given this mentality, Carroll's long-awaited retirement could seem like a legacy-erasing affront. Certain historians seem to take this view. In histories of stand-up comedy, members of Carroll's cohort—Milton Berle, Henny Youngman, and the like—loom large, while her name is omitted. In the rare occasions when historians do include her, it is as a novelty or after-thought. For instance, Kliph Nesteroff speaks dismissively of Carroll in his history of American comedy: "In a way she was a poster child for the independent working woman, but when her husband was named head of the massive talent agency General Amusement Corporation, she retreated. In typical 1950s fashion, after several appearances on *The Ed Sullivan Show*, she abandoned her trade and became a housewife."[78] To clarify, her "several appearances on *The Ed Sullivan Show*" was actually twenty-nine, to say nothing of her other television appearances and forty years of live performances. As so many comedy professionals will attest, Jean Carroll changed the game of stand-up comedy forever. Yet to hear male historians tell it (when they tell it at all), she was a brief flash in the pan who "abandoned" comedy to become a housewife. Moreover, nei-ther Nesteroff nor other men writing comedy history (Gerald Nachman, Richard Zoglin, Laurie Stone, John Limon, Eddie Tafoya) acknowledge the challenges of balancing the expectations of a career comedian with those of a family caretaker.[79]

The problem is that these challenges have not gone away—and are not going away any time soon. After the feminist movement of the 1960s and '70s, women have become more vocal about the challenges of negotiating motherhood and careers, including careers as comedians. Some stand-up comedians have reconciled their roles as comedian and caretaker by realizing Jean Carroll's dream of spending time with their children on camera. Joan Rivers, for instance, developed several televi-sion shows that starred her with her daughter, Melissa, by her side.[80] Ali Wong has developed two specials on the subject of pregnancy and motherhood, and Amy Schumer has made a franchise out of pregnancy with *Growing* and *Expecting Amy*.[81]

However, just as Carroll found that motherhood was both great comedy fodder and a major career obstacle, contemporary comedians have come to similar conclusions. Parenthood continues to be time-consuming—if not life-consuming. And the majority of parenthood responsibilities frequently fall to women. Although American gender norms have shifted since the midcentury, there is still a social pressure for women to serve as primary caregivers. And so the roles of mother and comedian are exclusive in a way that the roles of father and comedian are not. The stand-up superstar Sarah Silverman spoke to this difference in an interview on her longing to be a "fun dad":

> One of the other [male] comics on the tour said, "Why don't you just do it [have kids]? I have a 2-year-old and it's f—king great." And I go, "Yeah, who's watching your 2-year-old right now while you're on tour with me for two months?" It doesn't even occur to men that, more often than not, they're in a relationship with someone who's the primary caregiver of their kids and they get to be the fun dad. I'd f—king love to be a fun dad. I'd be the best fun dad. I'd come home and give 40-minute increments of the best of me when I'm not on the road. That's the f—king dream, but I love what I do. I don't want to stay home with a baby all day. I f—king love kids, and I'd love to have the traditional dad role of parenting. It'd be incredible.[82]

This interview is not from the 1950s—it is from 2017. And in it, Silverman articulates the underlying assumption that while fatherhood entails only brief increments of playful engagement, motherhood demands daily dedication. "Fun dad" may be a classic role, while "funny mom" is anything but.

This too, is part of Jean Carroll's legacy. The challenges that Jean Carroll faced as she tried to reconcile her roles as comedian and caretaker still loom large for women in a variety of career paths. But regardless of her place (or absence) in the history of stand-up, Carroll proved to thousands of viewers—many of them women—that there were new possibilities open to them. She showed that it was possible to command the attention of a nation, cracking jokes and changing minds, all while caring for her own beloved "rotten kid."

Conclusion

The pages of Jean Carroll's scrapbook are filled with attempts to define her in terms of her peers. Over the course of her career, press clippings from *Variety* referred to her as a "female Milton Berle," a "distaff Joey Faye," a "female Henny Youngman," and a "female counterpart of Sam Levenson."[1] The *Daily News* described her with comparisons to such disparate performers as Groucho Marx and female comic singers like Gracie Fields and Bea Lillie.[2] A British columnist noted wryly that Miss Carroll has "been described as a female version of every living comedian."[3] By 1961, the Carroll comparisons were almost a running joke, and Ramsdon Grieg printed a humorous column reading, "The American comedienne Jean Carroll has been described as a female Bob Hope, a female Charlie Chaplin, and a female Benny Hill. I have also seen her described as a female Tallulah Bankhead, which should give Miss Bankhead something to think about."[4] Clearly, it is difficult to describe someone who is the first of their kind.

As the first Jewish woman stand-up comedian, Jean Carroll is a historic figure in Jewish performance and stand-up comedy. Responding to personal and historical circumstances, she developed a comic persona that reflected a mixture of her reality and her aspirations. The version of Jean Carroll at the stand-up microphone was glamorous in a way that her alter ego, Sadie Zeigman, never was. Carroll's comedy occasionally dropped references to a college education that belied her actual high school equivalency degree. But her wit and insight were all her own. She took insulting stereotypes about parochial, undignified Jewish women and used her performance chops and comic savvy to render them ridiculous. She insisted on embodying traits that had not previously coexisted in comedy: she was pretty *and* funny, Jewish *and* all-American, opinionated *and* feminine. In sum, Jean Carroll expanded models of funny Jewish women through her assimilatory efforts portraying the comic persona of a white, heterosexual, upper-middle-class—or, as it was problematically called, "universal"—Jewess. To some audience members, Carroll's persona rendered her Jewishness illegible. But for others, it broadened their sense of what Jewish women were like.

The discussion of Jewish women in comedy—and media more broadly—has more recently again put *The Marvelous Mrs. Maisel* in the spotlight. This time, the media flurry was prompted by Sarah Silverman—a Jewish woman stand-up comic who could in many ways be seen as part of Jean Carroll's lineage. Silverman critiqued the casting of the non-Jewish actress Rachel Brosnahan as Miriam Maisel, citing a larger pattern that also includes the casting of Kathryn Hahn as Joan Rivers in an upcoming biopic and Felicity Jones in the (noncomedic) role of Ruth Bader Ginsburg in the film *On the Basis of Sex*. Silverman was unsettled by what this phenomenon—which she provocatively called "Jewface"—suggested about America's limited embrace of Jewish women, exclaiming, "If the Jewish female character is courageous or deserves love, she is never played by a Jew. Ever!"[5] The journalist Sam Litvin, taking up what he named "The Sarah Silverman Theory of American Antisemitism in Films and Roles," quantified some data, finding that in a sample of sixty-six Jewish films, if a Jewish woman was played by a non-Jewish actress, that role was depicted in a "positive" way 90 percent of the time. However, when the role of the Jewish woman was played by a Jewish actress, the role was depicted in a "positive" way only 67 percent of the time.[6] The Jewish popular culture scholar Jennifer Caplan presented a paper at the 2021 Association for Jewish Studies conference with *The Marvelous Mrs. Maisel* and *Transparent* as case studies for a broader trend in which "more 'desirable' and in most case younger Jewish women are played by non-Jewish actors, while Jewish actors are used to play older, less attractive, and more stereotyped Jewish women."[7]

This phenomenon is an interesting reversal of Jean Carroll's intervention. In the early and mid-twentieth century, Carroll's comedy coincided with a larger cultural project trying to expand the American perception of Jews to encompass white, upper-middle-class status. By the twenty-first century, the perception of Jewish people as white and upper middle class was so normalized that Jews became—from some perspectives—indistinguishable from other white people. In the 2020 pilot of Kenya Barris's comedy *Black AF*, a white Jewish character hems and haws, "Well, um, technically, Jews aren't like, white-white," before being swiftly shut down by the character of Barris's wife, Joya, who emphatically pronounces, "Jews are white. Jews. Are. White." Ironically, the actress playing Joya, who uttered the line so definitively, was Rashida Jones, a Black Jewish woman.[8] To a non-Jewish audience, the moment might be yet another argument in an endless negotiation of the perception of Jews in the United States. However, to in-group audience members aware of Jones's identity, it was a much-needed reminder of the Ashkenormative bias that discounts Jewish people of color. With her deadpan delivery, Rashida Jones took Jean Carroll's comic intervention—expanding limited conceptions of Jewish women—in a new and necessary direction.

Surveying contemporary Jewish women stand-up comedians, it is clear that many of them are doing comedy that, while dissimilar in content to Jean Carroll's, also does the cultural work of expanding representation of Jewish women to be more inclusive and accurate. Jewish women stand-up comics like Tiffany Haddish and Rainn Pryor, who are Black; Joanna Hausmann, who is Latina; and Anna Suzuki, who is Japanese, make brilliant comedy out of the discrimination they have faced as Jewish women of color. Stand-up comics like Judy Gold and Jessica Kirson, who are lesbians, break down heteronormative conceptions of the Jewish family. The work that these comedians are doing at the microphone can make a significant contribution to shifting attitudes toward Jewish women. In Lauren Feldman and Caty Borum's analysis of the social impact of comedy *A Comedian and an Activist Walk into a Bar*, the communications scholars conclude that the intimacy of the comic-audience relationship in stand-up can be a powerful engine for change: "Research in psychology has established the importance of self-disclosure for creating intimacy in interpersonal relationships, a process that can easily be extended to the interaction between stand-up comics and their audiences. The bond developed between a comic and audience is where stand-up comedy derives its greatest potential as an agent of social change and public engagement. Through this bond comes empathy and understanding, which can reduce stigma and foster more positive attitudes."[9]

Feldman and Borum's emphasis on intimacy and self-disclosure as defining features of stand-up comedy speak to the other key element of Jean Carroll's historical significance—which extends beyond the sphere of Jewish performance. As one of the earliest stand-up comics to move away from a presentational "joke-book" style and embrace the more anecdotal, conversational mode that I have called *confidant comedy*, she modeled a form of stand-up that would come to be the industry standard. In the coming years, stand-up comics of all ethnicities and identities would go even deeper into the well of personal and political self-disclosure.

* * *

In Jean Carroll's name, ten millennial comedians were gathered together by Carroll's granddaughter Susan Chatzky, both as a fundraising benefit for Planned Parenthood Hudson Peconic and as an embodied testament to Carroll's legacy. The event, "Dirty Mouths, Dirty Martinis Comedy Night," took place on January 11, 2016, which would have been Carroll's 105th birthday, at Irvington Town Hall Theater in upstate New York. On the cover of the program, under an image of a smiling woman's lips, was large text proclaiming, "This event is held in honor of comedian Jean Carroll."[10]

The evening began with Chatzky introducing and recognizing her grandmother by screening one of her early appearances on *The Ed Sullivan Show*. Following the video were performances by ten women—eight stand-up comics and one musical-comedy duo, all of whom performed with a feminist edge more explicit than anything Jean Carroll had exhibited.[11] For instance, the comedian Jena Friedman ridiculed then-President-Elect Donald Trump, joking that it was unfair for people to compare him to Adolf Hitler: "after all, Hitler served in his country's military and hired female directors." Another comic went after the Republican Party by likening it to "the uncle who says there is no money to go to Disneyworld, until you find out that he went without you." In spite of their more political material and varied ethnic backgrounds, many of the comedians spoke of strong feelings of kinship to Jean Carroll.

The benefit itself came out of Susan Chatzky's sense of social responsibility, a value that she connected directly to her grandmother's legacy.[12] And this philanthropic element of Carroll's legacy intertwined with her legacy as a pioneer of women in comedy, resisting representation by men by standing up and representing herself. "Dirty Mouths, Dirty Martinis" was a night of resisting another version of men representing women—as national policy makers. The event resisted an administration that threatened women's autonomy over their own bodies.

Jean Carroll shared in an interview toward the end of her life that it was not uncommon for women comics to approach her and say things like, "You are our inspiration. Not only your humor, but your courage." Then, she laughed, turning to the interviewer with a conspiratorial tone and guffawing, "Your courage? To go out there and do what I knew I could do as well as any man? Why should I not do it?"[13] But anyone who has ever performed stand-up can attest that it takes courage. Jean Carroll took on stand-up comedy, a strange new form of individual self-expression, unmasked by character or script. It is a form that grabs the audience by the collar and says, "Listen to me! *Show me* that you are listening with your laughter." Jean Carroll made it clear that women were worthy of that platform and of that attention. Stand-up is an empowering form—you might be being laughed at, but you are being seen and heard. In taking her place as "The First Lady of Laughs," Carroll was able to stand up, speak out, and pave the road for future comics. And then, amid the applause, she bid her audience good night, picked up her shopping bag, and took that freshly paved road all the way home.

ACKNOWLEDGMENTS

An analysis of Jean Carroll's "moving monologues" in chapter 5 was previously published in Grace Overbeke, "The Real Mrs. Maisel: Jean Carroll, the First Jewish Female Stand-Up Comedian," *SHOFAR: An Interdisciplinary Journal of Jewish Studies* 39, no. 3 (2021): 154–180; reprinted with permission of Purdue University Press.

This book began when my parents decided to name me Gracie, after Gracie Allen. They wrote a letter to George Burns sharing this news, and he returned it, letting them know that he loved children and was thinking of having a few more. He was only about ninety-five at the time. My parents raised me on cassette tapes of old Burns and Allen radio shows, and for most of my childhood, George Burns's memoir *Gracie: A Love Story* was my favorite bedtime story. Were it not for this unconventional namesake, I may not have found midcentury American comedy to be such a touchstone of Jewish identity. So my first and deepest thanks will always be to my mother, Kathy Kessler Overbeke, and my father, Ned Overbeke, for being such supportive comedy nerds.

The next step to this book came from the mentorship of Ron Jenkins, who oversaw my senior thesis on Jewish female stand-up comedians at Wesleyan University. It was there that I first learned about Jean Carroll from the irrepressible comic Corey Kahaney, in her homage to Jewish female stand-ups, *The J.A.P. Show*. In the years between undergraduate and graduate education, I was encouraged in my study of Jewish performance by illustrious Jewish artistic leaders like Joy Zinoman, Serge Seiden, Ari Roth, and Derek Goldman.

Much of the research for this project took place while I was pursuing an interdisciplinary PhD in theater and drama at Northwestern University. Innumerable thanks are due to my dissertation committee members. My advisor, Susan Manning, has been a force of inspiration, encouragement, critique, challenge, and clarity. She exemplifies the values of scholarship and mentorship, and I am grateful for her generous and insightful feedback. Barry Wimpfheimer has been immeasurably generous offering himself as a source of wisdom not only in Jewish studies but also in the study of comedy. Liz Son helped develop this project from its prospectus stage, pushing with positivity and energy to clarify its objectives and seek its significance. And Lilah Shapiro spent countless hours in her office, mentoring me in the field of sociology and history of Jews in the United States.

Northwestern also supported this work through a number of internal grants and fellowships, including the Mellon Foundation at Northwestern and the Northwestern University Ignition Grant for Graduate Research and the Crown Center for Jewish Studies at Northwestern, led by Claire Sufrin. Dr. Sufrin changed my life when she guided my exploration of the intersection of Jewish studies and feminism and introduced me to the work of Judith Plaskow and Riv-Ellen Prell. This research was greatly aided by Elizabeth Lenaghan and The Writing Place at Northwestern, which provided a number of indispensable services including Interdisciplinary Peer Writing Groups, Dissertation Boot Camps, and one-on-one review sessions with writing mentors.

Other Northwestern faculty who mentored me personally and professionally include Harvey Young, who taught me that "nice, hardworking people can accomplish anything"; Dassia Posner, who taught me to be a dramaturg; Laura Schellhardt, who taught me to work with fearlessness and ferocity; Tracy Davis, who taught me to be a scholar; and Rives Collins, who taught me to love others through storytelling.

This book weaves together stories told not just by documents but by people. I am so grateful to those who have lent their tales to this project. Key among them is Susan Chatzky, the granddaughter of Jean Carroll, who allowed me to photocopy her grandmother's scrapbook, a family heirloom and archival treasure. Moreover, she shared memories of her grandmother that helped bring this storied figure into focus. This work has benefited immeasurably from the generosity of Stephen Meredith Silverman and Diane Krausz, who shared the hard-won interview footage that they gathered for "I Made It Standing Up." Although the documentary was never produced, I hope to continue their great work with this book. The many interview subjects and survey participants who contributed their time and reflections to this book are also an invaluable element in its creation. Michael Kantor, the director, writer, and producer of PBS's documentary *Make 'Em Laugh*, generously shared the transcripts from his interview with Jean Carroll. While the interview may not have made it into his documentary, it was a great asset to this book. And Jane Wollman Rusoff, Jean Carroll's friend and a skilled journalist, was a dedicated email correspondent who generously shared her notes and memories.

This book came to fruition because of the Duke University Perilman Postdoctoral Fellowship. Laura Lieber and Serena Bazemore brought me onto the dream team that is Duke University's Jewish Studies program with such warmth. It was through this fellowship that I was able to facilitate a Manuscript Feedback session with Dr. Lieber as well as two other senior scholars whose writing I have long admired: Heather Nathans and Beth Holmgren. Their input and encouragement showed them to be not only estimable authors but kind and generous mentors.

I am indebted to the professional societies whose mentorship and faculty development initiatives have directly benefited this work. Through the Association for Theatre in Higher Education, the indefatigable Heather Nathans, Donatella Galella, and Kirsten Pullen created the First Book Bootcamp, where I had the great honor of being mentored by Henry Bial, whose work is largely responsible for my going into this field. He proved even more wonderful in "person" (online), helping me to wrestle an outline and book proposal into form with his inimitable wit, expertise, and dramatic flair. He has since been a wise mentor and generous colleague. I am also grateful to Heather Nathans—yes, I have named her twice already, but I could never thank her enough—for spearheading ATHE's many "Wacky" writing weeks.

Not to be outdone, the American Society for Theatre Research has been a consistent source of peer review and support, connecting me to brilliant scholars like Matthew McMahan, Maria DeSimone, and Katelyn Hale Wood, as well as all the other members of the working group in Comedy Studies. It is also through ASTR that I met the legendary editor Liane Fields from the University of Michigan Press, who offered characteristically savvy feedback on my book proposal and sample chapters.

The American Humor Studies Association has also championed my work from its earliest days, providing not only a forum for publication through *Studies in American Humor* but also a network of brilliant comedy scholars. I am especially grateful to Beck Krefting for her work facilitating the AHSA M. Thomas Inge First Book Workshop.

My first conference, and the place that convinced me that scholarship was my path, was the Association for Jewish Studies. I am inexpressibly grateful for the home and support that this conference has provided. Through the AJS's Jordan Schnitzer First Book Publication Award, I was able to work with the exemplary copy editor Beka Bryer and Constance Rosenblum, a development editor who is the rising tide that lifts all boats. Through AJS, I have connected about this book with role models like Riv-Ellen Prell; colleagues like Jennifer Caplan, Debra Caplan (no relation), Tahneer Oksman, Rachel Gordan, Joshua Lambert, and Hannah Schwadron; and exciting peers like Samantha Pickette, Jon Branfman, Thais Miller, and many more than I can name here.

It was also at an AJS conference that I met Jennifer Hammer, the extraordinary editor who shepherded this book to publication. Many, many thanks to her for her support of this project, her careful editing and wise guidance, and her enduring patience as I wrote through a pandemic, childbirth, and a new job. I also want to thank my readers from NYU Press for their astute, insightful, and inspiring feedback. Academic publishing is intense and difficult work, and I am forever grateful to Alexia Traganas, Andrew Katz, and everyone at NYU Press.

I also want to acknowledge my colleagues at Columbia College Chicago. Through Columbia College's faculty development programs, I was able to get a course release to support the completion of this book. My program coordinator, Anne Libera, and my chairs, Peter Carpenter, Carin Silkaitis, Susan Padveen, and Jimmy Noriega, have provided support in the form of both morale boosting and paperwork. Molly Schneider was a generous font of knowledge and readings on midcentury television and media. Khalid Long organized a writing group where he patiently listened as I read selections of this book out loud.

Last, but never least, great thanks to my family and friends, many of whom read messy drafts of large portions of this book, despite it being largely irrelevant to their professions. Karl Miller; my parents-in-love, Doug and Marianne McMunn; and my sister, Romy Overbeke Palan, have offered insightful readings and feedback, and I have been emotionally sustained by the moral support of the entire McKessThomRob-Mugler-Overbeke family. And to my husband, Matthew McMunn, I researched this book while falling in love with and marrying you, proposed it while pregnant with our first child, wrote it throughout his pandemic-ridden infancy, and share it with the world by your side, always mindful that my work does not exist without yours.

NOTES

INTRODUCTION

1 Stephen Silverman, "Print Intros."
2 Stephen Silverman, "I Made It Standing Up" raw footage.
3 Holden, "Laugh Bargains for a Summer Night."
4 Bill Smith, "Caught Again," n.d., Jean Carroll Scrapbook, 53.
5 David Martin, "Mayfair Merry-Go-Round," *London American*, October 26, 1960, Jean Carroll Scrapbook, 77.
6 Hal Boyle, "Feminine Comic Tells Her Woes," *New York Journal*, January 31, 1956, Jean Carroll Scrapbook, 69.
7 Charlie Dawn, "Comedienne Stars in Empire Room Revue," *Chicago American*, October 22, 1953, Jean Carroll Scrapbook, 59.
8 Wollman, "First Lady of Laughs Fifty Years Ago."
9 Quoted in "Moms Mabley."
10 Grossman, *Funny Woman*, 46.
11 Elie, "House Review: RKO, Boston."
12 George Bourke, "Night Life," *Miami Herald*, May 13, 1950, Jean Carroll Scrapbook, 35.
13 Turner Classic Movies, "Martha Raye."
14 Kay Gardella, "Carroll Keeps 'Em Laughing through Comic-Less Season," n.d., Jean Carroll Scrapbook, 49.
15 Carroll, interview by Michael Kantor, 84.
16 This "superiority theory of humor" is most commonly attributed to Thomas Hobbes, due to a few sentences in his *Elements of Law, Natural and Politic*. Specifically, he writes that "the passion of laughter is nothing else but a sudden glory arising from sudden conception of some eminency in ourselves, by comparison with the infirmities of others." Hobbes, *Elements of Law*, 42.
17 Boyle, "Feminine Comic Tells Her Woes."
18 "Jean Carroll to Star in Steel Pier Show."
19 Dorothy Kilgallen, "The Voice of Broadway," 1940, Jean Carroll Scrapbook, 4.
20 Wollman, "First Lady of Laughs Fifty Years Ago."
21 Diller and Buskin, *Like a Lampshade in a Whorehouse*, 131.
22 Diller and Buskin, 131.
23 Stephen Silverman, "Print Intros."
24 Stephen Silverman, "I Made It Standing Up" raw footage

25 Matheny, "Lily Tomlin."

26 Rusoff, "Milton Berle, with Charm and a Mink."

27 Painter Young, "Rap On, Sister."

28 Stephen Silverman, "I Made It Standing Up" raw footage

29 Silverman.

30 Rivers, "Joan Rivers on How Phyllis Diller Paved the Way."

31 Entertainment Buff, "Joan Rivers & Johnny Carson."

32 Kohen, *We Killed*; Fields, *Girl in the Show*.

33 analog36, "Jean Carroll (Stand-Up Comedy)."

34 Sherman-Palladino, "Pilot."

35 IMDb, "Rachel Brosnahan."

36 Soloski, "Did You Hear the One about the Housewife?" I was able to confirm that Brosnahan studied Carroll for the role in a conversation I had with her at a fundraiser for Chicago's Victory Gardens Theatre in 2018.

37 analog36, "Jean Carroll (Stand-Up Comedy)."

38 McGlynn, "What *The Marvelous Mrs. Maisel* Gets Right."

39 Thomas, "7 Female Comedians."

40 Soloski, "(Elegant, Brazen, Brainy) Pioneering Women."

41 Overbeke, "Meet the Real Mrs. Maisel."

42 Gardenswartz, interview by Grace Overbeke.

43 Soloski, "Did You Hear the One about the Housewife?"

44 Nesteroff, "Classic Television Showbiz."

45 Pickette, *Peak TV's Unapologetic Jewish Woman*, 60.

46 Carroll, interview by Stephen Silverman, 4-14.

47 Carroll, interview by Michael Kantor, 86.

48 Stember and American Jewish Committee, *Jews in the Mind of America*.

49 Rusoff, "Notes for Jean Carroll Memorial Service."

50 Spigel, *Make Room for TV*, 147.

51 Hammerman, "Dirty Jews"; Mock, *Jewish Women*.

52 Cohen, "Unkosher Comediennes," 105–106.

53 Antler, "One Clove Away," 123, 125.

54 On a personal note, this fusion of comedy and Jewish identity echoes my own experience. Although I have gone through periods feeling quite at odds with some elements of Jewish theology, my lifelong research on Jewish comedians has led me to identify with Judaism as a culture that binds me to the tradition of family, questioning, and, most importantly, laughter. This puts me in line with larger findings from Pew Research Center's "Portrait of Jewish Americans" study in 2013, which found that 42 percent of the nation's 5.3 million religious and cultural Jews said that a sense of humor is essential to their Jewish identity (as compared to only 19 percent who felt that observing Jewish law was essential to their Jewish identity).

55 Chatzky, interview by Grace Overbeke.

56 "Israel Bond Dinner Raises $175,000," November 1971, Jean Carroll Scrapbook, 73.

57 Chatzky, interview by Grace Overbeke.

58 My use and understanding of the term "recollections" here comes from Hastie, *Cupboards of Curiosity*. In this book, Hastie uses a broad definition of "recollection" that encompasses not only traditional autobiographical texts but also material collections like a dollhouse filled with miniatures, celebrity scrapbooks, and cookbooks by famous actresses and directors. In doing so, she is able to centralize "texts" that—like the women who authored them—had been deemed "tangential" to film history. Jean Carroll, who has been similarly marginalized in theater and comedy studies, "recollects" her story in a similar way, not through an autobiography proper but through a collection of press clippings and interviews.

59 Hastie, *Cupboards of Curiosity*, 30.

60 Hastie, 24.

61 Hastie, 14.

62 Hastie, 74.

63 Hastie, 87.

64 Ware, *Letter to the World*, xviii.

65 Ware, xviii.

66 Hastie, *Cupboards of Curiosity*, 76.

67 Hastie, 28.

68 Hastie, 89.

69 In chapter 6, I return to a more thorough examination of how the scrapbook's curation subtly but consistently documents ongoing tensions between Carroll's life as a "star" and her role as a mother.

70 In order to examine trade publications, I used ProQuest's Entertainment Industry Magazine Archive, which encompasses periodicals like *Variety*, *Billboard*, and several others from throughout the United States and the United Kingdom. In order to explore Jewish publications, I used a temporary membership to ProQuest's Historical Newspapers American Jewish Newspapers, which includes the *American Hebrew and Jewish Messenger*, the *Jewish Advocate*, the *American Israelite*, and the *Jewish Exponent*. I also made use of Carnegie Mellon University's Pittsburgh Jewish Newspaper Project, which offers over one hundred years of digitized, searchable copies of Pittsburgh-based Jewish newspapers. Additionally, I used the open-source online database Historical Jewish Press to examine English-language papers including *The Forward*, the *American Jewish Advocate*, and the *B'nai B'rith Messenger*, among others. And in order to research mainstream American publications, I used ProQuest's Historical Newspapers database, which includes the *New York Times*, the *Chicago Tribune*, the *Los Angeles Times*, the *Washington Post*, and more.

71 Manning, *Modern Dance*, xviii.

72 Alfred Albelli and Harry Schlegel, "Comedienne Caught with Mate, Says EX," March 1954, sec. News Daily, Lester Sweyd Collection; Gabriel Prevor, "The Love

Rivals Said: 'Let's Be Civilized'—Then Wham!," *Sunday Mirror Magazine*, October 28, 1954, Lester Sweyd Collection; "Ex-Model Loses $25,000 Action: Jury Votes Out Suit against Jean Carroll," n.d., Lester Sweyd Collection.

73 Novick, *Beyond the Golden Door*; Erdman, *Staging the Jew*; Nathans, *Hideous Characters*; Bial, *Acting Jewish*; Most, *Making Americans*.
74 "Actors' Temple Benefit."
75 Hammerman, "Dirty Jews," 65.
76 Mock, *Jewish Women*.
77 Laurie, "Review-Preview."
78 "Ashkenormative" is a term describing the normalization of eastern European Jews, as opposed to Jews coming from Sephardic or other backgrounds.

CHAPTER 1. "YOU'RE JEAN CARROLL"

1 Carroll, interview by Stephen Silverman, 1-6.
2 Carroll, 1-6.
3 Carroll, 1-6.
4 Carroll, interview by Michael Kantor, 63.
5 Carroll, interview by Stephen Silverman, 1-6.
6 Wollman, "First Lady of Laughs Fifty Years Ago."
7 Carroll, interview by Stephen Silverman, 1-7.
8 Carroll, 1-7.
9 Jewish Virtual Library, "New York City."
10 Roediger, *Working toward Whiteness*.
11 Zielonka and Wechman, *Eager Immigrants*, 78.
12 Wenger, *Jewish Americans*, 201.
13 Carroll, interview by Stephen Silverman, 1-12.
14 Wollman, "First Lady of Laughs Fifty Years Ago."
15 Carroll, interview by Michael Kantor, 1–2. Carroll gave an English approximation of this Yiddish expression, used when someone cannot stop laughing. Carroll said, "Actually, what she said was, 'the fool is pushing you.' That was in Yiddish. The translation comes out nonsense." Thanks to Paula Teitelbaum and the Facebook "Yiddish Research" group for their assistance in this query.
16 Carroll, interview by Stephen Silverman, 1-12–1-13.
17 Wollman, "First Lady of Laughs Fifty Years Ago."
18 Hyman, *Gender and Assimilation*.
19 Prell, *Fighting to Become Americans*, 37.
20 Carroll, interview by Stephen Silverman, 1-13.
21 Carroll, 1-13.
22 Carroll, 1-11.
23 Carroll, 1-11.
24 Carroll, 1-11.
25 Carroll, 1-11.

26 Glickman, *Consumer Society*, 154.

27 Carroll, interview by Stephen Silverman, 1-15–1-16.

28 Rusoff, "Milton Berle, with Charm and a Mink."

29 Limon, *Stand-Up Comedy in Theory*, 110.

30 Vaudeville lore often mentions that stage managers kept a large hook backstage that they would use to pull the bad performers off the stage.

31 Carroll, interview by Stephen Silverman, 1-17–1-19.

32 Carroll, 1-19–1-20.

33 Carroll, 1-20.

34 Smith, *Vaudevillians*.

35 Carroll, interview by Michael Kantor, 46.

36 Carroll, 47.

37 Carroll, interview by Stephen Silverman, 1-21.

38 Carroll, 1-21.

39 Nadell, *American Jewish Women's History*, 123.

40 Nadell, 122.

41 Wollman, "First Lady of Laughs Fifty Years Ago." Examining memoirs from early film stars like Lillian Gish, Mary Pickford, and Ethel Waters, Amelie Hastie's *Cupboards of Curiosity* notes a pattern of "a romantic, or at least classic, narrative of success out of poverty (interestingly, often to make up for the loss of the father)" (76). As examples, Hastie cites how Mary Pickford wrote (in her 1934 memoir) about being "cheated out of any real childhood" and Ethel Waters opened her 1951 memoir, "I never was a child" (77). So Carroll's declaration follows a tradition established by the women who were stars when Carroll was coming of age.

42 Snyder, *Voice of the City*.

43 According to the seasoned vaudevillean George Burns's memoir *All My Best Friends*, bookers tended to follow a set formula when setting up a show. First was a "dumb act," like trained animals or jugglers, which had no speaking. Next was a singing or dancing act, followed by a sketch. Fourth and fifth were the headlining spots, followed by an intermission. The sixth act, also called "opening intermission," was the largest act on the bill, sometimes called the "flash act." Seventh was the star spot, and eighth and final was another dumb act. See Burns and Fisher, *All My Best Friends*, 46–57.

44 Kibler, *Rank Ladies*, 85.

45 Bell, "New Shows This Week."

46 Con, "New Shows This Week."

47 Ibee, "New Shows This Week."

48 Ibee; Bell, "New Shows This Week."

49 Bell, "New Shows This Week."

50 "Plays and Photoplays."

51 Bell, "New Shows This Week"; Ibee, "New Shows This Week."

52 Rogin, *Blackface, White Noise*, 5.

53 Grossman, *Funny Woman*, 30.

54 Grossman, 30.

55 Rogin, *Blackface, White Noise*, 13.

56 Rogin, 56. While many scholars accepted his thesis, others did not; see Rosenberg, "Rogin's Noise."

57 Burns and Fisher, *All My Best Friends*, 53.

58 Dorinson, *Kvetching and Shpritzing*, 34.

59 Dorinson, 31.

60 Mintz, "Humor and Ethnic Stereotypes," 23.

61 Wollman, "First Lady of Laughs Fifty Years Ago."

62 Carroll, interview by Stephen Silverman, 1-7.

63 "Silberman Adds Three Acts."

64 Smith, *Vaudevillians*, 253–254.

65 Carroll, interview by Michael Kantor, 4.

66 Carroll, 6.

67 Carroll, 6.

68 Smith, *Vaudevillians*, 253–254.

69 Quoted in S. Levy, *In on the Joke*, 71.

70 Wollman, "First Lady of Laughs Fifty Years Ago."

71 Laurie, "Vaude-Nite Clubs."

72 Smith, *Vaudevillians*, 255–256.

73 The Yiddish term "chutzpah" means extreme self-confidence or audacity.

74 "Chicago" (1930).

75 "Vaude House Reviews: New Acts."

76 "Vaude House Reviews: New Acts."

77 Carroll, interview by Stephen Silverman, 2-1.

78 McConnell, "Pictures."

79 Odec, "Vaude House Reviews."

80 "Variety House Review"; "Vaude House Reviews: RKO Hillstreet, L.A."; Odec, "Vaude House Reviews."

81 Chic, "Reviews."

82 Odec, "Pictures."

83 "Vaude House Reviews: RKO Hillstreet, L.A."; "Variety House Review."

84 "Vaude House Reviews: New Acts."

85 "Advertisement."

86 Carroll, interview by Stephen Silverman, 2-3-2-4.

87 Land, "Film House Reviews."

88 Leny, "Variety House Reviews."

89 Char, "Outdoors"; Chic, "Reviews."

90 Land, "Film House Reviews."

91 "Vaude House Reviews: Orpheum, Denver"; Odac, "Variety House Reviews."

92 Odac, "Variety House Reviews."

93 Trav S.D., "Stars of Vaudeville #420,"

94 Trav S.D.

95 Carroll, interview by Stephen Silverman, 2-7.

96 Carroll, 2-8.

97 S. Levy, *In on the Joke*, 75.

98 Carroll, interview by Stephen Silverman, 2-8.

99 Carroll, 2-9.

100 Rusoff, "Notes for Jean Carroll Memorial Service."

101 Smith, *Vaudevillians*, 257.

102 Wollman, "First Lady of Laughs Fifty Years Ago."

103 Smith, *Vaudevillians*, 18.

104 Scho, "Vaudeville: New Acts."

105 Smith, *Vaudevillians*, 18.

106 Smith, 256.

107 Carroll, interview by Stephen Silverman, 2-21.

108 Chatzky, interview by Grace Overbeke.

109 Carroll, interview by Stephen Silverman, 2-23.

110 Smith, *Vaudevillians*, 257. In a separate interview with Stephen Silverman, Carroll gave more details of the journey's timeline, explaining, "Initially, we did the Palladium and one or two other places and came back. Went back four weeks later, four weeks later for what was supposed to be a two-week gig, stayed three and a half years." Carroll, interview by Stephen Silverman, 2-23.

111 Tunick, interview by Stephen Silverman, 2-2.

112 Burns, *Gracie*, 75–76.

113 Smith, *Vaudevillians*, 18.

114 Smith, 18.

115 Carroll, interview by Stephen Silverman, 2-19–2-20.

116 "Carroll and Howe (aka Garroll and Lowe)."

117 Burns, *Gracie*, 45–46.

118 Horowitz, *Queens of Comedy*.

119 Goldman, "Resurgence of Antisemitism."

120 Scho, "House Review"; "House Review."

121 Gold, "Vaudeville."

122 Loop, "House Review"; Scho, "House Review."

123 Burns, *Gracie*.

124 Burm, "House Review: Hipp, Balto" (1941).

125 United Service Organizations, "Our History."

126 Sahu, "Reviews."

127 "Vaudeville: USO-Camp Shows Casts."

128 Jean Carroll and Buddy Howe, "Comedy Team Sees USO Tour as Build-Up for Talent after War," *Billboard*, July 24, 1943, Jean Carroll Scrapbook, 5.

129 Smith, *Vaudevillians*.

130 Sahu, "Reviews."

131 Burm, "House Review: Hullabaloo."

132 Sahu, "Reviews."

133 Sahu.

134 "Uncle Sam's Callboard."

135 Carroll, interview by Stephen Silverman, 2-11.

136 Carroll, 2-12.

137 Hold, "House Review." Carroll's decision to perform stories in a Yiddish dialect is particularly notable given the success of Fanny Brice, who had become a successful comedienne largely through her parodic songs, delivered in a thick (and fake) Yiddish accent. However, it seems that this Yiddish storyteller persona was short-lived, for no other reviews of this period refer to a Yiddish dialect.

138 Burm, "House Review: Hipp. Balto" (1944).

139 Carroll, interview by Stephen Silverman, 2-12.

140 Unterbrink, *Funny Women*, 215.

141 Tafoya, *Legacy of the Wisecrack*, 203.

142 Nesteroff, *Comedians*.

143 "Pictures Grosses."

144 Kibler, *Rank Ladies*, 110.

CHAPTER 2. A WOMAN IN THE STAND-UP "FRATERNITY"

1 Laurie, "Review-Preview."

2 Hammerstein, "Pictures."

3 Laskow and Rosenberg, *Welcome to Kutsher's*.

4 Holson, "Catskills Are Back."

5 "Display Ad 7."

6 Nesteroff, *Comedians*, 74.

7 Nesteroff, 73.

8 "Display Ad 18"; "Stevensville Lake Hotel to Feature Name Talent"; "Laurel Club Plans Comics."

9 Carroll, interview by Stephen Silverman, 2-16.

10 "Photograph: Playhouse Foursome," n.d., Jean Carroll Scrapbook, 59.

11 Tunick, interview by Stephen Silverman, 2-8, 2-9.

12 Nesteroff, *Comedians*, 75.

13 Nesteroff, 74.

14 Carroll, interview by Stephen Silverman, 2-16.

15 Carroll, 2-17.

16 Carroll, interview by Michael Kantor, 32.

17 A "tummler" was a cross between a stand-up and an emcee who kept Catskills guests entertained.

18 Bennett, *Theatre Audiences*, 139.

19 Carroll, interview by Stephen Silverman, 2-16.

20 Carroll, 4-14.

21 Jarski, *Funniest Thing*; Unterbrink, *Funny Women*; M. Fox, "Jean Carroll."

22 Carroll, interview by Stephen Silverman, 4-14.

23 Carroll, 4-16, 4-17.

24 Quoted in Burns and Fisher, *All My Best Friends*, 178.

25 Weinstein, *Eddie Cantor Story*, 114.

26 "3 Jewish Groups Unite for Refugees." The United Jewish Appeal actually supported refugee relocation to a number of places other than Palestine. The UJA united three organizations that funded three different immigration paths for refugees. The United Palestine Appeal funded immigration and settlement in Palestine, the National Coordinating Committee Fund dealt with German refugees coming to the United States, and the Joint Distribution Committee dealt with German and Austrian refugees in other parts of Europe.

27 "Vaudeville: 'Night of Stars.'"

28 "Vaudeville: Talent Problem."

29 Weiss, "Bostonian on Broadway."

30 "Hillel Academy Celebration."

31 "Pictorial Picks."

32 "Extravaganza Aids Memorial Hospital"; "Photo Standalone 14."

33 "Talented New Comedienne to Appear at Carousel."

34 Carroll, interview by Stephen Silverman, 4-14.

35 Nesteroff, *Comedians*, 75.

36 Nesteroff, 26.

37 Burns, *Gracie*.

38 Carroll, interview by Stephen Silverman, 2-6.

39 Ben Gross, "Listening In," 1940, Jean Carroll Scrapbook, 4; Dorothy Kilgallen, "The Voice of Broadway," 1940, Jean Carroll Scrapbook, 4.

40 Gross, "Listening In."

41 Old Time Radio Catalog, "Sealtest Village Store."

42 Bea Pepan, "Jean Carroll: Nonstop Talker," *Milwaukee Journal*, January 8, 1961, Jean Carroll Scrapbook, 79.

43 "New York."

44 National Broadcasting Corporation, Inc., "NBC Western Program Service," July 15, 1945, Jean Carroll Scrapbook, 10.

45 Old Time Radio Catalog, "Sealtest Village Store."

46 Carroll, interview by Michael Kantor, 84.

47 Old Time Radio Catalog, "Sealtest Village Store."

48 Sands, "Too Funny"; Sands, "Great."

49 Nesteroff, *Comedians*, 76–77.

50 Berger, *Jewish Jesters*, 54–57.

51 For more on this, see Prell, *Fighting to Become Americans*.

52 Museum of Broadcasting, "Tomlin on Her Comedic Influences," December 19, 1990, Jean Carroll Scrapbook, 85.

53 Smith, "Night Clubs-Vaudeville."

54 Jose, "House Review: State. N.Y."

55 Edba, "House Review."

56 R.C.H., "Glenn Rendezvous," October 30, 1948, Jean Carroll Scrapbook, 27.

57 Mizejewski, *Pretty/Funny*, 5

58 In *Pretty/Funny: Women Comedians and Body Politics*, Mizejewski traces a lineage of female comics that begins with the Ziegfeld Follies, in which comedians like Fannie Brice and Sophie Tucker foregrounded their bodily abnormalities in their humor, alongside the Chitlin Circuit, where Moms Mabley used her Blackness and faux age to comic effect, and Mae West, whose transgressively abundant figure was central to her act. It is easy to draw a line from these performers, whose shortcomings in "prettiness" were prime comic fodder, to the women often credited with being the first female stand-up comics: Phyllis Diller and Joan Rivers. Both Diller and Rivers used humor based on a kind of flamboyant self-loathing, primarily appearance related. This narrative allows Mizejewski to position her millennial case studies—including Kathy Griffin, Tina Fey, Sarah Silverman, Margaret Cho, Wanda Sykes, and Ellen DeGeneres—as products of both second- and third-wave feminism, who "resisted and lampooned" the pretty/funny dynamic. Mizejewski also acknowledges Jean Carroll, mentioning her in several sentences of the introduction. She quotes Carroll's obituary asserting that doing comic monologues "in a shimmering evening dress, dripping diamonds and mink . . . was in itself subversive" and asserts that Carroll's brand of humor was a "shock tactic" that "relied on a belief that a glamorous woman was supposed to show up in a nightclub as a showgirl or singer, not a joker" (5). While "shock"—or at least incongruity—may have been part of Carroll's humor, I argue that her humor was less about the shock of incongruity than it was about resisting the binary, leveraging the power of "prettiness" into the power to be funny.

59 J.B.T., "Pin-Down Girl Steals Show at State," *Hartford Times*, n.d., Jean Carroll Scrapbook, 7.

60 "Varied Program Currently Offered on State's Stage," *Hartford Daily Courant*, March 11, 1944, Jean Carroll Scrapbook, 9.

61 H.K., "Temple's Show Wins Applause," n.d., Jean Carroll Scrapbook, 7; M.O.C., "Guy Lombardo and Crew Back on State Stage," n.d., Jean Carroll Scrapbook, 10.

62 M. Oakley Christoph, "Informing You," *Hartford Daily Courant*, March 11, 1944, Jean Carroll Scrapbook, 9.

63 "Jean Carroll Does a Man's Job as Comic," n.d., Jean Carroll Scrapbook, 3.

64 Mike, "Vaudeville."

65 Mal Hallett, "Mal Hallett at Earle," n.d., Jean Carroll Scrapbook, 8.

66 Stephen Silverman, "I Made It Standing Up" raw footage.

67 Jean Carroll headshot, n.d., Jean Carroll Scrapbook, 11.

68 A.D., "Chatter!," n.d., Jean Carroll Scrapbook, 3.

69 Rivers, *What Becomes a Semi-Legend Most?*

70 Quoted in A. McCracken, "Study of a Mad Housewife," 55.

71 Rothstein, "Henny Youngman."

72 Erickson, *From Radio to the Big Screen*, 130.

73 Arnold Russell, "Rapid Fire Wit," n.d., Jean Carroll Scrapbook, 61.

74 "Jean Carroll Does a Man's Job as Comic."

75 Herm, "House Review."

76 Nachman, *Seriously Funny*, 215.

77 This sexist inclination to gender stand-up comedy as an inherently masculine form has proven remarkably enduring. A (relatively) contemporary instance of its continuation is Christopher Hitchens's January 2007 article in *Vanity Fair* titled "Why Women Aren't Funny," in which he wrote, "Women do not find their own physical decay and absurdity to be so riotously amusing, which is why we admire Lucille Ball and Helen Fielding, who do see the funny side of it. But this is so rare as to be like Dr. Johnson's comparison of a woman preaching to a dog walking on its hind legs: the surprise is that it is done at all." His central thesis, that women are evolutionarily ill equipped for comedy because their attractive physical form does not require them to compensate with attributes like humor, is argued with the credibility and intellectual acumen of a Reddit troll.

78 Jose, "Pictures."

79 Riess, "Cyclical History of Horse Racing."

80 "Racing at Monticello," *Middletown Daily Record*, July 13, 1960, Jean Carroll Scrapbook, 77.

81 Assouly, "Gambling and Women Don't Mix."

82 Assouly.

83 Jose, "Pictures"; "Night Clubs-Vaudeville: Vaudeville Reviews"; Bill Smith, "Capitol, New York," n.d., Jean Carroll Scrapbook, 32.

84 Lary, "House Reviews"; Jose, "House Review: Paramount, N.Y."

85 As of the implementation of the Code in 1952, it specifically banned the advertising of "tip sheets" and "race track publications" and mandated that representations of gambling be restricted to "scenes necessary to the development of plot or as appropriate background" and only "when presented with discretion and in moderation, and in a manner which would not excite interest in, or foster betting, nor be instructional in nature." National Association of Radio and Television Broadcasters, "Television Code." Although Carroll's racetrack routine was far from instructional, it did not relegate gambling to "background," and it may well have excited interest.

86 *Toast of the Town*, January 30, 1949.

87 A "tout" is a person who gives tips on racehorses, usually with the expectation of reward.

88 *Toast of the Town*, January 16, 1949.

89 Jose, "Television Reviews."

90 *Toast of the Town*, January 16, 1949.

91 Lewis Funke, "Lauritz Melchior Heads New Bill of Variety at Palace Theatre," n.d., Jean Carroll Scrapbook, 57.

92 Nesteroff, *Comedians*, 79.

93 "London," n.d., Jean Carroll Scrapbook, 61.

94 "After Dark," n.d., Jean Carroll Scrapbook, <PAGE NO.>.

95 "Evening Express," n.d., Jean Carroll Scrapbook, 61; Russell, "Rapid Fire Wit."

96 Clifford Davis, "Six Laughs a Minute!," *Daily Mirror*, May 12, 1953, Jean Carroll Scrapbook, 61.

97 Wood, "House Review."

98 Jose, "House Review: Capitol, N.Y."

99 "The Olympia—A Review," n.d., Jean Carroll Scrapbook, 31.

100 "Comics Receive Awards."

101 "Jean Carroll Hits Handicap of Femininity."

CHAPTER 3. "THE FIRST LADY OF LAUGHS"

1 Davis, *Jews and Booze*.

2 Abel, "Dying Nite Clubs."

3 Abel.

4 "Cabarets"; "Chicago: All for Ike Bloom!"

5 Abel, "Night Clubs."

6 Nesteroff, *Comedians*, 58.

7 Nesteroff, 58.

8 "Night Clubs-Vaudeville: Night Club Reviews—La Conga"; "Miscellany: 'Bugsy' Siegel."

9 Sadowsky, *Wedded to Crime*.

10 G. Fox, "Writer Appalled by Jewish Gamblers."

11 Les Rees, "Chatter"; Greene, "My Favorite Jokes."

12 Valcourt, "Shecky Greene Discusses Frank Sinatra."

13 Nesteroff, *Comedians*, 67.

14 Nesteroff, 138.

15 Phillips, "Joe E. Lewis."

16 Kuntz, "Word for Word."

17 Greene, "My Favorite Jokes."

18 B. Weber, "Alan King."

19 King, *Alan King's Great Jewish Joke Book*, 35–36.

20 Carroll, interview by Michael Kantor, 10.

21 Cook, "Woman Comic."

22 Boyle, "Feminine Comic Tells Her Woes."

23 Hunt, "House Review."

24 Jose, "Vaudeville."

25 Nesteroff, *Comedians*, 55.

26 Carroll, interview by Stephen Silverman, 3-21–3-23.

27 "Night Clubs-Vaudeville: Night Club Reviews—Chez Paree."

28 Miller et al., *Entertainment Excerpts*. This is not a word-for-word transcript, because the policy at the New York Public Library for the Performing Arts, Dorothy and Lewis B. Cullman Center does not allow recordings, pausing the record, or playing records multiple times, so my notes had to come from hearing it twice through with no pausing.

29 Austin, "Great American Supper Club."

30 By the 1950s, Podell relaxed his "no-Black" policy as far as bookings went.

31 "Personal Appearances."

32 Abel, "Night Club Reviews."

33 Abel.

34 "Intersectionality," a term popularized by the legal scholar Kimberlé Crenshaw, was introduced in Crenshaw's "Mapping the Margins." It points out that social categories such as race, class, and gender are interconnected and overlapping.

35 Prell, *Fighting to Become Americans*, 146.

36 Prell, 163.

37 Prell, 165.

38 Antler, *Jewish Radical Feminism*, 243.

39 Nadell, *American Jewish Women's History*, 202.

40 Antler, *Jewish Radical Feminism*, 251.

41 Cited in Prell, *Fighting to Become Americans*, 173.

42 "Jean Carroll Hits Handicap of Femininity."

43 Boyle, "Feminine Comic Tells Her Woes."

44 George Bourke, "Night Life," *Miami Herald*, May 13, 1950, Jean Carroll Scrapbook, 35.

45 Kay Gardella, "Carroll Keeps 'Em Laughing through Comic-Less Season," n.d., Jean Carroll Scrapbook, 49.

46 Boyle, "Feminine Comic Tells Her Woes."

47 Dorothy Kilgallen, "The Voice of Broadway," 1940, Jean Carroll Scrapbook, 4.

48 James Green, "The First Lady of Laughs," October 13, 1960, Jean Carroll Scrapbook, 47.

49 Boyle, "Feminine Comic Tells Her Woes."

50 Edmund Leahy, "Jean Can Laugh at Herself," *New York World Telegram and Sun*, May 5, 1951, Jean Carroll Scrapbook, 52.

51 Jean Carroll, "The Voice of Broadway: Comedienne's Material Only Part of the Act," n.d., Jean Carroll Scrapbook, 72.

52 Boyle, "Feminine Comic Tells Her Woes"

53 Carroll, interview by Michael Kantor, 35–36.

54 The genealogy of the "buying a dress" routine could perhaps be a book unto itself. As a simple tale of a reluctant shopper falling victim to the

manipulations of an over-the-top shopkeeper, it shares a plot with a number of older comedy routines, ranging from the monologist Beatrice Hereford's *In the Hat Department* (1937) to Eddie Cantor's "Joe's Blue Front" in the *Midnight Rounders* vaudeville variety show where he and Carroll both launched their careers.

55 "Night Clubs-Vaudeville: Vaudeville Reviews."
56 "Jean Carroll Hits Handicap of Femininity."
57 Morreall, "Philosophy of Humor"; Boyle, "Feminine Comic Tells Her Woes."
58 Les, "Night Club Reviews.
59 Bill Smith, "Caught Again," n.d., Jean Carroll Scrapbook, 53.
60 Jack Smith, "Jean Carroll to Spice Harvest Moon Menu," *Daily News*, September 5, 1955, Jean Carroll Scrapbook, 59.
61 Tomlin, interview by Stephen Silverman, 7-1-12.
62 Zweibel, interview by Stephen Silverman.
63 Timothy White, quoted in Brodie, *Vulgar Art*, 164.
64 Brodie, 52.
65 Brodie, 52.
66 Simon, "After Years of Ranting."
67 "Night Clubs-Vaudeville: In Short."
68 Carroll, "Female of the Species."
69 "There's No Rattle in Jean's Skeleton," n.d., Jean Carroll Scrapbook, 46.
70 Charlie Dawn, "Comedienne Stars in Empire Room Revue," *Chicago American*, October 22, 1953, Jean Carroll Scrapbook, 59.
71 B. Smith, "Caught Again."
72 Spigel, *Make Room for TV*, back cover.
73 Pringle and Pringle, "Congress vs. the Plunging Neckline."
74 Murray, "Television Wipes Its Feet."
75 Murray, 131.
76 C. McCracken, "Regulating Swish," 363.
77 Rosen, "Television."
78 Nachman, *Right Here on Our Stage Tonight!*, 21.
79 Pringle and Pringle, "Congress vs. the Plunging Neckline," 49.
80 Corry, "American Censored."
81 Murray, "Television Wipes Its Feet," 129.
82 Pringle and Pringle, "Congress vs. the Plunging Neckline," 49.
83 Dale Stevens, "Amusements: The Funny Gal," *Dayton (OH) News*, January 2, 1954, Jean Carroll Scrapbook, 64.
84 "Personal Appearances."
85 "Untitled, 'TV Guest Shots,'" n.d., Jean Carroll Scrapbook, 12.
86 IMDb, "Jean Carroll"; "Television Review."
87 Untitled article, n.d., Jean Carroll Scrapbook, 12.
88 Spigel, *Make Room for TV*, 145.

89 However, Dinah Shore, another assimilated Jewish woman who was a singer and not a comedian, found great success with *The Dinah Shore Show*, which began on NBC in November 1951, just seven months after Carroll's failed pilot.

90 "Radio-Television: Jean Carroll to Have Own Show."

91 "Television: On-the-Air Audition."

92 Gilb, "Television Reviews."

93 Gilb.

94 Gilb.

95 Gilb.

96 Leahy, "Jean Can Laugh at Herself."

97 "Miscellany: Jean Carroll Pacts."

98 "Miscellany: Jean Carroll Pacts."

CHAPTER 4. "TAKE IT FROM ME" (AND THEY DID)

1 *Sunshine*, n.d., Jean Carroll Scrapbook, 6.

2 Carroll, interview by Stephen Silverman, 4-6.

3 Jane Wollman, "First Lady of Laughs," *Sunshine: The Magazine of South Florida*, June 16, 1991, Jean Carroll Scrapbook, 40–44.

4 Wollman.

5 Wollman.

6 Storrs, "McCarthyism and the Second Red Scare."

7 Storrs.

8 Nicholson, *Labor's Story*, 251.

9 Litvak, *Un-Americans*, 156.

10 Stabile, quoted in Berke, *Their Own Best Creations*, 33.

11 Lipsitz, "Meaning of Memory." In "The Meaning of Memory: Family, Class, and Ethnicity in Early Network Television Programs," the cultural anthropologist George Lipsitz points out that a handful of working-class ethnic sitcoms (*The Goldbergs, Mama, Life with Luigi*, and a few others) were popular on major networks. However, he notes that the ethnic dimensions of these programs had been largely sanitized, divorced from history and politics. Instead, these shows' ethnic dimensions functioned as a nostalgic invocation of the past, used to legitimize the program so that it could more effectively inculcate viewers into consumerism.

12 Spigel, *Make Room for TV*, 144.

13 Spigel, 152.

14 Gould, "TV's Top Comediennes."

15 Berke, *Their Own Best Creations*, 3.

16 Madelyn Pugh memoirs, quoted in Berke, 46.

17 Quoted in Berke, 55.

18 According to the *Encyclopedia Britannica*, Gertrude Berg took a playwriting extension course at Columbia University in December 1918. See "Gertrude

Berg." I am referencing Berg's decision to stand with her onscreen husband Philip Loeb, who was blacklisted. She threatened to criticize her sponsor, General Foods, unless it allowed her to keep Loeb, and in response, her show was canceled by CBS. For more on this, see Armstrong, *When Women Invented Television*.

19 Frank Brookhouser, "Jean Carroll Plans 'Casual' TV Show," 1952, Jean Carroll Scrapbook, 64.
20 Brookhouser.
21 Brookhouser.
22 "Radio-Television: Adams' ABC-TV Sponsored Quizzer."
23 Carroll, interview by Stephen Silverman, 4-6; "Radio-Television: Agronsky's 'At Issue.'"
24 Rusoff, "First Mrs. Maisel"; Wollman, "First Lady of Laughs Fifty Years Ago."
25 Carroll, interview by Michael Kantor, 59; Rusoff, "First Mrs. Maisel."
26 Rusoff, "First Mrs. Maisel."
27 "Radio-Television: Dick Linkroum Set."
28 "Radio-Television: Dick Linkroum Set."
29 Rusoff, "First Mrs. Maisel."
30 Ty Key, "Jean Carroll Wants Bigger, Better Show," *Scranton (PA) Tribune*, December 23, 1953, Jean Carroll Scrapbook, 66.
31 Carroll, interview by Stephen Silverman, 3-11.
32 Carroll, interview by Michael Kantor, 60.
33 Rusoff, "First Mrs. Maisel."
34 "Radio-Television: ABC Feels Way."
35 "Radio-Television: Jean Carroll Put on Ice."
36 Carroll, interview by Michael Kantor, 62.
37 Carroll, 59.
38 Gros, "Television Review."
39 "Script 11 'Take It from Me,'" November 11, 1953, 1–2, folder 11, box 377, Steven H. Scheuer Collection.
40 "Script 11 'Take It from Me,'" 21.
41 "Script 11 'Take It from Me,'" 36.
42 "Reviews: Program of the Week—Take It from Me," *TV Guide*, December 25, 1953, Jean Carroll Scrapbook, 65.
43 Gros, "Television Review."
44 Harriet Van Horne, "Jean Carroll Show Is Series of Jokes," n.d., Jean Carroll Scrapbook, 68.
45 Van Horne.
46 Gros, "Television Review."
47 Roland Lindbloom, "Wednesdays Packed with Good TV Fare," *Newark Evening News*, November 5, 1953, Jean Carroll Scrapbook, 67.
48 Gould, "Television in Review."

49 "Script 5 'Take It from Me,'" January 13, 1954, 8, folder 5, box 378, Steven H. Scheuer Collection.

50 Lindbloom, "Wednesdays Packed with Good TV Fare."

51 Herm, "Television Reviews."

52 Gardner, "Self-Referentiality in Art."

53 Bernie Harrison, "Scene and Heard: New Video Entries Feature Some Old Hands at Comedy," n.d., Jean Carroll Scrapbook, 67.

54 Gros, "Television Review."

55 "Reviews: Program of the Week—Take It from Me."

56 Bernstein, "Acting Live."

57 Gould, "Television in Review."

58 Gould.

59 Van Horne, "Jean Carroll Show Is Series of Jokes."

60 Harrison, "Scene and Heard."

61 "On the Television Scene," *Kansas City Star*, November 29, 1953, Jean Carroll Scrapbook, 68.

62 "Cue: Comedienne Jean Carroll Is Delightful in New Series," November 28, 1953, Jean Carroll Scrapbook, 62.

63 Spigel, *Make Room for TV*.

64 Martin and Segrave, *Women in Comedy*, 296.

65 Executives on network sitcoms went to great lengths to enforce gender norms regarding "appropriate" roles for women. In "The Meaning of Memory," Lipsitz notes that the novel on which the television program *Mama* was based depicted Mama using her skills as a cook to "make social connections that allow [her daughter] Katrin to pursue an untraditional career as a writer." However, in the televised version, "Mama instructs Katrin about cooking to help her land a husband, and Katrin becomes a secretary rather than a writer" (372). In 1956, the sitcom *Father Knows Best* featured an entire episode ("Betty, Girl Engineer") in which the eldest daughter learns to give up her passion for engineering (despite scoring well on aptitude tests) in order to be more attractive to a young man who believes that women ought not be engineers. Messages discouraging women from deviating from prescribed social roles were not just implicit; they were plotlines. In this media landscape, Jean Carroll's unconventional conceit of using direct address to broadcast her discontents about housewifery to viewers is shocking.

66 Spigel, *Make Room for TV*, 154.

67 "Script 11 'Take It from Me,'" 5.

68 In "The Meaning of Memory," Lipsitz offers an oppositional reading of midcentury sitcoms, pointing out that some of them *did* acknowledge familial tensions like the "father absent–mother present gender roles of the nuclear family" (367). Wives' frustrations with their husbands' inability to provide them with leisure time and luxury sometimes served as points of conflict or sources of comedy. Lipsitz posits that the historical shift from families as extended kinship networks

in the 1940s to nuclear units in the 1950s prompted anxiety that viewers appreci-
ated seeing reflected in television programming. However, the desire to speak to
the audiences' true circumstances had to be weighed against television's primary
job as a "mediator between the family and the economy." As Lipsitz concludes,
"the creators of television programs had to touch on real issues, albeit in truncated and idealized form" (368). And so even a show as combative as *The
Honeymooners* might end with "a humbled Ralph Kramden telling Alice, 'Baby,
you're the greatest'" (368).

69 Carroll, interview by Michael Kantor, 60.
70 "Script 11 'Take It from Me,'" 11.
71 "Script 2 'Take It from Me,'" December 9, 1953, 2, folder 2, box 378, Steven H.
    Scheuer Collection.
72 "Script 5 'Take It from Me.'"
73 "Script 11 'Take It from Me.'"
74 "Script 12 'Take It from Me,'" November 18, 1953, 12, folder 12, box 377, Steven H.
    Scheuer Collection.
75 Key, "Jean Carroll Wants Bigger, Better Show."
76 Key.
77 Key.
78 Tolstoy, *Anna Karenina*, 1.
79 Lipsitz, "Meaning of Memory," 362.
80 IMDb, "Arnie Rosen."
81 Grimes, "Coleman Jacoby."
82 YIVO Institute for Jewish Research, "ARTEF Arbeter Teater Farband."
83 Museum of Yiddish Theater, "Maurice Schwartz's Yiddish Art Theatre."
84 D. Caplan, "Six Degrees of Yankev Blayfer."
85 Feuer, "Laughter through Tears."
86 Dauber, *Jewish Comedy*, xvi.
87 Howe, "Nature of Jewish Laughter."
88 Kanfer, *Stardust Lost*. In 1939, Maurice Shwartz's Yiddish Art Theatre adapted
    Sholem Aleichem's stories of Tevye the Dairyman into a full-length play called
    Tevye, which was such a success that it was made into a Yiddish film that same
    year (Grinberg, "Rolling in Dust"). Ten years later, the Tevye stories were
    published in English translation as *Tevye's Daughters: Collected Stories of Sholom
    Aleichem*, making them available to non-Yiddish speakers (Liptzin, *History of
    Yiddish Literature*). And in 1953 (the same year that Rosen and Jacoby were
    writing *Take It from Me*), the unexpected smash of the off-Broadway world was
    an English adaptation of old Yiddish stories called *The World of Sholem
    Aleichem*. The play featured two of Aleichem's satirical stories, "A Tale of
    Chelm" and "The High School," as well as "Bontche the Silent" by I. L. Peretz. It
    was the highest-grossing off-Broadway show up to that time, playing for a year
    and touring for several more (Kanfer, *Stardust Lost*, 269). Although Sholem

Aleichem had received an underwhelming reception in the United States during his lifetime, he found himself the toast of American Jewry in the decades after his death.

89 Everitt, "Man behind the Chutzpah."

90 Contemporary Americans might believe themselves to be familiar with Aleichem's characters of Tevye and Golde from the 1964 musical *Fiddler on the Roof* (which was adapted from Aleichem's Tevye the Dairyman stories). However, the marriage of Tevye and Golde was substantially tenderized in *Fiddler on the Roof*. In *Fiddler*, Tevye's wife, Golde, mixes her invective with tender anthems like "Do You Love Me?" The Golde of the short story, however, has no such tempering influence. Instead, she is described, in Tevye's colorful language, as "an abscess on a blister on a boil" (Aleichem, *Tevye the Dairyman and Motl the Cantor's Son*, 64). The relationship between Aleichem's Tevye and Golde is clearly not a love match but an embattled partnership of labor and necessity. This same relationship dynamic drove the humor of the radio program *The Bickersons* (1946–1951) by the Jewish comic (and avowed Sholem Aleichem fan) Philip Rapp. Although Rapp claimed that deep down, the Bickersons loved each other, the comedy was driven by their vitriolic midnight spats.

91 Paley Center for Media, "Museum of Television and Radio."

92 Muñoz, "Feeling Brown," 69, quoted in Bial, *Acting Jewish*, 56.

93 Bial, *Acting Jewish*, 56.

94 "Script 2 'Take It from Me,'" 5.

95 Eisenhower, "Statement by the President."

96 "Script 2 'Take It from Me,'" 11.

97 Quoted in Albert, "11 Iconic Christmas Songs."

98 "Script 3 'Take It from Me,'" December 16, 1953, 18, folder 3, box 378, Steven H. Scheuer Collection.

99 "Script 3 'Take It from Me,'" 28.

100 "In the Simple Yet Impossible sketch, the protagonist attempts to do some basic, everyday, mundane task but irresistible obstacles arise that prevent the task from being successfully completed. The protagonist struggles against these obstacles but to no avail. The environment defeats our protagonist; he is not the master of his fate." mikegillettcomedy, "Sketch Archetypes."

101 "Script 3 'Take It from Me,'" 31.

102 "Script 3 'Take It from Me,'" 34.

103 Barnett, *American Christmas*, 129–130.

104 "Reviews: Program of the Week—Take It from Me."

105 Brook, "Americanization of Molly," 34.

106 Quoted in Spigel, *Make Room for TV*, 147.

107 Brook, "Americanization of Molly," 42.

108 Another factor contributing to the cancellation of *Amos 'n' Andy* was the objections of the National Association for the Advancement of Colored People

and other Black groups protesting the harmful representation. See Lipsitz, "Meaning of Memory," 376.

109 Howe, "Nature of Jewish Laughter," 19.

110 "Radio-Television: ABC Swings TV Axe"; "Radio-Television: Jean Carroll Put on Ice."

111 "Radio-Television: Jean Carroll Put on Ice."

112 Jack Gaver, "Radio and TV Today: Relatives Critical, Says Actress," *Dayton (OH) News*, November 23, 1953, Jean Carroll Scrapbook, 66.

113 Carroll, interview by Stephen Silverman, 4-6.

CHAPTER 5. *SULLIVAN* SPOTS AND PARTY RECORDS

1 Nachman, *Right Here on Our Stage*, 4.

2 Nachman, 36.

3 Quoted in Nachman, 6.

4 "Performers Who Appeared Most."

5 Carroll, interview by Michael Kantor, 33.

6 National Association of Radio and Television Broadcasters, "US Code of Practices."

7 Carroll, interview by Stephen Silverman, 3-8.

8 Carroll, 4-22.

9 Quoted in Nachman, *Right Here on Our Stage*, 225.

10 Quoted in Nachman, 208.

11 Quoted in Nachman, 208.

12 Carroll, interview by Stephen Silverman, 3-9.

13 Carroll, interview by Michael Kantor, 68.

14 Stember and American Jewish Committee, *Jews in the Mind of America*, 9.

15 Stember and American Jewish Committee, 110–111.

16 This language comes from Sollors, *Beyond Ethnicity*.

17 Bial, *Acting Jewish*, 50.

18 Bial, 31.

19 Rosten, *Joys of Yiddish*, xvi.

20 *Ed Sullivan Show*, January 15, 1956.

21 *Ed Sullivan Show*, January 15, 1956.

22 Rosten, *Joys of Yiddish*, xvi.

23 Rosten, xvi; *Toast of the Town*, January 16, 1949. The punch line—"Thirty dollars a day I should leave the room?"—not only conveys dismissal via interrogation but also demonstrates a convention of Yiddish-inflected English that Rosten does not include in this analytic: the increased use of the word "should." In Yiddish, one of the frequently used grammatical constructions is the "ich vill az zolstu" construction, which would be idiomatically translated as "I want you to" but directly translated as "I want that you should." For instance, when English speakers would say, "I want you *to go* to the store," the directly translated Yiddish structure would

be, "I want *that you should* go to the store." The frequent use of the word "should" was typically one of the more easily spotted markers of immigrant or non-native-English-speaking status, and therefore Carroll typically only used it in dialogue coming from other "characters" in her stand-up. Thanks to Asya Vaisman-Schulman for this information.

24 *Ed Sullivan Show*, November 30, 1958.
25 I recognize whiteness, and race in general, as social constructs governing the allotment of privilege and resources. This discussion of Jews and whiteness, which has a problematic tendency to erase Jewish people of color, is rooted largely in the excellent text by Brodkin, *How Jews Became White Folks*. See also Goldstein, *Price of Whiteness*; Jacobson, *Roots Too*; Bashi Treitler, *Ethnic Project*.
26 Jacobson, *Roots Too*, 133.
27 ClassicComedyCuts, "Alan King."
28 nealeo comedy, "'50s and '60s Comedians."
29 Jim G., "Sam Levenson."
30 "Alan King—1959—Standup Comedy."
31 nealeo comedy, "'50s and '60s Comedians."
32 "Jack Carter on The Ed Sullivan Show."
33 nealeo comedy, "'50s and '60s Comedians."
34 vintage video clips, "Myron Cohen."
35 Hyman, *Gender and Assimilation*.
36 Prell, *Fighting to Become Americans*.
37 Quoted in D. Weber, *Haunted in the New World*, 126.
38 Prell, *Fighting to Become Americans*, 157.
39 Horowitz and Kaplan, "Estimated Jewish Population."
40 Quoted in Antler, *You Never Call!*, 3.
41 Ravits, "Jewish Mother," 14.
42 In *Unheroic Conduct: The Rise of Heterosexuality and the Invention of the Jewish Man*, Daniel Boyarin helps to illuminate the curious phenomenon of Jewish artists using stereotypes of Jews as a way to signal to one another, in his formulation of "Jewissance," noting that when minorities invoke well-known stereotypes, it can help establish Jewish identity and make Jewish viewers feel "seen" by the larger culture.
43 *Toast of the Town*, September 17, 1950.
44 *Ed Sullivan Show*, March 2, 1958.
45 Preminger, "Jewish Nose."
46 *Ed Sullivan Show*, June 28, 1959.
47 Boyarin, *Unheroic Conduct*, 2.
48 Boyarin, 4.
49 Wisse, *Schlemiel as Modern Hero*, 5.
50 Steinberg, *Ethnic Myth*.
51 *Ed Sullivan Show*, January 17, 1960.

52 *Ed Sullivan Show*, April 5, 1959.
53 Prell, *Fighting to Become Americans*, 184.
54 *Ed Sullivan Show*, October 18, 1959.
55 *Ed Sullivan Show*, October 18, 1959.
56 Jacobson, *Roots Too*, 2. Jacobson acknowledges how the impulse to embrace one's cultural particularity may have animated the racist undertones of neoliberal sociologists like Nathan Glazer and Norman Podhoretz (*Roots Too*, 2).
57 Park, "Human Migration."
58 Carroll, interview by Stephen Silverman, 4-22.
59 It is worth noting that Carroll did not go to college. This line is a key example of how she used her comedy platform to create a fictionalized version of herself—a persona that embodied Carroll's aspirations of upper-middle-class status.
60 This usage of "Jewish shrugs" comes from Rossen, *Dancing Jewish*.
61 By playing up the contrast between the "Old World" furrier and her assimilated self, Carroll is practicing what Tahneer Oksman recognizes as a hallmark of Jewish self-representation: showing that Jews are not monolithic by focusing on "intra-ethnic" difference, rather than the difference between Jews and non-Jews. See Oksman, *"How Come Boys Get to Keep Their Noses?"*
62 Bowles, *Thousand Sundays*.
63 Jose, "Tele Follow-Up Comment."
64 Yente Telebende was a caricature of bossy Jewish women, known for loudly demanding that everyone do as she says, created in a humor column in *Der Forverts* by Jacob Adler. For more, see Kovner, "Yente at the Telephone."
65 Zweibel, interview by Stephen Silverman.
66 *Merv Griffin Show*, disc 2.
67 *Landsman* is a Yiddish term for someone from the same nation; it signals an "in-group member."
68 Rusoff, interview by Stephen Silverman.
69 Hammerman, "Dirty Jews," 65.
70 Hammerman, 60.
71 Cohen, *Jewish Wry*; Antler, "One Clove Away from a Pomander Ball."
72 Tomlin, interview by Stephen Silverman, 7-1-12.
73 Stephen Silverman, "I Made It Standing Up" raw footage.
74 MOR Music Clips, "Joan Rivers Interviews Lily Tomlin."
75 Sochen, "Dinah Shore."
76 Altman, "Ruth Mosko Handler."

CHAPTER 6. NOT WITHOUT MY "ROTTEN KID"
1 *Toast of the Town*, September 17, 1950.
2 In an interview with Stephen Silverman in 2007, Helen stated, "When she'd be on the 'Sullivan Show,' I wanted her to do well. . . . But mainly I wanted to notice the

time, because that would affect what time she got home." Tunick, interview by Stephen Silverman, 1-8.

3 Tunick, 1-2, 1-5.
4 Tunick, 1-5.
5 Tunick, 5-7.
6 Rusoff, "Notes for Jean Carroll Memorial Service."
7 Ravits, "Jewish Mother," 5.
8 Wylie, *Generation of Vipers*, 184–196.
9 Miller, *All My Sons*, 13.
10 Antler, *You Never Call!*, 47.
11 Ravits, "Jewish Mother," 1.
12 To draw from the fullest possible dialogue, I have supplemented the bits she did from this *Sullivan* appearance with bits from the *Girl in a Hot Steam Bath* record.
13 *Ed Sullivan Show*, April 5, 1959; Dobris et al., "Spockian Mother."
14 *Ed Sullivan Show*, April 5, 1959.
15 Bigner, "Parent Education," 315.
16 *Toast of the Town*, December 3, 1950.
17 *Ed Sullivan Show*, May 8, 1966.
18 Pratt, *I Learn from Children*.
19 *Ed Sullivan Show*, January 15, 1956.
20 Carroll, interview by Stephen Silverman, 3-21.
21 For comparable accounts of life as a comic in this period from a male perspective, see Marx, *Groucho and Me*; Berle and Frankel, *Milton Berle*; Hope and Hope, *Bob Hope*.
22 Carroll, interview by Stephen Silverman, 3-24.
23 "She Tells Tricks of the Trade," September 17, 1950, Jean Carroll Scrapbook, 38.
24 Jane Wollman, "First Lady of Laughs," *Sunshine: The Magazine of South Florida*, June 16, 1991, Jean Carroll Scrapbook, 40–44.
25 "Behind the Mike," May 29, 1950, Jean Carroll Scrapbook, 35.
26 Carroll, quoted in Rusoff, "Notes for Jean Carroll Memorial Service."
27 "Behind the Mike"; Dick Kleiner, "The Viewers Spoke, So Gene Kelly Is Back," *Kleiner TV Notebook*, n.d., Jean Carroll Scrapbook, 45; Sally Hammond, "Humanitarian Headliner," *New York Post*, April 5, 1968, Jean Carroll Scrapbook, 74.
28 John Mosedale, "Women Do Too Have a Real Sense of Humor, So One of Them Insists," *Milwaukee Journal*, May 26, 1958, Jean Carroll Scrapbook, 71.
29 Mosedale, 71.
30 Beth Judson, "Speaking of Families: They Talk Things Over," *Evening Bulletin*, January 23, 1956, Jean Carroll Scrapbook, 69.
31 Kay Gardella, "Carroll Keeps 'Em Laughing through Comic-Less Season," *New York Daily News*, n.d., Jean Carroll Scrapbook, 49.
32 Gardella.

33 "Fastest Female Talker Ever," May 16, 1953, Jean Carroll Scrapbook, 60.

34 Tunick, interview by Stephen Silverman, 2-14.

35 Vivian Brown, "Says Comedienne: Fun Is Serious," n.d., Jean Carroll Scrapbook, 47.

36 Kleiner, "Viewers Spoke."

37 Kleiner.

38 Tunick, interview by Stephen Silverman, 2-4.

39 "Garry Moore Show."

40 Harold Stein, "Jean Carroll in Series Swim," *Reporter Dispatch* (White Plains, NY), January 3, 1961, Jean Carroll Scrapbook, 79.

41 "Dream Contract," n.d., Jean Carroll Scrapbook, 75; Ramsden Grieg, "Talkative Miss Carroll Has a $50,000 Problem," *Evening Standard*, n.d., Jean Carroll Scrapbook, 75.

42 Grieg, "Talkative Miss Carroll."

43 Daily Mail Reporter, "$50,000 TV Offer, but Jean Thinks of Daughter," *Daily Mail*, n.d., Jean Carroll Scrapbook, 76.

44 Chatzky, interview by Grace Overbeke.

45 "Dream Contract."

46 "Dream Contract."

47 Stein, "Jean Carroll in Series Swim."

48 Daily Mail Reporter, "$50,000 TV Offer"; "With Jean It's the Family First, Show Biz Second," n.d., Jean Carroll Scrapbook, 78.

49 "With Jean It's the Family First."

50 Vandenberg-Daves, *Modern Motherhood*, 106.

51 Harriet Van Horne, "Jean Carroll Show Is Series of Jokes," n.d., Jean Carroll Scrapbook, 68.

52 Carroll, interview by Stephen Silverman, 4-6.

53 "Personal Appearances."

54 Wollman, "First Lady of Laughs."

55 "Vaudeville: Howe Joins Cri GAC."

56 Chatzky, interview by Grace Overbeke.

57 Tunick, interview by Stephen Silverman, 2-2.

58 Chatzky, interview by Grace Overbeke.

59 Rusoff, "Milton Berle, with Charm and a Mink."

60 Tunick, interview by Stephen Silverman, 1.

61 Chatzky, interview by Grace Overbeke.

62 "Ex-Model Loses $25,000 Action: Jury Votes Out Suit against Jean Carroll," n.d., Lester Sweyd Collection, Billy Rose Theatre Division, New York Public Library.

63 Alfred Albelli and Harry Schlegel, "Says Jean Made It a 2-Party Line, Told All," March 24, 1954, Lester Sweyd Collection, Billy Rose Theatre Division, New York Public Library.

64 Tunick, interview by Stephen Silverman, 2.

65 Rusoff, "Notes for Jean Carroll Memorial Service."

66 Carroll, interview by Stephen Silverman, 4-10.

67 Wollman, "First Lady of Laughs."

68 "Tay-Sachs Association Plans Benefit."

69 Hammond, "Humanitarian Headliner."

70 Taylor-Diehl, "Worth of Wives," 36.

71 "Foundation to Honor Wurtsboro Comedienne," *Times Herald*, March 21, 1968, Jean Carroll Scrapbook, 73.

72 Hammond, "Humanitarian Headliner."

73 Green, "Miscellany."

74 Chatzky, interview by Grace Overbeke.

75 "Fourteenth Annual Tay-Sachs and Allied Diseases Dinner Dance Honoring Buddy Howe," program, November 7, 1972, Jean Carroll Scrapbook, 90–91; E. B. Walzer, "Wild Burros Come Home to Yorktown," *Reporter Dispatch* (White Plains, NY), October 1, 1982, Jean Carroll Scrapbook, 92; "John Jay High School Dance Program," n.d., Jean Carroll Scrapbook, 93.

76 Quoted in Burns and Fisher, *All My Best Friends*, 228.

77 Burns and Fisher, 255.

78 Nesteroff, *Comedians*, 80.

79 Nachman, *Seriously Funny*; Zoglin, *Comedy at the Edge*; Stone, *Laughing in the Dark*; Limon, *Stand-Up Comedy in Theory*; Tafoya, *Legacy of the Wisecrack*.

80 Rivers and Rivers, *Joan & Melissa*.

81 Wong, *Ali Wong: Baby Cobra*; Wong, *Ali Wong: Hard Knock Wife*; Schumer, *Amy Schumer*; Cunningham and Hammer, *Expecting Amy*.

82 Bacardi, "Sarah Silverman."

CONCLUSION

1 Shal, "House Review"; Lowe, "House Review"; Bob, "Night Club Reviews"; Levy, "Radio-Television."

2 Jack Smith, "Jean Carroll to Spice Harvest Moon Menu," *Daily News*, September 5, 1955, Jean Carroll Scrapbook, 59.

3 J.B.T., "Sunday Night at the London Palladium," October 16 [no year], Jean Carroll Scrapbook, 76.

4 Ramsden Grieg, "Talkative Miss Carroll Has a $50,000 Problem," *Evening Standard*, n.d., Jean Carroll Scrapbook, 75.

5 Sarah Silverman, "Jewface, Iron Dome, Mr. Mom."

6 Litvin, "Hollywood Racism Extends to Jews."

7 J. Caplan, "When Jewish Bodies Are Not."

8 Barris, "because of slavery."

9 Chattoo and Feldman, *Comedian and an Activist*, 71.

10 Planned Parenthood Hudson Peconic, "Dirty Mouths, Dirty Martinis."

11 The performers were Rose Cohen, Regina Decicco, Teresa DeGaetano, Wanjiko Eke, Jena Friedman, Marcia Belsky and Isabel Martin (Free the Mind), Charlotte Gilbert, Corey Kahaney, and Cathy Ladman.
12 Chatzky, interview by Grace Overbeke.
13 Carroll, interview by Michael Kantor, 40.

BIBLIOGRAPHY

Abel. "The Dying Nite Clubs." *Variety* 89, no. 12 (January 4, 1928): 29.

———. "Night Club Reviews: Copacabana, N.Y." *Variety* 171, no. 11 (August 18, 1948): 40.

———. "Night Clubs: Chateau Madrid." *Variety* 88, no. 7 (August 31, 1927): 56.

"Actors' Temple Benefit; Many Celebrities Expected for Entertainment on Sunday." *New York Times*, December 9, 1949, Amusements, 37.

"Advertisement." *Variety* 104, no. 11 (November 24, 1931): 30, 54.

Albert, Maddie. "11 Iconic Christmas Songs That Were Written By Jews." *Kveller*, December 22, 2020. www.kveller.com.

Aleichem, Sholem. *Tevye the Dairyman and Motl the Cantor's Son*. Translated by Aliza Shevrin. New York: Penguin, 2009.

Altman, Julie. "Ruth Mosko Handler." *Shalvi/Hyman Encyclopedia of Jewish Women*. Jewish Women's Archive. Accessed September 1, 2023. https://jwa.org.

analog36. "Jean Carroll (Stand-Up Comedy)." YouTube, October 23, 2011. www.youtube.com/watch?v=PJvomZG8Wws&lc=UgjCRx-WgUD1pXgCoAEC.7-H0Z7-QVFx8f4RmKzDaRv.

Antler, Joyce. *Jewish Radical Feminism: Voices from the Women's Liberation Movement*. New York: New York University Press, 2018.

———. "One Clove Away from a Pomander Ball: The Subversive Tradition of Female Comedians." *Studies in American Jewish Literature* 29 (2010): 123–138.

———. *You Never Call! You Never Write! A History of the Jewish Mother*. New York: Oxford University Press, 2008.

Armstrong, Jennifer Keishin. *When Women Invented Television: The Untold Story of the Female Powerhouses Who Pioneered the Way We Watch Today*. New York: HarperCollins, 2021.

"ARTEF Arbeter Teater Farband (Workers Theater Association, 1925–1940)." YIVO Institute for Jewish Research. Accessed June 11, 2023. https://ataleoftwomuseums.yivo.org.

Assouly, Julie. "'Gambling and Women Don't Mix': Female Gamblers and the American Dream in Film." *Angles: New Perspectives on the Anglophone World*, no. 11 (2020). https://doi.org/10.4000/angles.2697.

Austin, Brie. "The Great American Supper Club." *Brie Austin*, December 31, 2004. www.brieaustin.com.

Bacardi, Francesca. "Sarah Silverman Would Rather Be a 'Fun Dad' than a Mom." *Page Six*, October 10, 2017. https://pagesix.com.

Barnett, James Harwood. *The American Christmas: A Study in National Culture*. New York: Arno, 1976.

Barris, Kenya, writer. "because of slavery." *#blackAF*. Khalabo Ink Society, Netflix, 2020. www.netflix.com.

Bashi Treitler, Vilna. *The Ethnic Project: Transforming Racial Fiction into Ethnic Factions*. Stanford, CA: Stanford University Press, 2013.

Bell. "New Shows This Week: Shuberts' New Style of Combination Show." *Variety* 65, no. 13 (February 17, 1922): 21.

Bennett, Susan. *Theatre Audiences: A Theory of Production and Reception*. London: Routledge, 1990.

Berger, Arthur Asa. *Jewish Jesters: A Study in American Popular Culture*. Cresskill, NJ: Hampton, 2001.

Berke, Annie. *Their Own Best Creations: Women Writers in Postwar Television*. Oakland: University of California Press, 2022.

Berle, Milton, and Haskel Frankel. *Milton Berle: An Autobiography*. New York: Delacorte, 1974.

Bernstein, Rhona J. "Acting Live: TV Performance, Intimacy, and Immediacy." In *Reality Squared: TV Discourse on the Real*, edited by James Friedman, 25–49. New Brunswick, NJ: Rutgers University Press, 2002.

Bial, Henry. *Acting Jewish: Negotiating Ethnicity on the American Stage and Screen*. Ann Arbor: University of Michigan Press, 2008.

Bigner, Jerry J. "Parent Education in Popular Literature: 1950–1970." *Family Coordinator* 21, no. 3 (1972): 313–319.

Bob. "Night Club Reviews: Sahara, Las Vegas." *Variety* 196, no. 4 (September 29, 1954): 57.

Bowles, Jerry G. *A Thousand Sundays: The Story of the Ed Sullivan Show*. New York: Putnam, 1980.

Boyarin, Daniel. *Unheroic Conduct: The Rise of Heterosexuality and the Invention of the Jewish Man*. Berkeley: University of California Press, 2000.

Brodie, Ian. *A Vulgar Art: A New Approach to Stand-Up Comedy*. Jackson: University Press of Mississippi, 2014.

Brodkin, Karen. *How Jews Became White Folks and What That Says about Race in America*. New Brunswick, NJ: Rutgers University Press, 1998.

Brook, Vincent. "The Americanization of Molly: How Mid-Fifties TV Homogenized 'The Goldbergs' (and Got 'Berg-larized' in the Process)." *Cinema Journal* 38, no. 4 (1999): 45–67.

Burm. "House Review: Hipp, Balto." *Variety* 145, no. 2 (December 17, 1941): 20.

———. "House Review: Hipp. Balto." *Variety* 153, no. 12 (March 1, 1944): 23.

———. "House Review: Hullabaloo." *Variety* 146, no. 12 (May 27, 1942): 46.

Burns, George. *Gracie: A Love Story*. New York: Signet, 1991.

Burns, George, and David Fisher. *All My Best Friends*. New York: Putnam, 1989.

"Cabarets: Ike Bloom's Deauville Popular in Chicago." *Variety* 78, no. 2 (February 25, 1925): 34.

Caplan, Debra. "Six Degrees of Yankev Blayfer." *Digital Yiddish Theatre Project*, December 4, 2015. https://web.uwm.edu.

Caplan, Jennifer. "When Jewish Bodies Are Not." Paper presented at Association for Jewish Studies, Chicago, IL, December 21, 2021.

Carroll, Jean. "Female of the Species." *New York Herald Tribune*, May 6, 1956, G18.

———. *Girl in a Hot Steam Bath.* New York: Columbia, 1960. LP.

———. Interview by Michael Kantor. *Make 'Em Laugh* interview transcripts. May 23, 2007. Email to author, February 11, 2022.

———. Interview by Stephen Silverman. Transcript. New York City, November 4 and 6, 2006. Personal collection of Stephen Silverman.

———. Scrapbook. Personal collection of Susan Chatzky.

"Carroll and Howe (aka Garroll and Lowe)." *British Pathé*, June 28, 1937. www.britishpathe.com.

Char. "Outdoors: Variety House Reviews—Albee, B'klyn." *Variety* 14, no. 5 (April 17, 1934): 63.

Chattoo, Caty Borum, and Lauren Feldman. *A Comedian and an Activist Walk into a Bar: The Serious Role of Comedy in Social Justice.* Oakland: University of California Press, 2020.

Chatzky, Susan. Interview by Grace Overbeke. October 7, 2016.

Chic. "Reviews: Met, Brooklyn." *Variety* 108, no. 6 (October 18, 1932): 34, 54.

"Chicago." *Variety* 99, no. 13 (July 9, 1930): 61.

"Chicago: All for Ike Bloom!" *Variety* 59, no. 12 (August 13, 1920): 9.

ClassicComedyCuts. "Alan King—1959—Standup Comedy." YouTube, July 5, 1959. www.youtube.com/watch?v=DUVWfYgIbcc.

Cohen, Sarah Blacher. *Jewish Wry: Essays on Jewish Humor.* Detroit: Wayne State University Press, 1990.

———. "The Unkosher Comediennes: From Sophie Tucker to Joan Rivers." In *Jewish Wry: Essays on Jewish Humor*, ed. Sarah Blacher Cohen, 105–124. Detroit: Wayne State University Press, 1990.

"Comics Receive Awards March 31." *Billboard* 61, no. 13 (March 26, 1949): 3.

Con. "New Shows This Week: Midnight Rounders." *Variety* 69, no. 9 (January 19, 1923): 25.

Cook, Joan. "Woman Comic Plays to 'Guy with a Sneer.'" *New York Herald Tribune*, March 5, 1952, 16.

Corry, John. "'American Censored,' on CBS Tonight." *New York Times*, May 28, 1985, C17.

Crenshaw, Kimberlé. "Mapping the Margins: Intersectionality, Identity Politics, and Violence against Women of Color." *Stanford Law Review* 43, no. 6 (1991): 1241–1299. https://doi.org/10.2307/1229039.

Cullen, Frank, with Florence Hackman and Donald McNeilly. *Vaudeville, Old and New: An Encyclopedia of Variety Performers in America.* New York: Routledge, 2007.

Cunningham, Ryan, and Alexander Hammer, dir. *Expecting Amy*. It's So Easy Productions, 2020. www.max.com.

Dauber, Jeremy. *Jewish Comedy: A Serious History*. New York: Norton, 2018.

Davis, Marni. *Jews and Booze: Becoming American in the Age of Prohibition*. New York: New York University Press, 2012.

Diller, Phyllis, and Richard Buskin. *Like a Lampshade in a Whorehouse: My Life in Comedy*. New York: Penguin, 2005.

"Display Ad 7—No Title." *Jewish Advocate*, August 3, 1967, 5.

"Display Ad 18—No Title." *Jewish Advocate*, August 24, 1950, 8.

Dobris, Catherine A., Kim White-Mills, Rachel D. Davidson, and Toula V. Wellbrook. "The Spockian Mother: Images of the 'Good' Mother in Dr. Spock's The Common Sense Book of Baby and Child Care, 1946–1992." *Communication Quarterly* 65, no. 1 (2017): 39–59.

Dorinson, Joseph. *Kvetching and Shpritzing: Jewish Humor in American Popular Culture*. Jefferson, NC: McFarland, 2015.

Edba. "House Review: Strand, N.Y." *Variety* 164, no. 5 (October 9, 1946): 26.

Ed Sullivan Show, The. CBS, January 15, 1956. SOFA Entertainment. DVD.

——. CBS, September 23, 1956. SOFA Entertainment. DVD.

——. CBS, March 2, 1958. SOFA Entertainment. DVD.

——. CBS, November 30, 1958. SOFA Entertainment. DVD.

——. CBS, April 5, 1959. SOFA Entertainment, DVD.

——. CBS, June 28, 1959. SOFA Entertainment. DVD.

——. CBS, October 18, 1959. SOFA Entertainment. DVD.

——. CBS, January 17, 1960. SOFA Entertainment. DVD.

——. CBS, July 24, 1960. SOFA Entertainment. DVD.

——. CBS, June 18, 1961. SOFA Entertainment. DVD.

——. CBS, October 11, 1964. SOFA Entertainment. DVD.

——. CBS, May 8, 1966. SOFA Entertainment. DVD.

Eisenhower, Dwight D. "Statement by the President upon Signing the Refugee Relief Act of 1953." August 7, 1953. American Presidency Project. Accessed September 24, 2022. www.presidency.ucsb.edu.

Elie. "House Review: RKO, Boston." *Variety* 157, no. 3 (December 27, 1944): 35.

Entertainment Buff. "Joan Rivers & Johnny Carson on a 'Tonight Show' Retrospective, 1984." YouTube, July 8, 2011. www.youtube.com/watch?v=C3dQYdttuiM.

Erdman, Harley. *Staging the Jew: The Performance of an American Ethnicity, 1860–1920*. New Brunswick, NJ: Rutgers University Press, 1997.

Erickson, Hal. *From Radio to the Big Screen: Hollywood Films Featuring Broadcast Personalities and Programs*. Jefferson, NC: McFarland, 2014.

Everitt, David. "The Man behind the Chutzpah of Master Sgt. Ernest Bilko." *New York Times*, April 14, 1996.

"Extravaganza Aids Memorial Hospital." *Jewish Advocate*, September 12, 1957, A3.

Feuer, Menachem. "Laughter through Tears or Tears through Laughter? Irving Howe and Ruth Wisse's Dialogue over Sholem Aleichem's Humor—Take 1." *Schlemiel Theory*, July 8, 2013. https://schlemielintheory.com.

Fields, Anna. *The Girl in the Show: Three Generations of Comedy, Culture, and Feminism*. New York: Arcade, 2017.

Fox, G. George. "Writer Appalled by Jewish Gamblers at Kefauver Committee Hearings." *Sentinel*, April 5, 1951, 11. Accessed July 6, 2022. National Library of Israel. www.nli.org.il.

Fox, Margalit. "Jean Carroll, 98, Is Dead; Blended Wit and Beauty." *New York Times*, January 3, 2010, A22.

Gardenswartz, Noah. Interview by Grace Overbeke. Telephone. January 15, 2018.

Gardner, Joann. "Self-Referentiality in Art: A Look at Three Television Situation-Comedies of the 1950s." *Studies in Popular Culture* 11, no. 1 (1988): 35–50.

"Garry Moore Show, The (Count Basie, Joe Williams, Jean Carroll)." CBS, January 3, 1961. Paley Center for Media. www.paleycenter.org.

"Gertrude Berg | American Actress, Producer, and Screenwriter." *Encyclopedia Britannica*. Accessed June 28, 2023. www.britannica.com.

Gilb. "Television Reviews: Jean Carroll Show." *Variety* 182, no. 8 (May 2, 1951): 34.

Glazer, Nathan. "Social Characteristics of American Jews, 1654–1954." *American Jewish Year Book* 56 (1955): 3–41.

Glickman, Lawrence B. *Consumer Society in American History: A Reader*. Ithaca, NY: Cornell University Press, 1999.

Gold. "Vaudeville: Unit Review—Pan-American Follies." *Variety* 142, no. 1 (March 12, 1941): 44.

Goldman, Aaron. "The Resurgence of Antisemitism in Britain during World War II." *Jewish Social Studies* 46, no. 1 (1984): 37–50.

Goldstein, Eric L. *The Price of Whiteness: Jews, Race, and American Identity*. Princeton, NJ: Princeton University Press, 2006.

Gould, Jack. "Television in Review: Jean Carroll, the Impressionist, Gets a Poor Shuffle in Shopworn Situation Comedy." *New York Times*, November 13, 1953.

———. "TV's Top Comediennes." *New York Times*, December 27, 1953, SM16.

Green, Abel. "Miscellany: Busy B's Fete: Benny, Burns, Block, Bishop; Big Name and Cash Draw." *Variety* 267, no. 1 (May 17, 1972): 2, 70.

Greene, Shecky. "My Favorite Jokes." *Jackson (MS) Clarion-Ledger*, May 21, 1961.

Grimes, William. "Coleman Jacoby, 95, TV Comedy Writer." *New York Times*, November 13, 2010, A21.

Grinberg, Marat. "Rolling in Dust: Maurice Shwartz's *Tevye* (1939) and Its Ambiguities." *Shofar* 32, no. 2 (2014): 49–72. www.jstor.org/stable/10.5703/shofar.32.2.49.

Gros. "Television Review: Take It from Me." *Variety* 192, no. 10 (November 11, 1953): 35.

Grossman, Barbara Wallace. *Funny Woman: The Life and Times of Fanny Brice*. Bloomington: Indiana University Press, 1992.

Hammerman, Shaina. "Dirty Jews: Amy Schumer and Other Vulgar Jewesses." In *From Shtetl to Stardom: Jews and Hollywood*, edited by Michael Renov and Vincent Brook, 49–72. West Lafayette, IN: Purdue University Press, 2017.

Hammerstein, Oscar. "Pictures: Talent Incubator." *Variety* 185, no. 4 (January 2, 1952): 11.

Handlin, Oscar. *Adventure in Freedom: Three Hundred Years of Jewish Life in America.* New York: McGraw-Hill, 1954.

Hastie, Amelie. *Cupboards of Curiosity: Women, Recollection, and Film History.* Durham, NC: Duke University Press, 2007.

Herm. "House Review: Paramount, N.Y." *Variety* 179, no. 13 (September 6, 1950): 55.

———. "Television Reviews: Burns & Allen Show." *Variety* 192, no. 5 (October 7, 1953): 45.

"Hillel Academy Celebration Has Spectacular Entertainment." *American Jewish Outlook* 33, no. 16 (February 9, 1951): 13.

Hitchens, Christopher. "Why Women Aren't Funny." *Vanity Fair* 557 (January 2007): 54.

Hobbes, Thomas. *The Elements of Law, Natural and Politic.* London: Simpkin, Marshall, 1889.

Hold. "House Review: National. L'ville." *Variety* 152, no. 10 (November 17, 1943): 46.

Holden, Stephen. "Laugh Bargains for a Summer Night." *New York Times*, July 24, 1987, C1.

Holson, Laura M. "The Catskills Are Back. Again. And Again." *New York Times*, June 21, 2019.

Hope, Bob, and Linda Hope. *Bob Hope: My Life in Jokes.* New York: Hyperion, 2003.

Horowitz, Morris C., and Lawrence J. Kaplan. "The Estimated Jewish Population of the New York Area 1900–1975." Federation of Jewish Philanthropies of New York, 1958. Jewishdatabank.org.

Horowitz, Susan. *Queens of Comedy: Lucille Ball, Phyllis Diller, Carol Burnett, Joan Rivers and the New Generation of Funny Women.* London: Routledge, 2005.

"House Review: Palace, Cleve." *Variety* 144, no. 1 (September 10, 1941): 38.

Howe, Irving. "The Nature of Jewish Laughter." *American Mercury*, February 1951.

Hunt. "House Review: Chicago, Chi." *Variety* 166, no. 7 (April 23, 1947): 48.

Hyman, Paula E. *Gender and Assimilation in Modern Jewish History: The Roles and Representation of Women.* Seattle: University of Washington Press, 1995.

Ibee. "New Shows This Week: Winter Garden." *Variety* 66, no. 1 (February 24, 1922): 18.

IMDb. "Arnie Rosen." Accessed June 11, 2023. www.imdb.com.

———. "Jean Carroll." Accessed September 23, 2022. www.imdb.com.

———. "Rachel Brosnahan." Accessed January 31, 2019. www.imdb.com.

"Jack Carter on The Ed Sullivan Show . . . A Classic—Video Dailymotion." *Dailymotion*, June 30, 2015. www.dailymotion.com.

Jacobson, Matthew Frye. *Roots Too: White Ethnic Revival in Post–Civil Rights America.* Cambridge, MA: Harvard University Press, 2009.

Jarski, Rosemarie. *The Funniest Thing You Never Said 2: The Ultimate Collection of Humorous Quotations*. London: Ebury, 2010.

"Jean Carroll Hits Handicap of Femininity." *Atlanta Journal-Constitution*, April 19, 1959, 19G.

"Jean Carroll to Star in Steel Pier Show." *Jewish Exponent*, July 30, 1954, 24.

Jewish Virtual Library. "New York City." Accessed October 23, 2018. www.jewishvirtuallibrary.org.

Jim G. "Sam Levenson—But Seriously Folks 1958." *Vintage Stand-Up Comedy*, May 9, 2013. www.vs-uc.com.

Jose. "House Review: Capitol, N.Y." *Variety* 171, no. 1 (June 9, 1948): 18.

———. "House Review: Palace, N.Y." *Variety* 185, no. 13 (March 5, 1952: 69.

———. "House Review: Paramount, N.Y." *Variety* 173, no. 6 (January 19, 1949): 47.

———. "House Review: State. N.Y." *Variety* 154, no. 4 (April 4, 1945): 20.

———. "Pictures: House Reviews—State N.Y." *Variety* 165, no. 6 (January 15, 1947): 23.

———. "Tele Follow-Up Comment: Ed Sullivan Show." *Variety* 223, no. 4 (June 21, 1961): 31.

———. "Television Reviews: Television Followup Comment—Bob Hope's." *Variety* 189, no. 1 (December 10, 1952): 30.

———. "Vaudeville: Night Club Reviews—La Martinique. N.Y." *Variety* 164, no. 13 (December 4, 1946): 46.

Kanfer, Stefan. *Stardust Lost: The Triumph, Tragedy, and Mishugas of the Yiddish Theater in America*. New York: Knopf, 2006.

Kibler, M. Alison. *Rank Ladies: Gender and Cultural Hierarchy in American Vaudeville*. Chapel Hill: University of North Carolina Press, 1999.

King, Alan. *Alan King's Great Jewish Joke Book*. New York: Crown, 2002.

Kohen, Yael. *We Killed: The Rise of Women in American Comedy*. New York: Picador, 2013.

Kovner, B. "Yente at the Telephone." *The Forward*, April 6, 2007. https://forward.com.

Krefting, Rebecca. *All Joking Aside: American Humor and Its Discontents*. Baltimore: Johns Hopkins University Press, 2014.

Kuntz, Tom. "Word for Word / Henny Youngman; He Delivered Deftly and Carried a Big Catskill Shtick." *New York Times*, March 1, 1998.

Land. "Film House Reviews: Palace, Chicago." *Variety* 107, no. 4 (July 5, 1932): 31, 47.

Lary. "House Reviews: Olympia, Miami." *Variety* 169, no. 11 (February 18, 1948): 47.

Laskow, Caroline, and Ian Rosenberg, dirs. *Welcome to Kutsher's: The Last Catskills Resort*. Menemsha Films, 2015. Film.

"Laurel Club Plans Comics." *American Jewish Outlook* 50, no. 14 (July 31, 1959): 10.

Laurie, Joe. "Review-Preview: The '39 Going on 50' Bracket." *Variety* 187, no. 6 (July 16, 1952): 41.

———. "Vaude-Nite Clubs: The Man and Woman Act." *Variety* 125, no. 4 (January 6, 1937): 198.

Leny. "Variety House Reviews: Paramount. L.A." *Variety* 112, no. 5 (October 10, 1933): 15.

Les. "Night Club Reviews: Palmer House, Chi." *Variety* 196, no. 8 (October 27, 1954): 71.

Levy. "Radio-Television: Chevalier Wows 'Em at Annual Radio-TV Correspondents Dinner." *Variety* 210, no. 5 (April 2, 1958): 30.

Levy, Shawn. *In on the Joke: The Original Queens of Stand-Up Comedy*. New York: Doubleday Books, 2022.

Limon, John. *Stand-Up Comedy in Theory, or, Abjection in America*. Durham, NC: Duke University Press, 2000.

Lipsitz, George. "The Meaning of Memory: Family, Class, and Ethnicity in Early Network Television Programs." *Cultural Anthropology: Journal of the Society for Cultural Anthropology* 1, no. 4 (1986): 355–387.

Liptzin, Solomon. *A History of Yiddish Literature*. Middle Village, NY: J. David, 1972.

Litvak, Joseph. *The Un-Americans: Jews, the BlackList, and Stoolpigeon Culture*. Durham, NC: Duke University Press, 2009.

Litvin, Sam. "Hollywood Racism Extends to Jews." *San Diego Jewish World*, December 29, 2021. www.sdjewishworld.com.

Loop. "House Review: Oriental, Chi." *Variety* 139, no. 10 (August 14, 1940): 39.

Lowe. "House Review: Capitol, Wash." *Variety* 165, no. 9 (February 5, 1947): 22.

Manning, Susan. *Modern Dance, Negro Dance: Race in Motion*. Minneapolis: University of Minnesota Press, 2008.

Martin, Linda, and Kerry Segrave. *Women in Comedy*. Secaucus, NJ: Citadel, 1986.

Marx, Groucho. *Groucho and Me: The Autobiography*. London: Virgin Books, 2009.

Matheny, Amy. "Lily Tomlin: An Icon Talks." *Windy City Times*, September 17, 2008, 13, 29.

McConnell. "Pictures: Variety House Reviews—Palace, Akron." *Variety* 3, no. 13 (September 5, 1933): 35.

McCracken, Allison. "Study of a Mad Housewife: Psychiatric Discourse, the Suburban Home, and the Case of Gracie Allen." In *Small Screens, Big Ideas: Television in the 1950s*, edited by Janet Thumim, 50–65. London: Tauris, 2002.

McCracken, Chelsea. "Regulating Swish: Early Television Censorship." *Media History Media History* 19, no. 3 (2013): 354–368.

McGlynn, Katla. "What *The Marvelous Mrs. Maisel* Gets Right about Early Stand-Up Comedy." *Vulture*, December 19, 2017. www.vulture.com.

Merv Griffin Show, The. Disc 2. Narberth, PA: Alpha Home Entertainment, 2006. DVD.

Mike. "Vaudeville: Chez Paree, Chi." *Variety* 161, no. 11 (February 20, 1946): 46.

mikegillettcomedy. "Sketch Archetypes: Simple Yet Impossible." *Tumblr*, October 2015. https://mikegillettcomedy.tumblr.com.

Miller, Arthur. *All My Sons: Drama in Three Acts*. New York: Dramatists Play Service, 1974.

Miller, Mitch, Jean Carroll, Jo Stafford, and Tennessee Ernie Ford. *Entertainment Excerpts from 11th Crystal Ball Dinner*. 1956. LP.

Mintz, Lawrence E. "Humor and Ethnic Stereotypes in Vaudeville and Burlesque." *MELUS* 21, no. 4 (1996): 19–28. https://doi.org/10.2307/467640.

"Miscellany: 'Bugsy' Siegel Said to Have Had Other Show Business Ties." *Variety* 167, no. 3 (June 25, 1947): 2.

"Miscellany: Jean Carroll Pacts 5-Year NBC-TV Deal." *Variety* 189, no. 10 (February 11, 1953): 2.

Mizejewski, Linda. *Pretty/Funny: Women Comedians and Body Politics*. Austin: University of Texas Press, 2014.

Mizejewski, Linda, and Victoria Sturtevant. *Hysterical! Women in American Comedy*. Austin: University of Texas Press, 2017.

Mock, Roberta. *Jewish Women on Stage, Film, and Television*. New York: Palgrave Macmillan, 2016.

"Moms Mabley—Agitation in Moderation by Kliph Nesteroff." *WFMU's Beware of the Blog*. August 26, 2007. https://blog.wfmu.org.

Morgan, Thomas. "The Vanishing American Jew." *Look Magazine* 28, no. 9 (May 5, 1964): 42.

MOR Music Clips. "Joan Rivers Interviews Lily Tomlin Part 1." *The Late Show*, 1981. YouTube, August 4, 2018. www.youtube.com/watch?v=PJP4docoqtE.

Morreall, John. "Philosophy of Humor." In *The Stanford Encyclopedia of Philosophy*, edited by Edward N. Zalta. Metaphysics Research Lab, Stanford University, 2020. https://plato.stanford.edu.

Most, Andrea. *Making Americans: Jews and the Broadway Musical*. Cambridge, MA: Harvard University Press, 2004.

Muñoz, José Esteban. "Feeling Brown: Ethnicity and Affect in Ricardo Bracho's 'The Sweetest Hangover (and Other STDs).'" *Theatre Journal* 52, no. 1 (2000): 67–79. https://doi.org/10.1353/tj.2000.0020.

Murray, Matthew. "Television Wipes Its Feet: The Commercial and Ethical Considerations." *Journal of Popular Film and Television Journal of Popular Film and Television* 21, no. 3 (1993): 128–138.

Museum of Yiddish Theater. "Maurice Schwartz's Yiddish Art Theatre." Accessed June 28, 2023. www.museumofyiddishtheater.org.

Nachman, Gerald. *Right Here on Our Stage Tonight! Ed Sullivan's America*. Berkeley: University of California Press, 2009.

———. *Seriously Funny: The Rebel Comedians of the 1950s and 1960s*. New York: Back Stage Books, 2004.

Nadell, Pamela S. *American Jewish Women's History: A Reader*. New York: New York University Press, 2003.

Nathans, Heather S. *Hideous Characters and Beautiful Pagans: Performing Jewish Identity on the Antebellum American Stage*. Ann Arbor: University of Michigan Press, 2017.

National Association of Radio and Television Broadcasters. "The Television Code: Effective March 1, 1952." 1952.

———. "US Code of Practices for Television Broadcasters." December 6, 1951. https://historymatters.gmu.edu.

nealeo comedy. "'50s and '60s Comedians." 1987. YouTube, August 8, 2021. www.youtube.com/watch?v=__cRLtVU4zg.

Nesteroff, Kliph. "Classic Television Showbiz: An Interview with Joey Bishop's Gag Writer—Don Sherman—Part Two." *Classic Television Showbiz*, June 4, 2011. http://classicshowbiz.blogspot.com.

———. *The Comedians: Drunks, Thieves, Scoundrels, and the History of American Comedy*. New York: Grove, 2016.

"New York.—Summer's Approach Brings Noticeable Signs of Contrasting . . ." *Hollywood Reporter* 83, no. 45 (June 6, 1945): 4.

Nicholson, Philip. *Labor's Story in the United States*. Philadelphia: Temple University Press, 2004.

"Night Clubs-Vaudeville: In Short." *Billboard* 57, no. 49 (December 8, 1945): 38.

"Night Clubs-Vaudeville: Night Club Reviews—Chez Paree, Chicago." *Billboard* 58, no. 7 (February 16, 1946): 41.

"Night Clubs-Vaudeville: Night Club Reviews—La Conga, New York." *Billboard* 58, no. 19 (May 11, 1946): 47.

"Night Clubs-Vaudeville: Vaudeville Reviews—Loew's State, New York." *Billboard* 59, no. 3 (January 18, 1947): 35.

Novick, Julius. *Beyond the Golden Door: Jewish American Drama and Jewish American Experience*. Basingstoke, UK: Palgrave Macmillan, 2009.

Odac. "Variety House Reviews: Palace, N.Y." *Variety* 113, no. 8 (February 6, 1934): 15.

Odec. "Pictures: Film House Reviews—Fox. Brooklyn." *Variety* 110, no. 13 (June 6, 1933): 29.

———. "Vaude House Reviews: State, N.Y." *Variety* 107, no. 9 (August 9, 1932): 28.

Oksman, Tahneer. *"How Come Boys Get to Keep Their Noses?": Women and Jewish American Identity in Contemporary Graphic Memoirs*. New York: Columbia University Press, 2016.

Old Time Radio Catalog. "The Sealtest Village Store." Accessed June 15, 2022. www.otrcat.com.

Overbeke, Grace Kessler. "Meet the Real Mrs. Maisel: Jean Carroll." *The Forward*, July 5, 2018. https://forward.com.

Painter Young, Jamie. "Rap On, Sister." *Backstage*, November 5, 2019. www.backstage.com.

Paley Center for Media. "The Museum of Television and Radio: The Original Honeymooners." 1993. www.paleycenter.org.

Park, Robert E. "Human Migration and the Marginal Man." *American Journal of Sociology* 33, no. 6 (1928): 881–893.

"Performers Who Appeared Most on The Ed Sullivan Show." *The Ed Sullivan Show Blog*, October 1, 2021. www.edsullivan.com.

"Personal Appearances: Buddy Howe Dead at 71; Helmed ICM, Was Dean of N.Y. Friars." *Variety* 302, no. 6 (March 11, 1981): 223.

Pew Research Center. "A Portrait of Jewish Americans." October 1, 2013. www
.pewforum.org.

Phillips, McCandlish. "Joe E. Lewis, Nightclub Comic Noted for Garrulousness, Dies."
New York Times, June 5, 1971, 32.

"Photo Standalone 14—No Title." *Jewish Advocate*, October 3, 1957, 9.

Pickette, Samantha. *Peak TV's Unapologetic Jewish Woman: Exploring Jewish Female
Representation in Contemporary Television Comedy*. Lanham, MD: Rowman and
Littlefield, 2022.

"Pictorial Picks." *Jewish Advocate*, April 12, 1951, 7.

"Pictures Grosses: 'Kismet' Okay 33g, Hub Ace." *Variety* 157, no. 3 (December 27, 1944): 13.

Planned Parenthood Hudson Peconic. "Dirty Mouths, Dirty Martinis." Program.
Irvington Town Hall Theater, January 11, 2016.

"Plays and Photoplays." *Jewish Criterion* 60, no. 12 (December 1, 1922): 24–26. Pittsburgh Jewish Newspaper Project.

Pratt, Caroline. *I Learn from Children: An Adventure in Progressive Education*. 1948.
New York: Grove Atlantic, 2014. ebook.

Prell, Riv-Ellen. *Fighting to Become Americans: Assimilation and the Trouble between
Jewish Women and Jewish Men*. Boston: Beacon, 2009.

Preminger, Beth. "The 'Jewish Nose' and Plastic Surgery: Origins and Implications."
JAMA: The Journal of the American Medical Association 286, no. 17 (2001): 2161.

Pringle, Henry F., and Katharine Pringle. "Congress vs. the Plunging Neckline." *Saturday Evening Post*, December 27, 1952, 49.

"Radio-Television: ABC Feels Way into Mag Concept Via Carroll TV'er." *Variety* 193,
no. 2 (December 16, 1953): 27.

"Radio-Television: ABC Swings TV Axe on 4 Shows; Jean Carroll Off." *Variety* 193, no.
3 (December 23, 1953): 25, 34.

"Radio-Television: Adams' ABC-TV Sponsored Quizzer." *Variety* 192, no. 6 (October
14, 1953): 29.

"Radio-Television: Agronsky's 'At Issue,' Soviet Series Take Up Wed. Slack on ABC-TV."
Variety 192, no. 7 (October 21, 1953): 46.

"Radio-Television: Dick Linkroum Set as 'Home' Exec Director." *Variety* 193, no. 1
(December 9, 1953): 30.

"Radio-Television: Jean Carroll Put on Ice Till Spring Sponsor Thaw; 18G to Sustain."
Variety 193, no. 4 (December 30, 1953): 25.

"Radio-Television: Jean Carroll to Have Own Show This Summer." *Variety* 182, no. 6
(April 18, 1951): 40.

Ravits, Martha A. "The Jewish Mother: Comedy and Controversy in American Popular
Culture." *MELUS* 25, no. 1 (April 1, 2000): 3–31. https://doi.org/10.2307/468149.

Rees, Les. "Chatter: Milan." *Variety* 188, no. 9 (November 5, 1952): 61.

Riess, Steven. "The Cyclical History of Horse Racing: The USA's Oldest and (Sometimes) Most Popular Spectator Sport." *International Journal of the History of Sport*
31, nos. 1–2 (January 22, 2014): 29–54. https://doi.org/10.1080/09523367.2013.862520.

Rivers, Joan. "Joan Rivers on How Phyllis Diller Paved the Way for Women in Comedy." *Washington Post*, August 24, 2012. www.washingtonpost.com.

———. *What Becomes a Semi-Legend Most?* Warner Bros. Records, David Geffen Co., 1983. LP.

Rivers, Joan, and Melissa Rivers, producers. *Joan & Melissa: Joan Knows Best?* Pie Town Production, 2011–2014.

Roediger, David R. *Working toward Whiteness: How America's Immigrants Became White*. New York: Basic Books, 2005.

Rogin, Michael Paul. *Blackface, White Noise: Jewish Immigrants in the Hollywood Melting Pot*. Berkeley: University of California Press, 1996.

Rosen, George. "Television: CBS Out on a Godfrey Limb." *Variety* 178, no. 2 (March 22, 1950): 29, 36.

Rosenberg, Joel. "Rogin's Noise: The Alleged Historical Crimes of The Jazz Singer." *Prooftexts* 22, no. 1 (2002): 221–239.

Rossen, Rebecca. *Dancing Jewish: Jewish Identity in American Modern and Postmodern Dance*. New York: Oxford University Press, 2014.

Rosten, Leo. *The Joys of Yiddish*. New York: Pocket Books, 2000.

Rothstein, Mervyn. "Henny Youngman, King of the One-Liners, Is Dead at 91 after 6 Decades of Laughter." *New York Times*, February 25, 1998, B9.

Rusoff, Jane Wollman. "The First Mrs. Maisel." Television Academy. Accessed January 25, 2022. www.emmys.com.

———. Interview by Stephen Silverman. Transcript. November 6, 2006. Personal collection of Stephen Silverman.

———. "Milton Berle, with Charm and a Mink." *New York Times*, November 5, 2006.

———. "Notes for Jean Carroll Memorial Service." 2010. Email to the author.

Sadowsky, Sandy. *Wedded to Crime: My Life in the Jewish Mafia*. New York: Putnam, 1992.

Sahu. "Reviews: USO Camp Shows—Looping the Loop." *Variety* 149, no. 2 (December 23, 1942): 46.

Sands, Karl. "Great." *Hollywood Reporter* 84, no. 33 (July 31, 1945): 4.

———. "Too Funny." *Hollywood Reporter* 84, no. 39 (August 8, 1945): 4.

Scheuer, Steven H. Collection of Television Program Scripts. YCAL MSS 266. Yale Collection of American Literature. Beinecke Rare Book and Manuscript Library.

Scho. "House Review: State, N.Y." *Variety* 137, no. 4 (January 3, 1940): 143.

———. "Vaudeville: New Acts—Carroll and Howe." *Variety*, May 20, 1936, 44.

Schumer, Amy, dir. *Amy Schumer: Growing*. It's So Easy Productions, 2019. www.netflix .com.

Shal. "House Review: Earle, Philly." *Variety* 154, no. 9 (May 10, 1944): 18, 38.

Sherman-Palladino, Amy, dir. "Pilot." *The Marvelous Mrs. Maisel*. Dorothy Parker Drank Here Productions, 2017.

"Silberman Adds Three Acts." *Billboard* 39, no. 19 (May 7, 1927): 13.

Silverman, Sarah. "Jewface, Iron Dome, Mr. Mom." *The Sarah Silverman Podcast*, September 30, 2021. https://podtail.com.

Silverman, Stephen, dir. "I Made It Standing Up" raw footage. 2006. Personal collection of Stephen Silverman.

———. "Print Intros." November 5, 2006. Personal collection of Stephen Silverman.

Simon, Jeff. "After Years of Ranting, He's Still the King of Comedy." *Buffalo News*, August 5, 2001. https://buffalonews.com.

Smith, Bill. "Night Clubs-Vaudeville: Vaudeville Reviews—Loew's State, New York." *Billboard* 56, no. 14 (April 1, 1944): 25.

———. *The Vaudevillians*. New York: Macmillan, 1976.

Snyder, Robert W. *The Voice of the City: Vaudeville and Popular Culture in New York*. New York: Oxford University Press, 1989.

Sochen, June. "Dinah Shore." *Shalvi/Hyman Encyclopedia of Jewish Women*. Jewish Women's Archive. Accessed September 1, 2023. https://jwa.org.

Sollors, Werner. *Beyond Ethnicity: Consent and Descent in American Culture*. New York: Oxford University Press, 1986.

Soloski, Alexis. "Did You Hear the One about the Housewife Who Walks into a Comedy Club?" *New York Times*, November 21, 2017, AR17.

———. "The (Elegant, Brazen, Brainy) Pioneering Women of Comedy." *New York Times*, November 21, 2017, AR17.

Spigel, Lynn. *Make Room for TV: Television and the Family Ideal in Postwar America*. Chicago: University of Chicago Press, 1992.

Spock, Benjamin. *The Common Sense Book of Baby and Child Care*. New York: Duell, Sloan, and Pearce, 1946.

Steinberg, Stephen. *The Ethnic Myth: Race, Ethnicity, and Class in America*. Boston: Beacon, 2001.

Stember, Charles Herbert, and the American Jewish Committee. *Jews in the Mind of America*. New York: Basic Books, 1966.

"Stevensville Lake Hotel to Feature Name Talent." *Jewish Advocate*. May 23, 1957, 9.

Stone, Laurie. *Laughing in the Dark: A Decade of Subversive Comedy*. Hopewell, NJ: Ecco, 1997.

Storrs, Landon R. Y. "McCarthyism and the Second Red Scare." *Oxford Research Encyclopedia of American History*, July 2, 2015. https://doi.org/10.1093/acrefore /9780199329175.013.6.

Sweyd, Lester. Collection. Billy Rose Theatre Division. New York Public Library.

Tafoya, Eddie. *The Legacy of the Wisecrack: Stand-Up Comedy as the Great American Literary Form*. Boca Raton, FL: BrownWalker, 2009.

"Talented New Comedienne to Appear at Carousel." *American Jewish Outlook* 28, no. 26 (November 19, 1948). Pittsburgh Jewish Newspaper Project.

Taylor-Diehl, Christiane. "The Worth of Wives: 1950s Corporate America 'Discovers' Spousal Social Capital." *Essays in Economic and Business History* 26, no. 1 (2008): 33–46.

"Tay-Sachs Association Plans Benefit at the Waldorf." *New York Times*, March 26, 1968, 36.

"Television: On-the-Air Audition for Jean Carroll TVer." *Variety* 182, no. 7 (April 25, 1951): 31.

"Television Review: Tele Follow-Up Comment." *Variety* 177, no. 6 (January 18, 1950): 26, 30.

Thomas, Leah Marilla. "7 Female Comedians That 'Marvelous Mrs. Maisel' Fans Should Check Out Right Now." *Bustle*, December 6, 2017. www.bustle.com.

"3 Jewish Groups Unite for Refugees: Combined Appeal to Be Offered to Nation for Fund of 3 or 4 Times That Given Year Heightened Crisis Cited Agencies to Retain Separate Duties in Pressing Common Cause for Victims." *New York Times*, January 13, 1939, 12.

Toast of the Town. CBS, January 16, 1949. SOFA Entertainment. DVD.

———. CBS, January 30, 1949. SOFA Entertainment. DVD.

———. CBS, September 17, 1950. SOFA Entertainment. DVD.

———. CBS, December 3, 1950. SOFA Entertainment. DVD.

Tolstoy, Leo. *Anna Karenina*. New York: Penguin Classics, 2004.

Tomlin, Lily. Interview by Stephen Silverman. Transcript. November 6, 2006. Personal collection of Stephen Silverman.

Trav S.D. "Stars of Vaudeville #420: Carroll and Howe." *Travalanche*, January 7, 2012. https://travsd.wordpress.com.

Tunick, Helen. Interview by Stephen Silverman. Transcript. November 6, 2006. Personal collection of Stephen Silverman.

Turner Classic Movies. "Martha Raye." Accessed June 22, 2023. www.tcm.com.

"Uncle Sam's Callboard: Carroll & Howe Broken Up." *Variety* 152, no. 4 (October 6, 1943: 4.

United Service Organizations. "Our History: About the USO." Accessed January 23, 2019. www.uso.org.

Unterbrink, Mary. *Funny Women: American Comediennes, 1860–1985*. Jefferson, NC: McFarland, 1987.

Valcourt, Keith. "Shecky Greene Discusses Frank Sinatra and Las Vegas in the Old Days." *Washington Times*, February 9, 2017. www.washingtontimes.com.

Vandenberg-Daves, Jodi. *Modern Motherhood: An American History*. New Brunswick, NJ: Rutgers University Press, 2014.

"Variety House Review: Palace, N.Y." *Variety* 115, no. 2 (June 26, 1934): 22.

"Vaude House Reviews: New Acts—R-K-O, L. A." *Variety* 100, no. 10 (September 17, 1930): 46.

"Vaude House Reviews: Orpheum, Denver." *Variety* 106, no. 8 (May 3, 1932): 30.

"Vaude House Reviews: RKO Hillstreet, L.A." *Variety* 106, no. 5 (April 12, 1932): 37.

"Vaudeville: Howe Joins Cri GAC." *Variety* 162, no. 4 (April 3, 1946): 51.

"Vaudeville: 'Night of Stars' Benefit Nets 110G for UJA." *Variety* 172, no. 11 (November 17, 1948): 52.

"Vaudeville: Talent Problem Vexes 'Night of Stars' Show but 125G Gross at Par." *Variety* 176, no. 10 (November 16, 1949): 63.

"Vaudeville: USO-Camp Shows Casts." *Variety* 148, no. 12 (November 25, 1942): 46.

vintage video clips. "Myron Cohen—Comedian (1951)." YouTube, March 12, 2013. www
.youtube.com/watch?v=WEcD5px35Lc.

Ware, Susan. *Letter to the World: Seven Women Who Shaped the American Century*.
Cambridge, MA: Harvard University Press, 2000.

Weber, Bruce. "Alan King, Comic with Chutzpah, Dies at 76." *New York Times*, May 9,
2004, B7.

Weber, Donald. *Haunted in the New World: Jewish American Culture from Cahan to
"The Goldbergs."* Bloomington: Indiana University Press, 2005.

Weinstein, David. *The Eddie Cantor Story: A Jewish Life in Performance and Politics*.
Waltham, MA: Brandeis University Press, 2017.

Weiss, Nathan Norman. "Bostonian on Broadway: The Benefit Circuit." *Jewish Advocate*, August 17, 1950, 13.

Wenger, Beth S. *The Jewish Americans: Three Centuries of Jewish Voices in America*.
New York: Doubleday, 2007.

Willett, Cynthia, and Julie Willett. *Uproarious: How Feminists and Other Subversive
Comics Speak Truth*. Minneapolis: University of Minnesota Press, 2019.

Wisse, Ruth R. *The Schlemiel as Modern Hero*. Chicago: University of Chicago Press, 1971.

Wollman, Jane. "First Lady of Laughs Fifty Years Ago, Jean Carroll Was America's
No. 1 Female Stand-Up Comic. But Comedy Wasn't Always a Funny Business." *Ft.
Lauderdale (FL) Sun-Sentinel*, June 16, 1991.

Wong, Ali, writer. *Ali Wong: Baby Cobra*. Comedy Dynamics, 2016. www.netflix.com.

———. *Ali Wong: Hard Knock Wife*. Comedy Dynamics, 2018. www.netflix.com.

Wood. "House Review: Capitol, N.Y." *Variety* 167, no. 1 (June 11, 1947): 50.

Wood, Katelyn Hale. *Cracking Up: Black Feminist Comedy in the Twentieth and Twenty-
First Century United States*. Iowa City: University of Iowa Press, 2021.

Wylie, Philip. *Generation of Vipers*. New York: Pocket Books, 1942.

YIVO Institute for Jewish Research. "ARTEF Arbeter Teater Farband (Workers Theater
Association, 1925–1940)—YIVO Online Exhibitions." Accessed June 11, 2023, https:
//ataleoftwomuseums.yivo.org.

Zielonka, David M., and Robert J. Wechman. *Eager Immigrants: A Survey of the Life
and Americanization of Jewish Immigrants to the United States*. Champaign, IL:
Stipes, 1972.

Zoglin, Richard. *Comedy at the Edge: How Stand-Up in the 1970s Changed America*.
New York: Bloomsbury, 2009.

Zweibel, Alan. Interview by Stephen Silverman. Transcript. November 6, 2006. Personal collection of Stephen Silverman.

INDEX

Page numbers in italics indicate Figures and Photos

men, Jewish: stand-up comedians, 104, 111; stereotypes of, 177, 181–83, 186, 188, 189, 190–94

merchant stereotype, Jewish, 186–88, 190–94, 195–96

methods, 18, 23; methodologies, 24–25; scrapbook, 19–22

Meyerson, Bess, 207

Miami Beach (Florida, US), 104

Michaels, Marilyn, 78

microphone, stand-up comedy changed by, 122–28

Middletown Daily Record, 95, 96

Midnight Frolics (Chicago, Illinois), 103

Midnight Rounders (variety theater touring musical revue), 45, 48

Miller, Arthur, 170, 207, 211

Milwaukee Journal, 85, 87, 218

mimicry, 37, 71, 98–100

Mintz, Lawrence, 47–48

Miriam Maisel (fictional character, in *The Marvelous Mrs. Maisel*), 12, 14–15, 18, 238

misogyny: in Carroll, Jean, reviews, 101–2; in stand-up comedy, 88–89, 259n77

Mizejewski, Linda: *Hysterical* by, 27; *Pretty/Funny* by, 258n58; on pretty women comedians, 90

mob: Chicago speakeasies owned by, 103; Greene, Shecky, attacked by, 105; Lewis, Joe E., attacked by, 104; stand-up comedy ran by, 103–6

Mock, Roberta, 17, 27

Modern Dance, Negro Dance (Manning), 25

Momism, 211

Montgomery Bus Boycott, 185

Moore, Colleen, 21

mordant syntax, 171

Morgan, Thomas, 202

Mosedale, John, 218

motherhood, 235; of Carroll, Jean, 217–19, 220, 221–25, 225, 226–27; comedic material about, 3–4, 210–15

mothers, Jewish: Carroll, Jean, persona of, 215; comedy routines on, 78–79, 184, 211–12; stereotypes of, 180–81, 194–95

Mother's Day, 213

"moving monologue" comedy routine, 174–78

Muñoz, José, 158

Murray, Jan, 95

Murray, Matthew, 128

My Favorite Husband (sitcom), 137

Nachman, Gerald, 166, 167

Nadell, Pam, 44

National Association for the Advancement of Colored People, 267n108

National Association of Radio and Television Broadcasters, "Television Code," 97, 128–29, 130, 167, 259n85

National Broadcasting Company (NBC): Carroll, Jean, promotional headshot, 86, 87; Carroll, Jean, sitcom contract with, 138–39; *The Dinah Shore Show* on, 263n89; *I Married Joan* sitcom on, 136, 137; *Perry Como Chesterfield Show* and *Tag the Gag* TV shows on, 131; radio comedies on, 84, 85; *Show of Shows* TV show on, 133; *Texaco Star Theater* TV show on, 129, 131, 140, 166; *The Village Store* TV show on, 85, 87, 88

National Coordinating Committee Fund, 257n26

National Desertion Bureau, 44

National Labor Relations Board, 135

National Tay Sachs, 232

NBC. *See* National Broadcasting Company

neckline hearings, congressional, 129–30

Nesteroff, Kliph, 13–14, 83, 101, 104; on
    The Ed Sullivan Show Carroll, Jean,
    appearances, 234; on nightclub stand-
    up act length, 107; on presentation
    houses, 88; on radio, 84
Newark Evening News, 147, 148
New York (United States): Bronx, 35–36;
    Capitol Theatre in, 88, 92, 94; Catskill
    Mountains in, 76–84, 102, 256n17;
    Chateau Madrid in, 103; Copacabana
    nightclub in, 105, 109–10; Friars Club
    in, *x*, 1–3, 8–9, 17, 23, 78, 165, 221,
    229; Irvington Town Hall Theater in,
    240; Jacoby and Rosen in, 156–57;
    La Conga in, 104; La Martinique
    in, 107; Madison Square Garden in,
    80–81; Paramount Theatre in, 88, 95;
    Physician's Hospital in, 230; presenta-
    tion houses in, 61, 88, 90, 92, 94, 95;
    Rainbow's End in, 230–33; Shubert
    Crescent, 45; Television Workshop in,
    163; Velvet Room in, 104; Westchester
    County, 178–79; Yiddish Art Theatre,
    157, 266n88
New York Daily News, 219
New York Post, 231
New York Public Library Performing Arts
    Research Collection, 23, 25, 261n28
New York Times, 251n70; Brosnahan in,
    12–13; "The (Elegant, Brazen, Brainy)
    Pioneering Women of Comedy"
    by, 13; on sitcoms and women, 137;
    Take It from Me reviewed by, 147, 151;
    Tomlin in, 10; Youngman's obituary
    in, 94
New York World-Telegram and Sun, 132
nightclubs: comedic material for, 107–9;
    comedy routines in, 23, 29; Copaca-
    bana, 105, 109–10; mob-run, 103–6;
    during Prohibition, 103
"Night of Stars," 82
"Night Side" (column), 131

"Night Spot" (column), 101
nose: cosmetic surgery on, 16, 111, 181;
    jokes about, 15–16, 80–81, 181
Nye, Louis, 139

Oakley, M., 91–92
obituaries: of Howe, Buddy, 110; of
    Youngman, 94
"Old Maid" one-liners, 109
On Suburbia (King), 173
On the Basis of Sex (film), 238
Oriental Theater (Chicago, Illinois), 57
Our Gal Sunday (radio drama), 84–85
Our Miss Brooks (sitcom), 87
Overbeke, Grace Kessler, 13

Packard, Vance, 111
Palace Theatre, 22, 47, 59, 61, 68, 101
Palestine, 257n26
Paley Center Media Archive, *The Gary
    Moore Show* at, 23
Palladino, Dan, 12
Palladium theater (London, UK), 62, 64,
    101, 224
Palmer House (Chicago, US), 4, 121, 124
Pantages, 61
Paramount Theatre (New York presenta-
    tion house), 88, 95
parenthood, 235. *See also* motherhood
parent teacher associations (PTAs), 179,
    222
party albums, 23, 125, 184–85, 192–93, 230,
    271n12
Pathé studios (London, UK), 64–65
Pathetone Presents Carroll & Howe, 65
PBS. *See* Public Broadcasting Service
Pennsylvania Tribune, 155
people of color, Jewish, 269n25
Pepan, Bea, 85, 87
performance analysis, 24
Perry Como Chesterfield Show (NBC TV
    show), 131

persona: of Brice, 5, 66, 256n137; "Dumb Dora," 66, 114

persona, Carroll, Jean, 41, 178, 189, 237–38, 270n59; in "beatnik daughter" comedy routine, 215; in "buying a fur coat" comedy routine, 189, 194–96; Carroll, Jean, *Take It from Me* character compared to, 30, 154; dignified, 6–7, 16–17, 30, 114, 122, 133; "Dumb Dora," 66; Jewish identity relationship with, 16–17, 18, 114, 133, 172; of Jewish mother, 215; Jewish stereotypes of, 194–95; relatable, 124–26; in "rotten kid" comedy routine, 213

Peter Pan (school play), 39

Pew Research Center, "Portrait of Jewish Americans" study by, 250n54

The Phil Silvers Show, 158

Physician's Hospital (Queens, New York), 230

Pickette, Samantha, 15

Pickford, Mary, 21, 253n41

"The (Elegant, Brazen, Brainy) Pioneering Women of Comedy" (*New York Times*) ,13

Pittsburgh Jewish Newspaper Project, by Carnegie Mellon University, 251n70

Planned Parenthood Hudson Peconic, 240

Podell, Jules, 109

Podhoretz, Norman, 270n56

pogroms, 34

Polaroid Electric Eye Camera commercial, 223–24

"Portrait of Jewish Americans" (Pew Research Center), 250n54

Pratt, Caroline, 213

Precht, Bob, 197

Prell, Riv-Ellen, 38, 111, 177

presentation houses, 89, 91, 93, 93, 96, 97–102; Capitol Theatre, 88, 92, 94;

Loew's State, 61, 88, 90; Paramount Theatre, 88, 95

Pretty/Funny (Mizejewski), 258n58

Procter & Gamble, 141

Prohibition era, 103

propaganda, against Jewish peoples, 80

ProQuest, 251n70

Proser, Monte, 109

Pryor, Rainn, 239

PTAs. *See* parent teacher associations

Public Broadcasting Service (PBS), 16, 37

Pugh, Madelyn, 137

rabbi: at Madison Square Garden, 80; wedding officiated by, 61, 62

"racetrack" comedy routine, 29, 95, 97–101, 259n85

radio, 86, 87–88; "Amos & Andy" show on, 84, 267n108; *The Bickersons* show on, 267n90; Burns on, 84, 123; *Father Knows Best* program on, 211, 265n65; NBC comedies on, 84, 85; *Stella Dallas* drama on, 83

Rainbow's End (Wurtsboro, New York), 230–33

Rapid Advancement (policy), 39

"Rapid Fire Wit" (column), 101

Rapp, Charles (The Ziegfeld of the Catskills), 77

Rapp, Philip, 267n90

Raye, Martha "The Mouth," 6, 113

recordings: of Crystal Ball Dinner, 23; of live performances, 23, 24, 106, 109

Redbook, 212

Red Channels (pamphlet), 135–36

Red Scare, 36, 135–36

Refugee Relief Act (1953), 159

"Regulating Swish" (McCracken), 129

Reporter Dispatch, 226

representation: Jewish, 27, 270n61; of Jewish women, 206–7, 237–38, 270n61; of Jewish women comedians, 239

Republican Party, 241

retirement, 231, 232–33, 234

reviews: of Carroll, Jean, and Howe, Buddy, comedy double act, 68; of Carroll, Jean, stand-up comedy act, 92, 95, 109, 110, 121; of May and Carroll, Jean, comedy double act, 55–56; misogyny in, 101–2; of solo comedy act, 71, 90, 92, 95, 109, 110; of *Take It from Me*, 144, 145, 147, 148, 149, *150*, 151–52, 163

Rivers, Joan, 11–12, 94, 122, 125, 166, 194, 206, 233, 234, 258n58

RKO theaters, 61

Robin Carroll (fictional character, of Howe, Helen Roberta), 217–18, 219, 222, 223; ATV sitcom integration of, 226–27; in *Take It from Me*, 143, *146*, 154, 156, 159, 161–62. *See also* Howe, Helen Roberta

the Rockettes, 26, 82

Rockwell, Tommy, 131

Rogin, Michael, 46

Roman, Freddy, 92

Roosevelt, Franklin D., 68–69, 84

Rosen, Arnie, 132, 140–41, 148, 149, 151–52, 156–57, 158, 162

Rosenberg, Ian, 77

Rosten, Leo, 171, 268n23

"rotten kid" comedy routine, 31; on *The Ed Sullivan Show* Carroll, Jean, appearances, 212–13; Howe, Helen Roberta, impacted by, 209, 210

routines, comedy: "beatnik daughter," 214–15; on body image, 125–27; "buying a dress," 118–21, 167, 261n54; "buying a fur coat," 185–96; on Jewish mothers, 78–79, 184, 211–12; of Leonard, 123–24; "moving monologue," 174–78; in nightclubs, 23, 29; "racetrack," 29, 95, 97–101, 259n85; "rotten kid," 31, 209, 210, 212–13; "swish," 129, 130

Rudner, Rita, 9

Rusoff, Jane Wollman, 38, 204–5

Sahl, Mort, 107

Saranoff the Violinist (Lipton), 50, 51

Saturday Evening Post: on congressional neckline hearings, 130; on Marx, 129

Saturday Night Live, 122, 203

Saxon, Pearl, 48, 49–50

"Scene and Heard" (column), 149

scholarships, 39

Schumer, Amy, 26–27, 235

Schwartz, Louis, 103

Schwartz, Maurice, 157

scrapbook, Carroll, Jean, 25, 138, 225, 237, 251n58; caretaking in, 31, 33, 216–18, 221, 227, 233, 251n69; fashion in, *116–17*; Howe, Helen Roberta, in, 218–19, *220*, 221; *The Jean Carroll Show* TV show ticket in, 131; *Middletown Daily Record* clipping in, *96*; NBC newsletter promotional headshot in, *86*; storytelling structure in, 21–22, 74; *Take It from Me* in, *146*, *150*

scrapbooks, 22; Hastie on, 19–20, 21, 251n58; storytelling structures in, 21

Segrave, Kerry, 152

segregationist policy, of Copacabana nightclub, 110

Sergeant Bilko (fictional character, on *The Phil Silvers Show*), 158

Serviceman's Readjustment Act (1944), 169

sexual harassment, 64

Shabbos, 37

Shane, Irwin, 163

Shaw, Carl (comic tanglefoot), 50

She, 111

Sherman, Don, 13–14

Sherman-Palladino, Amy, 12, 13–14, 18

Shore, Dinah, 207, 263n89

Show of Shows (NBC TV show), 133

Shubert Crescent (Brooklyn, New York), 45

Shubert Organization, 43

Siegel, Benjamin "Bugsy," 104

Silverman, Sarah, 235, 238

Silverman, Stephen M., 1, 22–23, 33–34, 71, 255n110, 270n2

Simon, Neil, 157

Simple Yet Impossible sketch, 161, 267n100

Sinatra, Frank, 26; *The Frank Sinatra Show* CBS TV show, 131; mob involvement of, 105

sitcoms, 30, 133, *150*, 263n11; ATV network offer of, 224–25, 226–27; cancellation of, 163–64, 165, 267n108; Carroll, Jean, ABC sitcom contract, 139–41; Carroll, Jean, NBC sitcom contract, 138–39; *Father Knows Best*, 211, 265n65; gender norms enforced in, 265n65; *The George Burns and Gracie Allen Show*, 137, 148–49, 152, 153; *I Love Lucy*, 134, 136, 137; Lipsitz on, 265n65, 265n68; *Make Room for Daddy*, 124; *Our Miss Brooks*, 87; stand-up comedy and, 147–49, 151; women in, 136–38; writers for, 132, 137–38, 140–41, 148, 149, 151–52, 156–57, 158, 162. See also *Take It from Me*

"Six Laughs a Minute" (column), 101

Smith, Bill: Carroll, Jean, stand-up comedy act reviewed by, 121; solo comedy act reviewed by, 90; *The Vaudevillians* by, 49–50

"Social Characteristics of American Jews, 1654–1954" (Glazer), 169

SOFA Entertainment, 2, 23

solo comedy act: comedic material of, 89, 109; costumes used in, 90–91, 115; husband jokes in, 73–74; impressions in, 71–72; reviews of, 71, 90, 92, 95, 109, 110

speakeasies, in Chicago, 103

Spigel, Lynn, 136, 148, 153

Spock, Dr., 210, 211, 212

Springer, Phil, 160

SS *Philadelphia*, 35

Stabile, Carol, 136

stand-up comedians, 75, 101; Jewish men, 104, 111; men, 112, 175

stand-up comedians, women, 2, 7, 9, 12, 31; "Dirty Mouths, Dirty Martinis Comedy Night" performances of, 240–41; double standards facing, 110. See also comedians, women; women

stand-up comedy, 72, 94–95, 241; in *The George Burns and Gracie Allen Show*, 148–49, 152, 153; husband jokes in, 183–84; Limon on, 41; microphone changing, 122–28; misogyny in, 88–89, 259n77; mob-run, 103–6; in nightclubs, 107–9; sitcoms and, 147–49, 151; storytelling humor style of, 30; vaudeville transitioning into, 75; white male bias in, 27–28

stand-up comedy act, Carroll, Jean: comedic material restrictions of, 112–13, 118, 133; on *The Ed Sullivan Show*, 165, 167, 174–77, 178–79, 185, 189–92, 194–96, 201–3, 207–8, 209, 212–13, 214; *Variety* reviewing, 92, 95, 109, 110, 121

Stand-Up Comedy in Theory (Limon), 41

Stanwyck, Barbara, 91, 92

"State of Israel Bonds Woman of the Year" (award), 18

State Theatre, 90, 91, 97

Steinberg, Stephen, 182

Stella Dallas (radio drama), 83

Stember, Charles, 168

stereotypes, 6–7, 29; as Jewish codes, 180–84, 269n42; of Jewish men, 177, 181–83, 186, 188, 189, 190–94; Jewish merchant, 186–88, 190–94, 195–96;

ABOUT THE AUTHOR

GRACE KESSLER OVERBEKE is Assistant Professor of Theatre at Columbia College Chicago. She received her BA from Wesleyan University and her MA and PhD from Northwestern University. She received the Graduate Fellowship from Northwestern's Crown Family Center for Jewish and Israel Studies and the Perilman Postdoctoral Fellowship from Duke University's Center for Jewish Studies.